Pinstripes & Pearls

THE WOMEN OF THE HARVARD LAW SCHOOL
CLASS OF '64 WHO FORGED AN OLD-GIRL NETWORK
AND PAVED THE WAY FOR FUTURE GENERATIONS

JUDITH RICHARDS HOPE

A LISA DREW BOOK

SCRIBNER
New York   London   Toronto   Sydney   Singapore

A LISA DREW BOOK/SCRIBNER
1230 Avenue of the Americas
New York, NY 10020

For information regarding special discounts for bulk purchases,
please contact Simon & Schuster Special Sales at 1-800-456-6798
or *business@simonandschuster.com*

DESIGNED BY ERICH HOBBING

Set in Goudy Oldstyle

Manufactured in the United States of America

1   3   5   7   9   10   8   6   4   2

Library of Congress Cataloging-in-Publication Data
Hope, Judith.
Pinstripes & pearls : the women of the Harvard Law School class of '64 who forged
an old-girl network and paved the way for future generations / Judith Richards Hope.
p. cm.
"A Lisa Drew book."
Includes bibliographical references and index.
1. Harvard Law School—Alumni and alumnae—Biography. 2. Women lawyers—United States—
Biography. 3. Law students—United States—Biography. I. Title: Pinstripes and pearls. II. Title.

KF372.H67 2003
340'.071'17444—dc21   2002030411

ISBN 0-7432-1482-X

Copyright page information continues on page 294.

For Miranda and Zachary

Acknowledgments

The idea for this book first came to me in the winter of 1997, when I was (as usual) racing to do battle with some adversary or other in my pinstripe suit and my beloved mother's three-strand pearl necklace. But the book itself was not really born until the spring of 2000. Washington superlawyer Bob Bennett, who at the time was defending President Bill Clinton in the Paula Jones lawsuit, and his talented photographer wife, Ellen, who had just finished a photo shoot in Northern Ireland, had invited me to dinner with some of their pals from the Democratic Party establishment. Bob Shrum, then presidential candidate Al Gore's top political strategist, and his wife, journalist and author Marylouise Oates, showed up, touting Vice President Gore's experience and likely victory. I, the lone Republican in the group, predicted that my candidate, then Governor George W. Bush of Texas, would be the winner. As the wine flowed, the debate became more and more heated. It was time to change the subject.

I began to talk about my long-postponed desire to write about the tribulations and the successes of the women in my law school class, which I referred to—then and now—as the legendary Harvard Law School class of 1964. The table became quiet, and Oatsie and Shrum, who had been listening intently, looked across the table at each other and, simultaneously, uttered a single word: "Mel!"

Despite what, from their point of view, must have been my political incorrectness, they soon introduced me to Mel Berger, the respected literary agent at the William Morris Agency. In a moment of obvious temporary insanity, he took on this green and unproven writer. He also gave me his own one-word recommendation: "Lisa!" A week or so after I met Mel, he called to tell me that Lisa Drew, Scribner's renowned editor, had bought the book. Now all I had to do was write it.

Lisa and Mel shepherded me through the discoveries and difficulties of the next two years with sympathy, encouragement, humor, and extraordinary patience. When I finished the first draft and sent it off, Mel left the shortest and likely the best message I've ever received on my answering machine: "I love what you have done so far. Please double space."

Lisa edited my manuscript with perceptiveness and a clear sense of the jugular of this story. There were a lot of "we don't need to know this" comments penciled in the margins and, fortunately, once in a while a "Great!" or a "Fantastic!" This book would never have seen the light of day without Lisa and Mel.

My classmates, professors, administrators, law partners, and colleagues, men and women from the forty years of my professional life, were extraordinarily generous in sharing their recollections, diaries, letters, and feelings about our era and our challenges. They reviewed the manuscript, making helpful suggestions for accuracy as well as tone. Some of my classmates, intensely private people, were uncomfortable with becoming a significant part of this book, even though their careers and accomplishments warrant such recognition. To the best of my ability, I have respected their wishes and am grateful for the information they were willing to share. It required an intense effort from everybody, but in the end it turned out to be an amazingly good experience, bringing us even closer together.

Harvard University opened its archives and its memory banks to me. I am particularly grateful to David Warrington, the Librarian for Special Collections of the Harvard Law School Library, for his guidance and his rigorous review of the final manuscript. His mill ground exceedingly fine: he even corrected my reference to the marble floors in the Harvard Law library of our day by reminding me that they were not marble but cork, and highly polished.

Professor Dan Coquillette, Harvard Law School's official historian, provided invaluable help and, even more important, historic documents and steady encouragement. Sandra Spanier, associate secretary to Harvard University's Office of the Governing Boards, gave me extraordinary assistance and encouragement in the documentation of the Harvard Corporation's history and deliberations on admitting women to the Law School. The archivists at Mount Holyoke College and at Wellesley College were unfailingly generous with their time and their assistance.

Having never published even a lengthy scholarly article, much less a book, I needed—and, fortunately, received—marvelous help from friends and family who are real pros in the writing business. Just weeks before his untimely death in the spring of 2001, the great journalist Rowland Evans read my outline and revised it, giving me sound advice on how to proceed. *Newsweek* editor, journalist, and author Evan Thomas never let up on me. When, in his view, I finally got the beginning right after a dozen attempts (all of which he had rejected with a simple "Not right yet"), all he said was "Bingo!" My colleague and friend Harvard Law Professor Charles Fried read the manuscript and, with gentle firmness, shifted the tone just the right amount. My longtime pal Marc Leland read it, too, encouraging me to take a few risks and, yes, to loosen up a bit. My dear friend Ellis Wisner, a brilliant, caring teacher of English and the classics, worked with me hour after hour on syntax and style, not to mention logic.

For keeping my facts, statistics, and history straight, I am deeply indebted to Kelly Brion, Paul, Hastings's gifted librarian; Margaret Smith, my stellar researcher; and Amy Beth Horowitz, a talented third-year law student at Georgetown University Law Center.

For whatever reason—and there were many—I went through innumerable drafts of this story. My amazingly patient assistants at Paul, Hastings— Doreen Wood, Charlotte Stewart, and Rosie Daniels—never gave up on me: they typed and retyped, read and reread, and commented again and again not only on the progress, but also—gently—on the flaws. Ann Jones ably coordinated the production of the manuscript, bringing together the notes, the fragments, and all the scribbles. We ate a lot of Chinese food as we pulled more than a few all-nighters together. At home, Elvira Johnson kept things running smoothly for me and my family throughout the long months when I was writing. This book would never have been completed in my lifetime without all of them.

I owe a deep debt of gratitude to my parents, who loved me and backed me every step of my way in life. My mother, Eve Kemp Richards, who died too young in 1983, was and still is my role model: she was a talented professional woman, and also the best cook, homemaker, and mother I could ever have known. My father, Joseph Coleman Richards, has provided unstinting support for my dreams for more than sixty years, and, at age ninety-six, encouraged me to write this book, offering perceptive comments on the many drafts of the manuscript. My son, Zachary, cheered me on, but also pushed me to tell it like it was, not like I wanted to think it was.

There would have been no book worthy of the name, however, without the insights and persistence of my daughter, Miranda. When, in 1998, I showed her the first outline for this book, her reaction was swift and sharp: "Mom, it's not right. You've made what you did sound easy. You haven't told the whole story." I interpreted Miranda's comments to mean the book was a disaster. Wounded to the core, I packed up my notes, interview transcripts, and outlines in a large cardboard box, sealed it with an entire roll of strapping tape, and shoved it into the back of the attic for nearly two years. When, with Lisa and Mel's encouragement, I started writing again, I lacked the courage to show Miranda my drafts for a year and a half. Only near the end of the process did I mail her the almost finished manuscript. Her insistence that the book be honest and open never flagged: from commenting that "this is known—and not interesting," to questions like "Okay, okay, but why *you* at Harvard and not the other forty million American women?" She was relentless. Finally, she scribbled in the margin "Now this is interesting—this is a new story that only you can tell." I knew then that I was at last on the right track. Of all the extraordinary help I received in writing this book— from so many gifted people over such a long time—Miranda's directness, incisiveness, candor, clarity, and tough love, from the very beginning to the very end, proved to be at once the most painful and the most helpful. I might have been able to write this story without her help, but I suspect it would never have rung true.

Contents

PART ONE
Beginnings   I

PART TWO
Law School   27

Part Three
The Real World: June 1964 Forward   149

PART FOUR

Bumps in the Road   205

PART FIVE

At the Table   225

PART SIX

Exit from the Fast Lane? (September 2001)   237

Coda   255

List of Participants

Women of the Class of 1964

Alice Pasachoff Wegman, Counsel to the Environmental Appeals Board, EPA. Grandmother. Bethesda, Maryland

Ann Dudley Cronkhite Goldblatt, Assistant Director, MacLean Center for Clinical Medical Ethics, and Lecturer in the Social Sciences, Biological Sciences, and Humanities Divisions, Department of Medicine, University of Chicago. Chicago, Illinois

Arlene Lezberg Bernstein, solo practitioner, family law. Grandmother. Wellesley, Massachusetts

Aurelle Joyce Smoot Locke, Professor and Assistant Dean, University of Hartford Business School (retired). Grandmother. Granby, Connecticut

Barbara Margulies Rossotti, Partner, Shaw, Pittman, Potts & Trowbridge; Chair, Mount Holyoke Board of Trustees (Emerita). Washington, D.C.

Diana R. Gordon, author, Professor Emerita of Political Science and Senior Research Scholar in the Ph.D. Program in Criminal Justice, City University of New York. Surrogate grandmother. New York, New York

Eleanor Rosenthal,* retired lawyer; teacher, the Alexander Technique. San Francisco, California

Grace Weiner Wolf, community volunteer. Grandmother. Chicago, Illinois

Judith Richards Hope, Partner, Paul, Hastings, Janofsky & Walker. Corporate director. Chairman, National Housing Partnership Foundation. Washington, D.C., and Rappahannock County, Virginia

Judith W. Rogers, Judge, U.S. Court of Appeals for the District of Columbia Circuit. Washington, D.C.

*Graduated from Columbia Law School, 1964.

June Freeman Berkowitz,* mediator, community volunteer. Grandmother. Gloucester, Massachusetts

Katherine K. Huff O'Neil,† founding partner, Graff & O'Neil; founder, Oregon Women Lawyers. Grandmother. Portland, Oregon

Liz Daldy Dyson,‡ Office of General Counsel, U.S. Office of Personnel Management (retired). Accompanist, Washington School of Ballet. Grandmother. Washington, D.C.

Marjory Freincle Haskell, former Vice Mayor and City Council Member. Arbitrator. Oakland, California

Nancy Kuhn Kirkpatrick, Partner, Cohen, Swados, Wright, Hanifin, Bradford & Brett (retired). Grandmother. Buffalo, New York

Pat Scott Schroeder, former Congresswoman. President, Association of American Publishers, Alexandria, Virginia

Rosemary Cox Masters, Manhattan psychotherapist. Grandmother. New York, New York

Sheila Rush, Executive Director, East Palo Alto Community Law Project, Palo Alto, California (retired). Former General Counsel and current Communications Director, Ananda Church of Self-Realization. Nevada City, California

Sonia Faust, Assistant Attorney General for Land and Transportation. Honolulu, Hawaii

Susan Wall Stokinger. Deceased

Other Members of the Class of 1964

Anthony H. Bloom, Investment Banker. London, England

Thomas Boodell, Partner, Boodell, LeBaron & Trinka. Chicago, Illinois

Michael Boudin, Chief Judge of the U.S. Court of Appeals for the First Circuit. Boston, Massachusetts

Stephen Breyer, Associate Justice, United States Supreme Court. Washington, D.C.

Charles Buffon, Esq., Partner, Covington & Burling. Washington, D.C.

Kevin Conwick, Partner, Holme, Roberts & Owen LLP. Denver, Colorado

Paul Dodyk, Esq., Partner, Cravath, Swaine and Moore. New York, New York

---

*Graduated with the Harvard Law School class of 1975.
†Graduated from Lewis and Clark University Law School, 1977.
‡Graduated from the University of Kansas Law School, 1964.

Dan Emmett, Esq., Chairman and CEO, Douglas-Emmett Realty Corporation. Los Angeles, California

Eric Fox, Esq., Managing Partner, Ivins, Phillips and Barker. Washington, D.C.

Stanley Futterman, Esq., founder, Managing Partner, Law Offices of Stanley N. Futterman. New York, New York

Frederick Hitz, Esq., Professor, Princeton University. First Statutory Inspector General, CIA. Princeton, New Jersey

Thomas Penfield Jackson, Judge, U.S. District Court for the District of Columbia Circuit. Washington, D.C.

Joshua Hubbard Lane, Esq., Bond Portfolio Manager, Salomon Smith Barney (retired). New York, New York

Jon Masters, Esq., Chairman, Masters Governance Consulting. New York, New York

James Schroeder, Esq., former Deputy Undersecretary of Agriculture (retired). Arlington, Virginia

Donald Speuler, Esq., Partner, O'Melvany & Meyers (retired). Los Angeles, California

Faculty

Judith Areen, Dean, Georgetown University Law Center. Washington, D.C.

Barbara Allen Babcock, Professor, Stanford Law School, Palo Alto, California

Derek Bok, former President, Harvard University, former Dean and Professor, Harvard Law School. Cambridge, Massachusetts

Ernest Brown, Langdell Professor of Law, Emeritus, Harvard Law School, Senior Attorney, U.S. Department of Justice (retired). Washington, D.C.

Martha Field, Langdell Professor of Constitutional Law, Harvard Law School. Cambridge, Massachusetts

Charles Fried, Beneficial Professor of Law, Harvard Law School. Former Justice, Massachusetts Supreme Judicial Court. Former Solicitor General of the United States of America. Cambridge, Massachusetts

Benjamin Kaplan, Justice, Massachusetts Supreme Judicial Court. Former Royall Professor of Law, Harvard Law School. Cambridge, Massachusetts

John Mansfield, John H. Watson Professor of Law, Harvard Law School. Cambridge, Massachusetts

Henry Steiner, Jeremiah Smith, Jr. Professor of Law, Harvard Law School. Cambridge, Massachusetts

Kathleen Sullivan, Dean, Stanford University Law School. Palo Alto, California

Louis Toepfer, Vice Dean, Professor of Admiralty, Harvard Law School; inventor of the LSAT; Harvard Law School Director of Admissions, 1950–67. Saxtons River, Vermont

Friends

Mary Elizabeth Hanford Dole, candidate for U.S. Senate. Salisburg, North Carolina

Ruth Bader Ginsburg, Associate Justice, United States Supreme Court. Washington, D.C.

Olivia Barclay Jones, Harvard Law School '65, financial adviser and general contractor. Washington, D.C.

Ruth Drinkard Knouse, Director, Office of Executive Secretariat, U.S. Department of Labor. Washington, D.C.

Sandra Day O'Connor, Associate Justice, United States Supreme Court. Washington, D.C.

Betsy L. Pond, President, Pond Roofing. McLean, Virginia

David Souter, Harvard Law School '66, Associate Justice, United States Supreme Court. Washington, D.C.

Calvin Trillin, author. New York, New York

Offspring and Family

Mordecai Berkowitz, M.D., orthopedic surgeon. Gloucester, Massachusetts

Jeremy Goldblatt. Chicago, Illinois

Miranda Townes Hope, teacher, singer, and poet. Scarborough, Maine

Zachary Richards Hope, hedge fund manager, entrepreneur. Santa Monica, California

Brooke Masters, reporter, the *Washington Post*. Arlington, Virginia

Joseph Coleman Richards, Pastor, Church Without Walls. Waterville, Ohio

Jamie Schroeder, Professor, Montana State University. Bozeman, Montana

Foreword

Stephen G. Breyer, Associate Justice,
United States Supreme Court, Harvard Law School '64

When Judy Richards and I graduated from Harvard Law School in 1964, fifteen of my classmates (in a class of 513) were women. Only a few years before, two of my present colleagues, Sandra Day O'Connor and Ruth Bader Ginsburg, had been unable to find firms to hire them—because they were women. The federal bench at the time had only three female members, the first three ever appointed. That was our law school and professional world then. We took it as a given, though we understood that it should, and would, change for the better.

Today, of course, much has changed. At the Harvard Law School women now make up about half the class. The profession is one in which women make up about 30 percent of all lawyers. The National Association of Women Judges has grown in size from 100 in 1979 when it was founded to more than 1,300. Today, it is not "surprising" to find a woman law student, lawyer, or judge. It is normal.

Will we now forget the pioneers, like those spirited and courageous women of the class of 1964 who, through their own work, helped to bring women, professionally speaking, "to the table"? Willa Cather tells us that once pioneers succeed they are often forgotten. How often do those who drive on a Nebraska superhighway, shop at a mall, or buy dinner at a gourmet delicatessen contemplate the fact that only a few generations earlier Nebraskans had traveled west in a wagon or went hungry when the snow became too deep? She says of that earlier life (in My Ántonia) that no one who did not live through it could know anything about it.

I am glad indeed then that Judith Richards Hope helps us to discover, to remember, what the lives of those women lawyers of '64 were, are, have been like and what they have accomplished. For one thing, Judy and her classmates deserve recognition. Life as a woman at Harvard Law School forty years ago was not easy—as the reader will soon discover. And life in the profession thereafter posed special challenges that, one way or another, these fifteen women met and overcame. For another thing, their goals are not yet achieved. Even today, only 15 percent of all equity partners in major law firms are women—despite the fact that women account for close to one-third of all lawyers. And many women today struggle with the same structural problems as did that earlier generation: how to balance the demands of family, community, and the profession; how to create a life that makes sense in a world of competing demands on time. Though women traditionally have felt the resulting stresses more strongly, that problem today confronts men and women alike. And both men and women now must find a way to resolve it.

Finally, I am glad that Judy has written this book because it tells a marvelous story, or rather, a set of stories, about a group of intelligent, enthusiastic, persevering, enterprising women, who managed not only to survive trials many never face, but to do so with a sense of humor and a smile. They were my classmates; they are my friends. Their stories are honest, poignant—teaching by example, as our professors used to say. And their professional and personal lives have bridged the temporal gap that began with considerable prejudice, barriers, closed doors and closed minds, and finishes at a time when the road ahead, though not without bumps, is a smoother one because of them and others like them. That is why I want to say thank you to them, and to you, Judy, for writing this book.

Introduction

This is not quite the book I expected to write when I first started reflecting on the remarkable and gutsy handful of women who entered Harvard Law School in September 1961. When I began, I wanted to relate the folklore of our class—all the stories we've told each other over the years: how we made it in the malest of male bastions in the early 1960s; how our law school professors and early mentors, almost all men, quietly—often secretly—helped us; how we juggled the encrustation of our confusing, often conflicting roles: dutiful daughter, loving wife, devoted mother, fierce competitor, extraordinary achiever. I thought that some stroke of great good luck had brought us together in 1961. It was much more than that.

The Law School's director of admissions, Louis Toepfer, who invented the Law School Admissions Test (LSAT), took special delight in finding people who would prove out. He told me the Admissions Committee picked us one by one: "The women who decided to go to law school back then were a special breed. You were smarter and tougher and better organized, and you could look after yourselves. We knew that, in spite of the biases and prejudices in those days, you would get jobs and that you would do well. And we were right."

As I talked with my classmates, men as well as women, I began to understand not only why we were picked and the reasons for our grit and willingness to buck tradition, but also why we became some of the most prominent women of our generation. Although Harvard Law School was, for each of us in different ways, a defining experience, each of us was also shaped by the events that forged the will and dedication of our era. Our view of the world developed from our parents' stories about the Great Depression, and from the reality of our fathers and uncles going off to war in Europe and the Pacific while our mothers went to work outside the home or served as home-front volunteers. Our memories of the Second World War, the Cold War, and the wars at home—for civil rights and against poverty—gave us our courage and our dreams. The bookends of the sixty years of our personal histories are compelling: from September 11, 1941, when the United States began construction of the Pentagon, in preparation for what became, on December 7, 1941, the U.S. entry into World War II, to September 11, 2001, when terrorist pilots blew up the World Trade Center and hit the Pentagon, we have lived with ultimate threats to our security and our country. These sixty years of challenges to our security, of growing social unrest, and enormous political change parallel and have molded our lives.

With the privilege of studying law at Harvard in the early 1960s came the enduring obligation to engage ourselves in the challenges of the time, to dedicate ourselves to working on the very threats and inequities that had so profoundly affected us throughout our lives. Perhaps it is this, more than anything else, that sets us apart and accounts for our drive and dedication— this sense of responsibility, already within us when we arrived at Harvard Law School, which grew in strength and commitment during our three years there. The women in my class took on many of these challenges, as did the men we studied with. No one asked us to do it and no one stopped us when we tried. Our professors, classmates, parents, husbands, and even our children helped us in our quest.

As it has turned out, many of the women and the men in the Harvard Law School class of 1964 went on to do extraordinary things in the law and other professions. We include leading members of the bar, respected political figures, a United States Supreme Court justice, federal and state court judges, professors, poverty lawyers, spymasters, entrepreneurs, ministers, venture capitalists, business moguls, private eyes, corporate directors, psychoanalysts, real estate barons, and military men.

The women in my class arrived at Harvard Law School in 1961 from across the United States, and across the economic and political spectrum, at what was a deceptively calm time: despite the intensity of the Cold War, the world was at peace. On TV Ozzie went to work while Harriet stayed home with their charming, zany children. People were reading John Kenneth Galbraith's *The Affluent Society*, a bestseller published in 1958, which reflected the prosperity and optimism of that time. It seemed to be a time of tranquillity. During our three years at Harvard Law School there was a seismic shift and our society and our world changed forever. My classmates and I were standing directly on those moving tectonic plates and became part of those profound changes.

In 1960, the U.S. Food and Drug Administration approved Enovid, the first oral contraceptive for women. In 1961, at the Bay of Pigs, volunteer soldiers secretly backed by the U.S. government tried unsuccessfully to depose Cuba's president, Fidel Castro, who only three years earlier had been received at Harvard as a liberator and hero. In 1962, Betty Friedan's *The Feminine Mystique* was excerpted in several American magazines, launching the movement for women's liberation. By the summer of 1963, my classmates and I were sitting in, marching for civil rights, and cheering Martin Luther King's "I Have a Dream" speech at the Lincoln Memorial in the nation's capital. Many of us were reading Michael Harrington's *The Other America: Poverty in the United States*, a bestseller that revealed another side of America, one mired in generations of poverty, lack of opportunity, and widespread discrimination. The Equal Pay Act passed in 1963. In November 1963, President Kennedy was assassinated in Dallas, and what we now think of as the real "sixties" began. The following summer, just after we graduated from law school, both the Civil Rights Act and the Economic Opportunity Act became the law of the land. That same summer, Attorney General Robert Kennedy spearheaded the first massive government-led drive for civil rights in the South, Freedom Summer. At the same time, after the Tonkin Gulf incident, the conflict in Vietnam escalated: our friends and classmates who had deferred their obligatory military service until after law school shipped out as "military advisers," risking their lives because their government told them it was imperative to our freedom to stop the spread of Communism in Southeast Asia. Before most of us had tested our mettle in the world of work, the enhanced sense of justice inculcated in us both before we arrived and during out three years at Harvard Law School had strengthened our resolve to add whatever talents we had to the nation's crusades for freedom and equal opportunity.

In the face of these profound upheavals, the modest revolution of a handful of women at Harvard Law School went unnoticed by the country, and even by ourselves. But, as it has turned out, we were on the cusp of a fundamental change not only in the legal community but also of women's place in the professional world.

For the women in my class to postpone or forsake lives as homemakers to attend law school, commonplace today, was almost unheard of in 1961. Nationwide, only 316 women earned law degrees that year, as compared to 10,904 men. Most of our female college classmates were engaged or already married, with some having already given birth to their first child. In 1960, the median age of females marrying for the first time was 20.3. Of all women aged 20–24, 3,833,956 were married; less than half that number, 1,567,622, were still single. The median interval between marriage and first birth was 14.5 months. At the time that we decided to pursue careers in the law, women who worked outside the home were predominantly poor—often single moms struggling in low-paying jobs to support their children. That

women who didn't "have to work" would voluntarily choose to train themselves to work seemed peculiar—as the admissions director, Dean Louis
Toepfer, told me, "It was like a male nurse in those days."

Our fathers were supportive of our decision, but concerned. They knew
that the workplace was not open to us—they imagined that our journey
would be difficult and perhaps impossible. Many of our mothers were worried that legal training would ruin our personal lives: "What man would
want to marry a lawyer, especially one who went to Harvard?" As it turned
out, twelve of the women who began at Harvard Law in September 1961
were married during law school or within a few months of graduation. We
were part of the first wave of women who would try to do it all, have it all,
be it all, living well in the law as well as at home.

Forty-eight women applied for admission to Harvard Law School in the
spring of 1961. Twenty-seven of us were accepted; 20 started in a class of 560;
15 graduated three years later in a class of 513. (There were also 5 women
lawyers from abroad who were in the Masters of Law Program.) Dean
Toepfer and his Admissions Committee had handpicked us not only because
of our outstanding academic records, but because they thought we had the
grit and the stamina to run the gauntlet at Harvard Law School and to stay
the course in the legal profession after we graduated. Against what were
overwhelming odds at that time, and contrary to many predictions that we
would drop out when the going got too tough or when we married (or that
we would never marry at all), ultimately not one of us gave up, not one of us
dropped out, and most of us married. Each of us, in her own way, kept going,
jumping (or sometimes just crawling under) the barriers, not understanding
that people would try to block us or why, or that we should be choosing
between career and family. We pulled our weight while simultaneously trying to hold our marriages together, rear our children, drive car pools, sometimes darn our family's socks, and get dinner on the table by seven o'clock
every night. We didn't know how hard it was going to be, so we just did it.

It is probably a good thing that we didn't fully understand what we were
getting into—what obstacles we would encounter, what trails we would blaze,
the price that we and particularly our families would pay, or even the good
we would do and, yes, the fun we would have. We just knew, from an early
age, that we wanted both to serve our country, help make our world a little
better and a little safer—just like our fathers and our brothers—and to marry;
rear honest, happy children; and lead fulfilling personal lives—just like our
mothers.

Decades later, when first Pat and then Liddy, in the class of 1965, ran for
president of the United States, their stump speeches always contained a men-

tion of their challenging years at Harvard Law School, their shorthand for "We have been in the kitchen and we can stand the heat." When Janet, in the class ahead of us, became the Attorney General of the United States, then ran for governor of Florida, her speeches never failed to acknowledge that, after surviving Harvard Law in the early sixties, she could tackle anything.

One way or another, we have somehow managed to solve many of the problems women still face today, without losing our nerve, our femininity, or our minds. For starters, we didn't—and still don't—whine. We haven't allowed ourselves to feel put down or be put down. We have not asked for or counted on or been the beneficiaries of government mandated affirmative action. To the contrary. We have made our way through without that supposed boost up. We have tried not to internalize the inevitable gibes, whether from classmates, professors, colleagues, or bosses. Of course we have struggled, and of course we have often failed. We were not as good as we thought we would be at juggling all the roles we tried to play, and looking back, we would do a lot of it differently and, probably, just do a lot less, period. But our duck's backs, our belief in ourselves, the unwavering backing from our families, and our abiding friendship with each other have sustained us and carried us ahead.

We have no magic formulas, no seven or ten rules for success, no twelve-step programs. Ours are just war stories from forty years on the women's front. They offer a few clues about what it still takes for women to make it to the top. Each of us has done it her own way, but we have kept sight of each other out of the corners of our eyes—watching what works and what doesn't, cheering the successes and mourning (and learning from) the failures, seeking each other out when things go wrong. We have never clustered, but having each other for support and advice over the years has saved—and comforted—us again and again.

Having moved fast for six decades, hit our stride and reached the top of our game, we are somewhat surprised to find that we are sixty, a time when the law permits us to retire, to lead a more leisurely life, to begin to draw down our IRAs. Now what are we supposed to do?

We are, in Ellen Goodman's phrase, the "go-for-the-prize generation," the trailblazers, the glass-ceiling shatterers. We have accomplished a lot, much more than even we ever dreamed when we began. We are also the "suck it up" generation—almost never showing the pain we often felt at the slights and insults we encountered, never admitting how tired we often were, never quitting—even when those who loved us thought we should. Now we find ourselves looking ahead to the next quarter century, wanting to stay involved but also yearning for a little time off for good behavior.

As we set new goals and contemplate whether and how and when to exit from the fast lane, we know that the professional playing field is infinitely better than it was forty years ago, but it is still not level. As Kathleen Sullivan, former Harvard Law School professor and now dean of Stanford Law School, reminds us in her "Closing Legal Brief," there is still a long way to go—for women law professors and deans, for women partners and managing partners, for women general counsels and executives in corporations. Women still need every skill, every brain cell, every subtlety, and every inch of their old-girl network to realize their goals. The trails we blazed appear wide and open, but age-old forces continue to lurk and those trails can narrow again.

This book comes from our hope that our stories and the history of our era at law school and in the complicated professional and personal worlds we have navigated may be of help to women today, their husbands, partners, parents, and children. It is based on hundreds of hours of interviews—with classmates from what, at least for us, has become the legendary Harvard Law School class of 1964; with some of the extraordinary professors who taught us during our time in Cambridge; and with employers, mentors, partners, and colleagues who offered help and encouragement along the way. It draws from the archives of the Harvard Corporation, Harvard Law School, and the colleges that the fifteen women graduates in the class of 1964 attended, including Wellesley, Mount Holyoke, and Radcliffe.

Today, we face new challenges. We know that our world still values wise old men more than wise old women. We have learned a lot and still have a lot to contribute. So, we keep on, trusting, verifying, and working, for ourselves, for those who follow. Perhaps in exploring what happens next, we will find ourselves pioneers once more.

Even more than we did forty years ago, we watch each other's back, knowing without any question that we can count on each other "no matter what." When all else fails us, we still leap into the abyss separately or together, playing our hunches. When we're blocked, we find another route. Even now, if we have to back down temporarily or take a demotion to find a better opportunity, we do it. Our goal is always to reach the destination, not just to avoid humiliation on the way.

PART ONE

Beginnings

CHAPTER I

The First Female Fellow

Judith Richards Hope

Madam, I beg to inform you that at a meeting of the President and Fellows held February 5, 1989 you were elected FELLOW OF HARVARD COLLEGE to serve from February 7, 1989, and that consent to this election was duly given by the Board of Overseers at their meeting of February 5, 1989.

Your obedient servant,
Robert Shenton
Secretary

Twenty-five years after graduating from Harvard Law School, one of 15 women in a class of 513 who finished in 1964, I was at the table. It was historic: I was the first woman in Harvard's 350-plus year history to be elected to the University's seven-person senior governing board, The President and Fellows of Harvard College, usually referred to as "the Corporation," the oldest corporation in the Western Hemisphere. My election came after a year-long search by the members of the Corporation for a new fellow who, they hoped, would be a lawyer (preferably a Harvard Law graduate), a woman, and someone with experience in management and decision-making at a senior level. Government service was thought to be a plus. Given those criteria, the pool of candidates was small: relatively few women had graduated from Harvard Law School by 1989, and even fewer had been able to fight their way to the top of a profession that, for generations, had been a male preserve.

Early in the search, my great friend and law school classmate Judith Wilson Rogers, at that time Chief Judge of the District of Columbia Court of Appeals, a trustee of Radcliffe, and a member of the Visiting Committee to Harvard Law School, and I were approached separately and confidentially: "Who would you recommend for this important position?" They said that

3

they only wanted our advice, but we knew that they were also looking us over. We called each other immediately. We each knew it would be both a great honor and a singular responsibility to be selected; we also discovered that we'd already recommended each other for the job. I added the name of my Harvard Law School friend and colleague Jamie Gorelich (later Deputy Attorney General of the United States and now Vice Chair of Fannie Mae) to the pool. Throughout the search, we supported each other's candidacy and, unbeknownst to the search committee, quietly shared the information we picked up on how things were going. We hoped one of us would be chosen. The best chance we had to have this happen, we thought, was to stick together rather than to cut each others' throats.

As we came down to the wire in the search, the three finalists were the three J's: Judy, Jamie, and me. Just before Christmas 1988, law school classmate Stephen Breyer (then Judge of the U.S. Court of Appeals for the First Circuit, and a professor at Harvard Law School) called to give me a heads-up that Harvard President Derek Bok had called him and two other Harvard friends to check me out. I learned much later what they'd said: Stephen had stressed my management experience as a member of the Executive Committee of my law firm, Paul, Hastings, and as a corporate director; Charles Fried (a professor at Harvard Law, and later Solicitor General of the United States and Justice of the Massachusetts Supreme Judicial Court) had given me high marks as a lawyer and a lecturer in trial law at Harvard; Marc Leland (a lawyer, venture capitalist, and Assistant Secretary of the Treasury in the first Reagan administration) had vouched for my high standing with the Reagan and Bush I administrations.

I called Judy and Jamie right away to report in. Each of them told me that friends of theirs had also been receiving due-diligence calls and, so far as they knew, had been giving them excellent references. Judy said she was concerned whether her position as a judge would allow her to serve on the board of a corporation, even a nonprofit one, and that she'd passed those concerns on to the search committee. It looked as if one of us would be selected. A few days later, Judy called me: "I have just one question. Do you really want to do this job?" I said that I did. All she said was "Okay."

In early January, President Bok telephoned to propose that we meet in person. We met in my law firm's office in Midtown Manhattan. He told me that the Corporation "knows more about you than you know about yourself," and that the final decision had been "very, very close." The clincher had apparently come when Judy Rogers withdrew her name from consideration because of her judgeship and "recommended you as an outstanding candidate." I was speechless. A few years earlier, I had gone to bat for her with the

Reagan administration, urging her appointment to a seat on the D.C. Court of Appeals, even though she was a Democrat. I told them that she was fair, judicious, and wise, that she'd do a great job. As she did, being selected shortly thereafter to be the Court's Chief Judge. Now, in her typical quiet, selfless way, she had returned the favor, and then some. It was an extraordinary act of friendship.

The next month I was back at Harvard.

I arrived on Sunday, February 19, 1989, the night before my first meeting. It was a raw Cambridge night, replete with sleet and a bone-chilling cold. There was no welcoming committee or reception. I ate dinner by myself at a dingy Chinese restaurant near Harvard Square and scurried back through the icy drizzle to Dana Palmer House, Harvard University's six-bedroom official guest house located next door to the Faculty Club and directly across Quincy Street from what is now called Loeb House, the imposing redbrick Georgian mansion that houses the Office of Harvard's Governing Boards. I put my predecessor Andrew Heiskell's key into the lock of the door to Room 3 on the second floor and entered the crimson-toile-and-antiques-decorated bedroom he had occupied for ten years. It would be mine for the next eleven years.

At 8:45 A.M. the next morning I crossed Quincy Street, passed through the massive black iron gates into Harvard Yard, and rang the bell at Loeb House. The security camera swiveled toward me. After a brief pause, a buzzer sounded, releasing the lock, and I was in. I struggled out of my slicker, boots, and rain hat, fluffed my hair with my fingers, slipped on my high heels, and purposefully climbed the sweeping, crimson-carpeted stairway to the second floor. With a shiver that came as much from anticipation as from the bitter weather I had just navigated, I entered the Cabot Room, where the Harvard Corporation meets every other Monday except in July.

Five men were seated in high-backed, brown leather chairs at the Corporation table, twelve feet of highly polished mahogany, probably made by Hepplewhite or Duncan Phyfe a couple of hundred years ago. There were three empty chairs. The men smiled and said, "Good morning." They seemed glad to see me, and I was definitely glad to be there. President Bok was at the head of the table, facing the door, the adjacent fireplace, and the Gilbert Stuart portrait of George Washington hanging above the mantelpiece. Charlie Schlichter, an acclaimed physicist from the University of Illinois, was on Bok's left, the chair I soon learned was reserved for the Fellow with the greatest seniority and power, "the Senior Fellow." The chair opposite Charlie and to the right of Derek was empty. Bob Stone, a shipping magnate and oil tycoon from Greenwich, Connecticut, whose father was a cofounder of the Hayden-Stone investment firm, and whose wife's maiden name is Rockefeller, sat to the right of that empty chair. Harvard's revered economist and former dean of the Faculty of Arts and Sciences, Henry Rosovsky, whose family had fled Poland as the Nazis arrived, sat next to Bob. Coleman Mockler, then Chairman and CEO of Gillette, sat across from Bob. The chair to the left of Coleman was empty, as was the chair at the foot of the table, which I ultimately found out was reserved for deans, vice presidents, and others who were to make reports to the Corporation. Robert Shenton, the Corporation's Secretary, a distinguished lawyer and Ph.D., sat at a small antique desk behind the left side of the table. He never spoke during the meetings unless asked.

Even though I was within reach of the table, I didn't know the customs of that table or quite the right way to travel the last few feet and take my place. No one told me where to sit and there were no place cards. Not wanting to reveal my ignorance of the inner sanctum, I sauntered toward the chair to the right of President Bok, reasoning that it was probably set aside, at least for the first meeting, so that I, as the newcomer, would feel welcome. Just as I was easing my way into that seat, Bob shook his head no and said, "That's the Treasurer's chair." The Treasurer had died some months before. They told me later that, by unspoken tradition, each chair at that table remains empty until someone is chosen to fill it.

I jumped up and looked around nervously. I decided to move to the chair at the foot of the table: it was, like me, the lowest-ranking one in the room and the farthest from the power end of the table where the President, Senior Fellow, and Treasurer sat. This time, everyone shook his head no. Uncharacteristically, I was confused and uncertain about what to do next. Henry finally took pity on me, wagged his finger, and, with a twinkle in his eye, pointed to the chair next to Coleman. With relief, I sank into "my" chair, the one next to the foot of the table and nearest the door. For 350 or so years, that chair had been reserved for the Junior Fellow, who is responsible for opening and closing the door when the Secretary isn't present. I decided that deducing where to sit was some sort of initiation rite into membership on the Corporation.[1] "My" chair had descended through twenty-one men, including Henry Flynt, who had occupied it for sixty years, from 1700 to 1760; John Quincy Adams (oldest son of Charles Francis Adams, brother of Henry, and grandson of the U.S. President), from 1877 to 1894; Henry James (Pulitzer Prize–winning son of William James), from 1936 to 1947; and my predecessor, Andrew Heiskell, the former Chairman and CEO of *Time* magazine, from 1979 to 1989.

There I was in my navy coatdress and black patent-leather, sling-back heels, wearing my mother's pearl necklace and my mother-in-law's pearl earrings for luck. The first female Fellow. A kid from Defiance, Ohio, who had worn homemade clothes through law school, who had started working at the age of twelve pressing coats in a dry-cleaning plant for twenty-five cents an hour. There they were, in their pinstripe suits, regiment striped ties, and highly polished, black wing-tipped lace-ups, some of the most powerful men in America. We were sitting together at the top of the educational ladder surrounded by historic paintings of famous men in what had been, until I arrived, the most exclusive men's club in the world.

The Corporation's leather-bound archives were arranged chronologically, starting with 1652, on floor-to-ceiling shelves on the two long sides of the Cabot Room. I decided that first morning to dig into those archives to learn the history of women at Harvard, and to figure out why Harvard was one of the last universities in the United States to admit women to its law school.

CHAPTER 2

Big Dreams

The Dean [Erwin Griswold] stated his view to the effect that the present number of applicants for admission was so great that it was necessary each year to deny admission to well qualified men students. He hazarded a guess that not one in ten women who study law remains a practitioner for any significant length of time so that, in his opinion, as long as the first year class was limited in numbers, every woman admitted would keep out a man and thereby reduce the number of graduates who would follow careers as lawyers.

—Minutes of Harvard Law School Faculty Meeting, January 11, 1949

Summer 1943. Wahiawa, Hawaii. Sonia Faust, age seven, had just returned home to Honolulu from Indiana, where she, her mother, and her baby brother had been evacuated shortly after the Japanese attack on Pearl Harbor. Her father, a motion-picture engineer with the U.S. Army, had stayed behind at his job at Schofield Barracks. In preparation for the second grade, Sonia read a small book about Abraham Lincoln. Even though she didn't know any lawyers or what lawyers did, she decided right then to be a lawyer. The University of Hawaii didn't have a law school then, so she knew she would have to go to the mainland to study law. She'd heard of Harvard, but didn't know much about it.

Fall 1953. Defiance, Ohio. I was twelve, almost thirteen years old. Although I didn't know it at the time, only fifteen of the seven thousand or so women lawyers in the United States had graduated from Harvard Law School. For months, my father, the local Methodist minister, and his board of trustees had been locked in a rancorous and very public court battle in the Defiance County Court of Common Pleas with the Methodist bishop of Ohio over who controlled the local church and had the power to name its pastor.

It was, I suppose, a great show for the local folks, but for me it was devastating: people were lying about my family, retaliating against me, shunning me in school, sending anonymous hate letters to the parsonage, and making crank calls to us at two in the morning. Seeking a way to even the score, I finagled my way into the boys' section of Career Day at Defiance Junior High. I knew I had found the right path when one of the two lawyers in town described his job in court as a way to fight for what was right. I went home and told my mother and my father that I was going to be a trial lawyer. When they asked me where I would go to law school and whether I'd like to make a modest wager on whether I would graduate, I bet them the biggest thing I could think of, a 1964 Thunderbird, that I would graduate from Harvard Law School in 1964.

Fall 1956. New York City. Judith Ann Wilson, whose father was a prominent architect and whose mother was a concert pianist, was a junior at the Dalton School, then a private all-girls school that encouraged its students not only to progress at their own rate, subject to minimum requirements, but also to have a strong commitment to community service. One afternoon a week, Judy worked in a settlement house or a hospital. Seeing the desperation of the families she was trying to help, she decided to devote her talents to making a difference for the underprivileged, particularly for children: "I realized that sitting in a hospital or a settlement house just trying to entertain children wasn't going to have much impact on their lives. So I thought I would go to law school and be able really to affect the laws and affect their lives in a significant way. I was interested both from the point of view of any child who is affected by laws and of children who had special problems, especially children who were involved in delinquency. I thought I should be a lawyer to do all of that."

In her senior year at Radcliffe College, Judy was admitted to both Yale and Harvard Law Schools. "I said to my dad, 'I've got a full scholarship to Yale.' And he said, 'But where do you want to go?' I said, 'Either place would be great, but Harvard will open more doors for me.' And he said, 'Well, go to Harvard.' So I did. Somehow, they managed to pay for it. I had summer jobs, of course, but you know summer jobs paid virtually nothing in those days."

Summer 1960. Pasadena, California. Ann Dudley Cronkhite, twenty, had just finished her junior year at Radcliffe College. There were approximately forty women and seventeen hundred men enrolled at Harvard Law School at the time. Ann Dudley had taken an aptitude test in high school that concluded she should be either a librarian or a lawyer. But when she went home that summer, she announced to her father that she wanted to get a Ph.D. and be an academic. He told her, "I really don't think I can afford it.

I know you'll get to graduate school and you'll just stay there forever because that's what I would like to do." She immediately countered, "Okay. Can I go to law school?" Her father agreed, "That's okay. It's only three years. And I've always wanted someone to prove the income tax is unconstitutional." Even though she thought that would be difficult because the income tax was itself a constitutional amendment, she decided not to press her luck: "If that was his price for sending me to law school, that was fine with me." Her father's only advice was to do as much as she could to overcome the handicap she would have as a woman in a man's profession: "A woman lawyer is going to have a reasonably hard time of it. You really should get as much clout as you can from your law school."

Ann Dudley applied to Yale and Harvard Law Schools. The morning of the LSATs she stepped on her only pair of glasses. She did terribly on the exam and was rejected by Yale, but "Harvard sent me a short letter of acceptance, with a three-by-five card in it to return. It wasn't 'I accept' or 'I decline.' It was 'I want a single room' or 'I want a double.' There was absolutely not a single indication that anyone would turn Harvard down."

Early fall 1960. Cambridge, Massachusetts. Diana R. ("Dinni") Lorenz, twenty-three, was an English teacher at Concord Academy, a girls' prep school that Caroline Kennedy later attended. Dinni loved literature but didn't want to do intense research into it. Since growing up in a politically liberal family in Pasadena, California, she had been deeply involved in social and political issues. She decided that law school would give her the most effective tools with which to redress some of the inequities she observed in the society around her. Her father encouraged her, but also warned her, "It's very hard for a woman. There aren't many women lawyers. I think if you don't go to Harvard, you'll have three strikes against you. If you go to Harvard, you'll only have two strikes against you. So if you get into Harvard, I'll send you. But if you don't, you should think of something else."

Dinni had to get into Harvard. It was the only place she applied.

October 20, 1960. South Hadley, Massachusetts. Rosemary Cox, twenty-one, was a senior at Mount Holyoke College. When she started to think about law school, the head of the political science department told her to go to Cambridge and talk to Professor Arthur Sutherland at Harvard Law School. When she met him, he gave her what he thought was the best practical advice: "He told me, in a very kindly, sweet way, 'Well, you'll never get a job, and probably not even an offer at a big Wall Street firm. I suggest that what you do is get secretarial training along with your law degree and that you then become the secretary to a very senior law partner. You'll have far more influence with a John Foster Dulles kind of person than you ever will

as an estates and trusts lawyer, which will probably be all that's open to you."
On October 20, 1961, Rosemary wrote her parents about her visit with Professor Sutherland: "Sutherland proved to be a very delightful and witty person, who talked at some length on the nature of law as a field where you deal with imperfect people, find imperfect solutions, and get fairly little thanks or glamour . . . but . . . if you have a concern for the good order of society and government and a pleasure in seeing that order perfected, law is a rewarding field.[2]" She also mentioned his suggestion that she hone her typing and shorthand: "He said that whatever firm a women [sic] goes into, she is bound to become absolutely invaluable and irreplaceable to the top bosses . . . and that more doors would be opened through this sort of training than by any other approach." For Rosemary, Sutherland's advice was useless. She had a learning disability and, among other things, couldn't spell very well: "I knew I could never become a secretary. It's one of the reasons I had to go to law school, so I could have a secretary."[3]

Winter 1960. Minneapolis, Minnesota. Patricia Nell Scott, twenty, a pilot and the daughter of a flight instructor and a teacher, was a senior at the University of Minnesota. She decided to become a lawyer because it was more broad-gauged than anything else she could think of: "I really started out wanting to be an aerodynamic engineer, but at Minnesota, they talked me out of it. They said that nobody hires women aerodynamic engineers. They forgot to tell me that almost nobody hired women lawyers either, at that time. When I started thinking about being a lawyer, I decided I wasn't about to be talked out of anything again. I thought, 'I need to go to a national law school.' And Harvard was a national law school. By process of elimination, that's why I decided to apply there. I didn't apply to any other place."

It was a time of big dreams, for us and, as it turned out, for the nation.

CHAPTER 3

History

The Corporation will not receive women as students into the College proper, nor into any school whose discipline requires residence near the school. The difficulties involved in a common residence of hundreds of young men and women of immature character and marriageable age are very grave. The necessary police regulations are exceedingly burdensome. The Corporation are not influenced to this decision, however, by any crude notions about the innate capacities of women. The world knows next to nothing about the natural mental capacities of the female sex. Only after generations of civil freedom and social equality will it be possible to obtain the data necessary for an adequate discussion of woman's natural tendencies, tastes, and capabilities.

—Inaugural address of Charles Eliot
as president of Harvard (1869)[4]

When the women in my class set course for Harvard's law school, we knew little or nothing of the University's centuries-long opposition to women students in general or to women law students in particular. The relevant portions of Harvard's archives reveal that, despite the occasional support of the Law School faculty for women applicants, the seven members of the Harvard Corporation repeatedly overruled them, with little discussion and no apparent criteria whatsoever. Their concerns were not flattering to either women or men: the Corporation claimed to have no knowledge as to whether female students could handle the rigorous intellectual challenges of law school, and no confidence that the male students could control themselves with young women close by. Harvard's archives do not indicate that the President and Fellows troubled themselves to obtain any objective information about any of their expressed reservations.

In 1869, Belle A. Mansfield was admitted to the state bar of Iowa, reputedly the first woman lawyer admitted to practice in the United States.[5] That same year, Myra Bradwell was denied admission to the bar of Illinois on the grounds that "the natural and proper timidity and delicacy which belongs to the female sex evidently unfits it for many of the occupations of civil life."[6]

In 1870, Christopher Columbus Langdell became Harvard Law School's first dean. A visionary when it came to inventing the case method and "scientific" legal-research procedures, Langdell suffered from myopia where women law students were concerned. In 1871, he opposed the admission of Helen M. Sayer, the daughter of a former justice of the New Hampshire Supreme Court, who had studied law in her father's office for a year. After two days of heated discussion by the law faculty and subsequently by President Eliot and the Fellows of Harvard College, Sayer's application was rejected because she was a woman.

That same year, just twelve miles from Cambridge, Henry Fowle Durant and his wife established the charter for Wellesley College: "Women can do the work. We give them the chance."

In 1878, another woman law school applicant was turned away from Harvard. The Corporation's minutes do not even reflect her name: "A request for the admission of a woman to the Law School was considered and denied" (October 7, 1878).

In 1886, Alice Jordan became the first woman to graduate from Yale Law School.

Sometime between 1896 and 1897, the Harvard Law School faculty reluctantly voted that graduate women registered in Radcliffe could take law classes at Harvard, but could not receive a degree. The dean voted "yes— but personally would regret it if it happened." Professors Thayer, Gray, and Wambaugh also voted yes, but noted that they "personally didn't want them to come, did not advise it, and preferred not to have women in the school." Langdell, who had stepped down as dean, "decline[d] to express an opinion—the question not being before us." Only Professor Smith voted "yes . . . some women would make good lawyers."[7]

In 1899, a gifted scholar from Bryn Mawr, Frances A. Keay, applied to Harvard Law School. After an acrimonious debate, the Law School faculty, by a split vote, conditionally approved her application, reasoning that they could not "deny the inherent justice of the claim." Their approval depended upon her admission by Radcliffe College, then an independent women's school that shared professors and classes with Harvard College, as a "graduate student" so that it would be clear that her law degree would *not* come from Harvard. This stipulation presumably ensured that a law degree from Harvard would have no female taint. Yet something more than gender or capability was at stake: even this demeaning condition did not pass muster. The Corporation continued to balk, stating without further elaboration: "The President and Fellows are not prepared to admit women to the instruction of the Law School."[8]

In 1909, Inez Milholland applied for admission to Harvard Law School. Her sponsor, Henry L. Higginson, a Boston lawyer and Harvard Law alumnus, wrote, tongue in cheek, to President Lowell on October 8, 1909:

> I do not know whether it is within our charter to admit her as a student, and I do not know how much it would interfere with our work. I have always supposed that this thing must come some day—that we must admit women to our law school. How much self-restraint on the part of the students it would call for, the professors will have to determine. If we are to begin at all with women, we certainly can do no better than with this young lady. It is, however, to be remembered that men are being gradually displaced by women, and if they are all like this young lady, it would merely hasten our banishment.[9]

The law faculty, led by Dean James Barr Ames, debated whether to admit Miss Milholland. Renowned Professor Edward "Bull" Warren was opposed: "But my teaching technique will have to change." Dean Ames is reported to have answered, "Is that an argument for or against?"[10] The faculty ultimately voted in favor of admitting her, but the Harvard Corporation immediately overruled them, voting unanimously "to inform the Faculty of Law that this Board is not willing to consent to the matriculation of women in the Law School."[11] President Lowell added, with scanty explanation and in garbled syntax, "Personally, I do not believe that it is wise now to admit them. There are other law schools which they can now attend, and I feel by no means sure that we should not imperil somewhat the peculiar efficiency of our law school if women were admitted."[12]

Inez Milholland matriculated elsewhere and became a noted lawyer, feminist, and suffragist.

On March 8, 1915, the Harvard Corporation voted against the petition of fifteen women applicants from the Seven Sisters of the Ivy League schools as "contrary to the best interests of the law school." When a group of Radcliffe alumnae applied in the 1920s, the Law School dean wrote them: "I can find no argument which my reason respects but I intend to vote against you."

In 1920, women won the right to vote.

In 1945, the Harvard Corporation, noting the shortage of male doctors and medical students following World War II, voted to permit Harvard Medical School to admit women.

In 1947, Dean Erwin Griswold appointed the first woman to the Harvard Law faculty, Soia Mentschikoff, as visiting professor of commercial law. It was, perhaps, part of his long-range strategy to persuade the Corporation to reverse its historical opposition to women at the Law School. Her appointment was a great success and had an unexpected benefit: she single-handedly integrated the Harvard Faculty Club. As former Professor, Vice Dean, and Director of Law School Admissions Louis Toepfer remembers it, "One day, she just walked in the front door and came and sat at the round table in the men's dining room. Well, everyone was astonished . . . we were astonished that she did it . . . we were astonished that nobody asked her to remove herself. And with that it was done."

At a Law School faculty meeting in August 1947, Professor Lon Fuller "suggested that serious consideration should be given to admitting women into the Law School beginning with the fall of 1948."[13] According to Professor Ernest Brown, the Law School sought permission to admit women, but the Corporation deferred the decision on the basis that veterans returning from World War II needed to be accommodated first.[14]

At about that time, Dean Griswold started talking quietly with a few members of the faculty about admitting women: "I found, as expected, that there was sharply divided opinion. . . . [Even] some of the younger members of the faculty did not think well of the proposal. On the other hand, there were a number, apparently a majority, who thought that the time had come."[15] Griswold asked Professor Mark deWolfe Howe, a great teacher and a respected Harvard College alumnus from a prominent Boston family, to "do a little proselytizing," advising him that the proposal shouldn't move before the fall of 1948 because of the large number of returning veterans seeking admission.

Finally on January 11, 1949, at the end of a particularly long Law School faculty meeting, Dean Griswold called for "any other business." Professor Mark deWolfe Howe piped up, "Is this the proper time to bring up the question of admitting girls to the School? I feel rather strongly that we should do so."[16]

Dean Griswold said that he thought the Corporation might at last adopt such a recommendation if the law faculty supported it, but that every woman admitted would take the place of a man who was more likely to use his legal education. The minutes of that faculty meeting reveal that finding support for having women students at Harvard Law School was not going to be easy.

Mr. Casner suggested as an intermediate plan, the admission of women to graduate work only. Mr. Bowie suggested there might be a higher standard of admission required for women than for men, only those outstandingly qualified being
admitted. He thought this might improve the general standard of the class. Mr.
Dodd thought that it was an appalling fact that only one law school in the six
New England states [Yale] admitted women. Mr. Howe said that "about
15% of our [male] students do not go into practice" and that he thought there
was an obligation to provide an opportunity for women, noting that it was possible that more women remained in practice than the Dean thought.[17]

The faculty voted to appoint a committee to study the matter. Dean
Griswold immediately named Professor Howe chairman.
Howe asked Professors Austin Scott, John Maguire, and
Ernest J. Brown, and Vice Dean and Professor Louis
Toepfer, to join the committee. They never met.[18] Howe
drafted a crafty report, covering everything from women's
talents to the need for and cost of a separate women's toilet, ultimately recommending women's admission despite
uncertainties about their stick-to-it-tiveness.

Professor Mark
de Wolfe Howe

Time has shown, as President Eliot believed that it might [in
1869, only eighty years before], that women's tendencies and
capabilities entitle her to equality of educational opportunity within the
Harvard community. . . . Perhaps the most serious justification for the exclusion of women is based upon the probability that a relatively small proportion
would make professional use of their training for a significant period of time,
and that for each woman admitted a qualified man, somewhat more likely to
use his training in his career, would have to be excluded. . . . The Committee
is not persuaded that the mortality rate justifies the complete exclusion of
qualified women from the Law School. . . .

It is, of course, true that the woman at the bar has always faced special difficulties and obstacles. It is likely that that situation will continue for some
time to come and that on graduation she will find the initial problems of placement and the later problems of advancement far more difficult to solve than
will her male classmate.

The fact that the woman lawyer is under special handicaps in securing the
fullest opportunity for professional success is hardly sufficient justification for
the preservation of a rule of exclusion which forbids her from attempting to
overcome them and denies her the right to secure what we like to consider the
best education in the law which the nation offers.

The cumulative effect of these considerations leads the Committee to recommend that beginning in the Fall of 1950 qualified women be admitted to the Law School.[19]

The faculty voted twenty-two to two to approve the report. On May 11, 1949, Dean Griswold forwarded it to the Harvard Corporation for final decision, noting that, if approved, the recommendation would not take effect until September 1950:

> . . . we are still receiving a substantial proportion of applications from veterans . . . the actual admission of women should not occur until a year from this fall . . . it would be desirable not to make any announcement of the change, if it is adopted, until next fall.[20]

Louis Toepfer told me, "It was unnatural not to have women. We all wanted women in the law school—well, most of us did. We expected, however, the Corporation to turn us down—because it always had."

On June 22, 1949, the Corporation unanimously and with no fanfare approved the admission of women to Harvard Law School starting in the fall of 1950. After eight decades of women knocking on the door to Harvard Law School, it was about to open. I had just finished the third grade in Ohio. I had no idea that a decision made in Massachusetts would change my life.

CHAPTER 4

Collective Consciousness

Long before we arrived in Cambridge, both I and the women in my law school class had become untethered from our pasts. There were no Harvard legacies among us, and no fathers—or mothers—who were lawyers. We were doing something our parents had not done in a place they had not been. In one sense, we were out of place for our time—we weren't supposed to be there; our brothers were. Yet we were exactly where we should have been, doing what we had always done: the unexpected.

Most of us were firstborn or only children. Many of us had gone to nursery school when that was unusual for young children, and then on to public school before going to college. We had totally supportive parents who were ahead of their time and who encouraged us to try our wings, to follow untrodden paths. By the time we were teenagers, we were already out of the traditional female roles of that time. We had learned the feminine arts—cooking, sewing, and needlework, and how to serve tea—but many of us had also learned how to shoot and hunt, how to play poker as well as musical instruments, and how to bet successfully on horse races. Pat Scott (Schroeder) was already a pilot. Our parents helped us every step of the way, urging us to dream our big dreams, and to use our talents to serve our country. In college, many of us had female role models who were our college presidents, deans, and professors.

Most of us came from the middle of the socioeconomic spectrum: perhaps for that very reason we had less of a stake in preserving traditions, including women's traditional roles. Some of us were first-generation Americans.

We came from different backgrounds, regions, economic circumstances, and colleges, but we had a lot in common. We were born at the end of the Depression, just before the start of World War II—historic events that shaped our personalities and our will. We were in a hurry—many of us were twenty or twenty-one years old when we started law school. We all had and still have the same collective consciousness of America during our growing up, a deeply embedded, shared perception of a world that was uncertain, threatening, and unequal, a world that we wanted to make secure, fairer, and more egalitarian.

Although I was four and a half years old when World War II ended, I still have clear images of that time. I remember my father's parishioners coming to our parsonage in tears because they had lost a family member in the fighting in Europe or the Pacific. I remember walking with my parents across the lawn to the church to attend funerals, and seeing flag-draped coffins in the sanctuary. I remember crying every time I saw a khaki-clad Western Union delivery boy in our neighborhood: as far as I knew, his stack of bitter yellow telegrams meant that someone we knew had been injured or, more likely, killed at the front.

My classmate Sonia Faust was born in Honolulu in 1936. Her father, Alfred, an Armenian who had fled Russia during the Revolution, had come to Hawaii as an enlisted man in the U.S. Army, based at the Schofield Barracks. Her mother, Geneve, was a schoolteacher from Indiana who had married him while attending the University of Hawaii.

Sonia was five years old when the Japanese bombed the American ships lying at anchor in Pearl Harbor not far from her home:

"I remember December seventh, 1941, but as a little child, I wasn't picking up on all the sounds of war that the adults heard. I just knew that things were very different. There was no paper delivered and people were restricted: we couldn't travel even down to Wahiawa town. Even on that first night there was a blackout, which, since nobody's windows were painted, was achieved by not turning on anything electrical—lights, stoves, anything.

"For quite a while after December seventh, we had a lot of people staying at our house who had evacuated from the Pearl Harbor housing area. It was very tense. We had been taken so totally by surprise that people believed that an invasion was well within the possibilities, and being in the military, they knew that we didn't have much defense against it. Later, everyone had bomb shelters built in their yards. . . . I was afraid a lot of the time, but it wasn't a complete sense of terror. It was just really not knowing what was happening, and the constant worry about invasion. We had air raids all the time—not just drills, but real air raids. I would be playing in the yard or grocery shopping with my mother or asleep in bed and then the sirens would go off. I ran to our bomb shelter. I had to do that a lot."

As the battle for Midway Island loomed, many mothers and children left Hawaii for the mainland, including Sonia, her mother, and her baby brother. They sailed for the West Coast on a Matson liner that had been converted into a troop carrier, escorted by a blimp all the way from Honolulu to San Francisco. "We saw whales sometimes and people were terrified. They thought they were submarines. When we got to San Francisco, most of us did not have any warm clothing. But the Red Cross was there and the ladies had knitted things for us. I remember I got a maroon sweater and I was very grateful for it."

After the United States won at Midway, Sonia returned to Hawaii and entered second grade. It was about that time that she decided to be a lawyer, even though she had no idea what that meant:

"Abraham Lincoln made me want to do it. The very first book I borrowed when I got my very first library card in Wahiawa was a child's book about Abe Lincoln. I thought he was wonderful. He saved the Union."

Classmate Nancy Kuhn (Kirkpatrick) remembers listening to the radio at night and bursting into tears when the news reported American casualties. "Being on a street full of row houses, I remember a lot of gold stars in the windows of, it seemed, nearly every house. The stars were awarded by the government to the mothers who had lost sons in the war. My brothers had paper routes, and without telling our parents, they would let me sell their extra papers on the corner. I was in kindergarten on the day the war ended in Europe. I can remember standing there on the corner, selling the papers with the news that the war there was over, and being so excited that we had won. It is one of my earliest memories."

Pat Scott's father, an aviator and flying instructor who'd been called back into military service shortly after the attack on Pearl Harbor, gave her a toy airplane with wheels that she could sit in, steer, and pedal. Pat remembers pedaling it around their house playing "bombing the Japanese." She was three and a half years old. When her daughter, Jamie, got married, she asked for her mom's pedal plane as a wedding present. Pat gave her the family's antique grandfather clock instead: her pedal plane was too precious, too much a reminder of how she'd started and whom she has become.

I remember going to black-and-white movies at the Valentine Theatre in Defiance, Ohio, on Saturday afternoons (it was, after all, before television), seeing feature films like *Guadalcanal Diary* and the *Sands of Iwo Jima*, depicting war as exciting and virtuous, Americans as heroes, and the allies as inevitable victors. But I also remember being riveted to the grim Movietone News reports of real war, and squinting at the screen, searching for a glimpse of someone I knew among the mud-spattered soldiers slogging to the front lines. I remember the rationing of sugar, gasoline, soap, and ice cream; weeding our family's backyard victory garden; helping my mother stamp down on emptied tin cans to save them for the scrap drives; and closing the mandatory blackout curtains tight each night so the enemy could not find our house or our town to bomb it. Later, in the 1950s, I remember diving under my school desk when the air-raid siren screamed, crouching there until the all-clear sounded. In 1953, the year I finished the eighth grade, my high school yearbook was dedicated "to all the alumni of Defiance High School who are serving, or have served, their country in the Korean Conflict."

At the end of these wars, when most of the soldiers and sailors I knew came home and took up their civilian lives again, my friends' mothers quit their jobs and became housewives again. But we never forgot the courage of the fighting men, and of our mothers, who also won the wars.

I and most of my Law School classmates took the wars personally. Pat Scott, Rosemary Cox, Judy Wilson, and I wanted to be heroes and swash-bucklers, too. We saw plenty around us: Ike and Patton and MacArthur and Churchill and De Gaulle and our fighting men had won World War II. Except for Eleanor Roosevelt, Rosie the Riveter, and a few WAFS, WACS, and WAVES, the heroes were all men. At the movies, Errol Flynn and John Wayne had saved us from the bad guys. Bing Crosby had brought us a white Christmas year after year, and Bob Hope had made us all laugh, no matter how scary our world was. That was it: the greatest excitement and the best chance to make a difference was, it seemed to us, in activities occupied at that time almost exclusively by men. We didn't want to be or act like men, we just wanted the chance to do the things they were doing.

Radio sharpened our imaginations, transporting us every week from danger to safety in the company of the Lone Ranger and his faithful sidekick Tonto, Roy Rogers and his gallant palomino Trigger, and Gene Autry and his brave chestnut gelding Champion. Sergeant Preston enforced the law in the Yukon with his valiant lead dog King and his team of huskies sledding across the tundra. The Green Hornet ferreted out crime, and of course the Shadow always saved us because he really did know what evil lurked in the hearts of men. We suffered with Helen Trent, who never quite seemed to catch Gil, the man of her dreams, and we agonized over whether "our gal Sunday, a girl from a little mining town in the West," would ever "find happiness as the wife of a wealthy and titled Englishman," Lord Henry Brinthrop. On Saturday mornings I had listened religiously to Uncle Bill and the Cream of Wheat radio gang on *Let's Pretend,* carrying me to fantastic lands of make-believe, of castles and fairies and princesses and very tall bean stalks—where folks always lived happily ever after. Most of my classmates remember Ike's election—and how much safer we felt that the man who had brought us victory in Europe would be there to lead us through the perils of the Communist threat. We were inspired by JFK's election and the promise of what later became immortalized as Camelot.

In our mind's eyes, we became all of those characters: crime fighters, horsewomen, lovelorn wives, princesses, and presidents. In law school and afterward, we never lost those images—it was why and how we thought, and still think, we could do it all.

From these early threads of meaning and shared culture, each of us developed clear and uncomplicated notions of ourselves and our obligations to our family, our society, and our country. Early on, we questioned the widespread anti-Semitism, racism, and sexual stereotyping in our society that was almost taken for granted at that time. We were completely traditional and completely comfortable in the quiescent 1950s, yet we were also planning to do things with our lives that most women of our parents' generation had never done.

Those of us who attended the Seven Sisters—the seven women's colleges founded in the late nineteenth century to provide girls with an education comparable to that offered boys in the Ivy League schools—had studied more than physics and philosophy and economics. We were required to dress for dinner each night in skirts, stockings, and high heels in order to steep ourselves in the life it was assumed we would live. We wore white gloves to the mandatory weekly chapel services and to "formals"—the dances we attended with boys from Ivy League colleges (if we knew a boy willing to invite us). We dressed up for mixers, the weekend dances (cattle drives) where we were supposed to meet eligible boys, and they were supposed to find "appropriate" girls to marry.

Pearl necklaces and white gloves, which we had started wearing as children, were powerful symbols: we didn't work with our hands, and at a deeper level, we were pure, virginal.

At my school, Wellesley College, we had formal teas in the dorms at four o'clock on Tuesday and Thursday afternoons. In what has been described as "a kind of touchstone for registering the uneven evolution of attitudes toward body, race, and gender in the past half-century," we also nervously but routinely stood naked in front of the camera for the "bizarre ritual" of posture pictures. I, along with thousands of freshmen at other Ivy League schools, were required to pose nude for a supposedly scientific study to determine whether body type was predictive of personality, intelligence, moral worth, and likely success later in life.[21] Even then, posture pictures seemed strange and embarrassing, but I, and all my classmates, went through with it: by and large, we were a compliant generation. Then.

I bought Wellesley's required freshman course, Fundamentals of Movement, in which I learned how to enter a car "appropriately," without sticking my rear end in my date's face when he held the door open for me, how to place a suitcase on the overhead rack of a train or look sufficiently help-less that some man or other would leap up to assist me, how to walk with a book on my head, how to shed an overcoat gracefully, how to give my pre-sumed future husband a backrub after a hard day's work, and how to relax for twenty minutes a day even on the hard floor of the gymnasium.

In retrospect, some of that training, which seems so arcane today, has been of enormous benefit to me personally and professionally. The grace and poise I developed as a required part of my college curriculum eventually helped me remain at ease in a professional environment where I was an oddity. The relaxation techniques I learned and still use now have a more scientific name, the relaxation response, and of course they came from a thousand years of the Zen practice of meditation.

While the memory of posture pictures is amusing, and even frightening, today, the coaching on charm continues to smooth the way for me—neither I nor my female Law School classmates ever wanted to be, nor could we be, the female "bully bosses" of the eighties and nineties, who are now taking de-assertiveness training to get in touch with their feminine sides and thereby become more effective in the workplace.[22] Still, for those of us who had aspirations of achieving more than grace, charm, marriage, moth-erhood, and community involvement, it would have helped to have some practical training on how to succeed in the male world of the professions as well.

The inaugural address of Richard Glenn Gettell as president of Mount Holyoke College on Saturday November 9, 1957, the year most of us entered college, including Law School classmates Rosemary Cox, Grace Weiner, and Barbara Margulies at Mount Holyoke, captures the dual, con-fusing messages being delivered to us as young women just starting out:

> In an earlier day, woman's life was . . . considered two-phased: first, a growing-up period requiring some training, generally in the home, then an adult lifetime of homemaking, devoted and subservient to the husband and the family. This concept of the role of women is vastly outdated—particularly so for the uncommon woman. . . . Another principle has been established, though it cannot yet be said that it is as fully accepted in practice: the right of women to careers outside, or inside, of marriage. . . . Most must still do battle uphill against lingering prejudice and masculine assumptions of superiority, but notable successes have been recorded and acknowledged. The able and determined woman—the uncommon woman—can win out. . . . The prac-tices of going steady, of early marriage, and of larger families have led to an increased partnership among young men and women, a more equal sharing of

family duties, and more equal contributions to the family earnings. In most cases, except for the unmarried independent woman careerist whose life follows the masculine two-phased pattern, there is a middle phase between schooling and work, or between stages in a career, a score of years occupied primarily by homemaking. No one will deny that this is a wonderful time— vital to the individual, to the family, and to society. The fact remains that it can be followed by the third phase. . . . [We must] face squarely the fact of the middle phase in the life of most of our women graduates. We must devise means to help them keep intellectually alive during the childbearing and child-raising period when most of their time is consumed with homemaking. Another area where society can, and does in part, use the well-educated woman to good effect is in avocational and unpaid work. . . . In the world of the future, where greater leisure is predicted, we have the option of frustration, boredom, and meaningless time-killing for many able women, or a richer, fuller, more cultured life for themselves, their families, and for all of society. The uncommon woman has much to offer. If some of our institutions of higher learning can help her develop to the fullest, and if our society will learn how to make the most of her, she need no longer be underutilized.[23]

Classmate Rosemary Cox quietly rebelled against some of the obligations implied by Mount Holyoke's notion of "the uncommon woman." She was interested in intellectual things, in going on to graduate school and a career, yet, at Mount Holyoke, there was intense pressure to marry, stay home, keep the house, and raise children.

"For me, it was very complex and very troubling: I was writing my thesis, applying to law school, and surrounded by expectations that the only way to be an 'uncommon woman' was to marry, have children, and be a community volunteer. Have a family! That was the ideal. Think about the press attention Jackie Kennedy got for being this beautiful intelligent ornament, with her pillbox hat and her white gloves. We got the same confusing message at Mount Holyoke. Most of the women professors were single. So you could have a career and be single or not have a career and be married and have a family and have sex. Either way seemed barren."

Our classmate Grace Weiner also spent her freshman year at Mount Holyoke, before transferring to the University of Michigan. For her Mount Holyoke's "uncommon women" were diverse only insofar as they came from different geographic regions. Mostly, they were upper-middle-class girls from proper white families who weren't inclined to stick their necks out: "Our then mortal enemies, the Russians, launched the first [orbiting space object] *Sputnik* in the fall of 1957, which should have indicated to us that the

U.S. was far behind in the space race. It was a riveting, frightening accomplishment but I remember that the girls at Mount Holyoke hardly seemed to notice. There was a sense of total isolation there."

As Rosemary observed of that era, "At Mount Holyoke, a great deal of effort and organizing time went into acquiring social skills in order to be 'acceptable' women. But there was no campus-wide commitment to an intellectual night. There was no idea that we might get together for an evening and learn the skills of negotiating with an automobile mechanic about the price to fix our car. None of that. It didn't even cross the screen. There was a split consciousness: on the one hand there were very high expectations of achievement of the students, from wonderful, wonderful women teachers who, in those days, could never have gotten a job (because of her gender) at Harvard or Yale. On the other hand, most of the students and many in the administration seemed obsessed with virginity and with marriage."

Regardless of which college we attended, one or another of our college professors and deans imbued us with the belief that we were out of the ordinary—a somewhat elitist notion that we had been blessed with intellectual gifts and were destined to do important and difficult things while also fulfilling our traditional roles as the wives of prominent men, the mothers of accomplished children, and the pillars of our communities. Their vision of who we were helped spur our nascent rebellion against the usual expectation for women of our era: that we would ultimately play only one role in life—second fiddle.

Our shared vision of a world of dangers and heroes and patriots and ladies in white gloves confused us, but it shaped our lives and our dedication to what would become our profession. It also inspired the dreams of our male classmates.

Classmate Stephen Breyer remembers, "My parents—many of our parents—were very involved in civic life. My father was the lawyer for the school board. His life was in city government. My mother liked to work for United Nations causes or the League of Women Voters. When I graduated from college and went to Oxford on a Marshall scholarship, our country had done some pretty important things for democracy—fighting and helping win World War Two and the Korean Conflict. It was before Vietnam engulfed us and we came to question whether it was our government or the protesters who had it right. We—and by 'we' I mean our generation—were not exactly chauvinistic, but we had a tremendous pride in the United States and what the United States could accomplish. To promote democracy and good government, to help prevent war—things that perhaps now have a slightly trite tone to them, didn't to us then. They inspired us. We quietly believed in ourselves and what we could and would do to further those objectives. The atmosphere was such that we were ready to believe in the importance of the mission of the United States as a country that could spread democracy and freedom, and the importance of our helping.

"People believed that John Kennedy embodied the ideal that the country could accomplish positive steps, very concrete, to achieve the objectives of freedom and equality. We knew about all the Harvard Law faculty who had gone to Washington to work for this exciting government that was going to make things better. That just seemed like a dream. I wanted to be part of that, to be a lawyer who would make a difference. So I applied to Harvard Law School."

On January 20, 1961, our senior year in college, President Kennedy asked us what we would do for our country. We answered—to ourselves and to him—"as much as we can." As for the women in my class, each of us knew that it would be harder for us than for men our age: we would need the best possible training and the most powerful network of people to keep that promise. We—and our parents—believed, at that time, that Harvard was the best place in the United States to study law, to earn the credentials we needed, to access that most powerful of networks, and, of course, at the same time, to survey a promising field of eligible men.

So, unlike our girlfriends and sorority sisters in college, we set our caps not only for a Harvard man but for Harvard itself.

PART TWO

Law School

CHAPTER 5

Admission (1961)

Harvard University
Law School

February 28, 1961

Dear Miss Richards:

I am pleased to report that the Admissions Committee has accepted your application for admission to the Harvard Law School. This acceptance is for the class entering in September 1961 only and cannot be deferred or held over for a later year. In order to hold your place in the class, we are asking you to complete the enclosed acceptance card and return it to us with a $50 deposit and two passport sized photographs of yourself. . . . This deposit will be credited against the tuition fee for the first quarter of the school year and is not refundable unless military service should prevent you from taking your place in the entering class. . . . We are very glad that we can offer you a place in our next entering class and hope that you will let us know if you have any questions or problems.

> Sincerely,
> Louis A. Toepfer
> Director of Admissions

I was IN! And even though the form letter of acceptance hadn't been revised to account for women, I was elated and relieved. Harvard Law School was the legal equivalent of Mount Everest. It was the toughest law school in the world at that time, with a legendary faculty who prided themselves not only on their scholarship but also on their showmanship. It was an absolute meritocracy: no amount of money, no pedigree, no social connections, would make a difference in whether you were admitted, how well you did there, or how far you would go after graduation. I and the other women in the entering class had all done well in college; that, we thought, would be enough. We thought we knew what we were getting into, and that we could handle it. But we underestimated both how demanding it would be, and how much fun we would have once we figured the place out. Law school would prove to be a sharp, almost violent change from the farm clubs where we'd prepared ourselves for the big leagues in Cambridge. Our undergraduate teachers believed that learning should be rigorous but civil and had gently shepherded us into our presumed adult lives of family and community. Harvard Law School was the exact opposite. Convinced that conquering hardship was a big morale booster, our professors administered hardship evenhandedly and with a kind of precision we had never before experienced. Their questions probed into every crevasse of our minds, ferreting out the last bit of information that might be lurking there. It was, at the same time, exhilarating, terrifying, and—on a bad day—not unlike unanesthetized root-canal surgery.

Classmate Kevin Conwick, now a highly regarded sports and entertainment lawyer in Denver, Colorado, had four years in the U.S. Marine Corps under his belt when he entered Harvard Law School in September 1961. He remembers his initial law school struggles: "First year was more frightening than boot camp and more humbling than officers' training school."

Calvin Trillin described the Law School of that era as "a high-pressure manufacturer of high-powered lawyers—a place where students were happy only in the sense that some Parris Island recruits found cheer in contemplating which of their number might collapse on the obstacle course in a particularly spectacular way."[1]

The Law School promised to teach us to "think like lawyers." By the second day, most of the women students understood that we had a much more urgent challenge: survival in a demanding, quintessentially male academic boot camp. Everybody was smart—the proverbial cream of the cream—so previous academic achievement and sheer brainpower weren't going to carry us through. We needed to hone our psychological IQs as well: to develop our confidence, resourcefulness, and thick skins while struggling to maintain our ingrained irreverence and sense of humor. We had a few other advantages as well: at least our mothers thought we were attractive— well, not unattractive; we liked to flirt at a time when flirtation was an art and not sexual harassment; and perhaps unexpectedly, most of us knew how to cook and were pretty good at it.

There is no question that there was intense pressure and, not infrequently, public humiliation at the hands of the professors, and that both were applied to men and women alike. (If anything, they went a little easier on the women.) But there is another side. Harvard Law School in the early sixties had probably the greatest collection of legal scholars and thinkers ever assembled in one place in the history of legal education. It was, in the words of Arthur Sutherland, our teacher and the official Law School historian of that time, one of the school's "golden eras." Our professors not only taught the law but also wrote and rewrote it, in Restatements of the Law, in federal and state legislation. They were also extraordinary performers, with the timing and delivery of stand-up comics. Our classmates—a collection of overachievers who included Rhodes, Marshall, and Fulbright scholars; an Olympic gold medalist; football captains; professional actors and musicians; published authors; and helicopter pilots who'd already served as "military advisers" in Vietnam—were not only brilliant but creative, mischievous, irreverent, and destined to do great things. Students who learned to play the game with the teachers, and who gave as good as they got, found the place exhilarating. The sound I remember most from classes is laughter.

It would turn out to be one of the hardest—and one of the best—times of our lives. Our class, the class of 1964, would become one of the most accomplished ever, with most of the women of the class eventually reaching the first ranks in the private practice of law, the judiciary, politics, the academy, and the professions. In his 1992 memoir, *Ould Fields, New Corne,* Dean Erwin Griswold named six women graduates of Harvard Law School who "have had distinguished records," three of whom were in the class of 1964: Pat Schroeder, Judith W. Rogers, and me. A fourth, Elizabeth Dole, almost entered with us, but decided to begin a year later, graduating with the class of 1965.[2]

CHAPTER 6

Arrival

The fifteen women who ultimately graduated with the class of 1964 first met on a muggy Saturday afternoon in early September 1961 when we arrived in Cambridge to register for classes. It wasn't hard to spot each other: there were only a handful of us among the 560 or so boys waiting in line.

My first stop was Wyeth Hall, the gloomy women's dormitory for Harvard's education school, law school, and Ph.D. candidates, where I dropped my gear before heading over to the Law School quadrangle to register. The first impression was not encouraging: Wyeth's windows were small and grimy, its floors dark and dull. What was worse, all the walls and ceilings were painted a glaring orange enamel, the least restful, most dismal color imaginable. It was probably somebody's idea of brightening the place up.

Housing women law students had been a problem for the Law School from the time they first decided to admit us. The 1949 "Report of the Committee on the Admission of Women" touched on the issue but brushed it aside: "The Committee realizes that it will be impossible for the University to provide housing, and medical and athletic facilities to women students. Yet the Committee believes that if women applicants are made aware in advance that they are largely on their own in Cambridge, the problem will not be serious."[3]

Eleven years later, it was only a little better: there were still so few of us that devoting an entire dormitory to women law students was out of the question. Nor could we live in the regular law school dormitories: the same number of male students were enrolled as before, there were no vacancies, and even if there had been, coed campus housing was unthought of and unthinkable in the early 1960s.

We were assigned to three-room, one-bath suites in Wyeth Hall. My room, on the third floor, had one window, which looked out on an alley and another building a few feet away. Our suite was down the hall from a tiny kitchenette with a two-burner stove and a small refrigerator. My new suite-

32

mates, Arlene Lezberg, from Radcliffe, and Marge Freincle, from Brooklyn College, were both entering law students.

Despite the grim decor and isolation from the rest of the law students, our assignment to Wyeth Hall turned out to be a lucky break. Most of us had felt out of step, a little odd, in college: we wanted professional lives, as well as husbands, and were focused on learning and getting good grades. By contrast, the vast majority of our female college classmates had marriage as their primary goal: they felt they had failed if they didn't have their diamond engagement ring by Christmas of their senior year.

In law school our professional dreams were normal and we didn't try to hide our intelligence, ambition, and competitiveness in order to lull some boy into a false sense of superiority. From the very beginning, I and the women in my class developed our own network, relying on each other for academic and personal help. Unlike many of our male counterparts at the Law School, we were not ferociously competitive with each other. We backed each other, shared our class notes, and exchanged course outlines. Women from the classes ahead of us, including Janet Reno (later Attorney General of the United States), Jeannine Jacobs, and Marie Driscoll, coached us on the professors' techniques, classroom recitation, and how to handle those professors and male classmates who were openly antagonistic to women in the Law School. They advised us that we possessed a certain distraction quotient, that our femininity could be a big advantage if we knew how to play it. We talked about cases and strategies while we cooked together in our tiny kitchens. We complained to each other about the appalling decor. Nobody dared to do anything about that until the next year when Olivia Barclay (now Washington, D.C., financial adviser and general contractor Olivia Barclay Jones) from California showed up. She immediately repainted her walls light blue and her ceiling white. Over the Thanksgiving holiday, the Law School repainted the entire room bright orange and billed her for it. She never paid the bill: "So sue me."

In Wyeth, and in our usual meeting place, the ladies' room in the building that housed the cafeteria, Harkness Commons, we could share our dreams for big careers without threatening the egos of the male students we were dating. We could talk to each other about having a family, without confirming the conventional wisdom that we would soon give up the law to stay home to raise our children. At law school, we were a female bubble on an ocean of testosterone, but in Wyeth Hall and the Harkness Commons' ladies' room, we were a critical mass of women figuring out

Olivia Barclay

how to deal both with an unfamiliar arena and with our more traditional roles as women. It was the beginning of our alliance, our old-girl network, that still exists today.

After I had introduced myself and gotten acquainted with my new room-mates, Arlene and Marge, and unpacked my books, I changed into a skirt, blazer, pearls, and high heels to make what I thought was the right first impression and headed over to the Law School to pick up my schedule and receive my first assignments—due to be completed, I discovered, by the time classes began, 8 A.M. the following Monday. I took my place in the seemingly endless line of overdressed law students waiting to register for classes. Dark oil paintings of stern men in black robes, and, often, white-powdered wigs, peered down from the walls, appearing to transmit their dis-approval of any female presence in that male bastion. "Okay!" I thought. "I'm gonna show 'em."

Registration that Saturday was something of an ordeal, as classmate Rosemary Cox noted at the time: "Mobs and mobs of boys, all talking at the top of their lungs. Upper classmen thrusting various documents and peti-tions and money requests at you."[4]

Even though it was hot and there was no air-conditioning, most of the boys wore ties and the pinstripe suits their parents had bought them for law school. The more confident boys wore sport jackets and khakis. They were in training for a profession and had decided to dress the part from the very first day. The girls wore dresses or skirts and blouses, pearl necklaces, nylon stockings, and high-heeled shoes. Except for Pat Scott, who, to the concern of many, showed up in shorts.

First-year law students register for classes, September 1961

CHAPTER 7

Classmates

I liked applicants with spirit and a sense of
adventure and a little boldness. I was dealing
a lot with paper people. So, when somebody
broke the mold and stood out, that was fine.
The women who applied in the early sixties
were like that. And I would say: "Look at her.
She's something. We ought to pick her." We
started with a lot of wonderful raw material.
You couldn't go wrong.

—Harvard Law School Vice Dean
and Director of Admissions Louis Toepfer,
personal interview with the author,
August 9, 1999

Patricia Nell Scott (University of Minnesota)

Pat arrived in Cambridge in early September 1961 driving
the bright aqua Lincoln Continental she had bought herself with the money left over from working her way
through the University of Minnesota. She was a breath of
fresh air from the Midwest and she dressed the part: "I
wore Bermuda shorts and knee-highs and a cotton
sweater tied over my shoulders. I remember when I
walked to the library to study—Langdell Hall, with all

those huge pillars running the length of the building—several people came
up to me and told me that I was not dressed properly for the most prestigious law library in the country. After the fourth student talked to me
sternly about my wardrobe, I said to myself, 'Who *are* these people?' There
was no dress code for studying in the library as far as I knew."

Pat, the older of the two Scott children, was born in Portland, Oregon, on July 30, 1940. Her mother, Bernice, was a schoolteacher; her father, a pilot who ran a private airport and flying school. When the United States entered World War II in December 1941, the federal government immediately nationalized his airport and called him up to military service to train pilots. Pat's family moved out of Portland and became vagabonds. They lived wherever the government sent them—the East Coast, the Midwest, and the West.

After the war ended, the Scotts moved to Hamilton, Ohio, living there from 1948 to 1955. Pat's dad had been devastated by the Great Depression, and made sure his children learned its lessons. When Pat was in the second grade, he started teaching her to be independent. He gave her $150 a month to manage; with it, she was required to support herself totally (except for rent), paying for her lunches, clothes, music lessons, and whatever else she needed out of her stipend. She learned fast that if she spent it all at the beginning, she didn't eat lunch for a month.

Pat's dad took her across the Ohio River into Kentucky to the gambling places, even though gambling was illegal there. He wanted her to see and experience everything. (My dad did the same thing with me, taking me from Cincinnati to show me the gambling parlors at the Lookout House in Kentucky, although I was only four years old.) As soon as Pat's feet could reach the pedals in a small propeller aircraft, her dad taught her to fly, coaching her on how to take care of herself in the air as well as on the ground. She got her pilot's license when she was fifteen, a year before she was allowed to drive a car. After graduating from high school, Pat worked her way through the University of Minnesota, graduating in three years at the top of her class. She was twenty years old.

Pat paid for college by using her pilot's license and renting the University's planes (which were owned by the U.S. government for ROTC) in order to do work for an insurance company. The University wouldn't let her fly the planes free: she wasn't male or in ROTC, so she didn't meet federal regulations. But they finally agreed that she could rent their airplanes for $10 an hour. She talked her way into a job adjusting aviation losses for an insurance company in Minneapolis: "When there was a crash, I would fly to the scene, investigate, write a report, and be back in the library in a couple of hours. . . . I made so much money in college that I not only paid all my way, but I was also driving a Lincoln I bought myself. I probably made more money on a pro rata basis, comparatively, than I do now. I was magna cum laude, I was Phi Beta Kappa, I was in a sorority, I was in the Student Senate. I was going a hundred miles an hour. I did it all. I had a wonderful time."

Pat wanted to go to graduate school, but hadn't decided exactly what to do when she "grew up." She was living fast, which left little time for reflection: "My father always said that if I took all my ammunition and went one way, I could be a rocket instead of a sparkler—trying everything. Which was probably true. But I always thought I was much broader than just being a 'rocket,' whatever that was."

In deciding on graduate training, Pat knew she wanted something broad-based: she had already been talked out of being an aeronautical engineer and had briefly thought of medicine, but decided it was fairly narrow. She finally decided that if she were a lawyer, she could be in business or teach, or even go into politics: "Frankly, I just didn't think about how I'd use law. I just wanted to do something and go to the best place I could."

Her adviser at the University of Minnesota urged her on—she had good grades, good test scores, and impressive leadership positions in student government. Because of her vagabond roots, she decided that she should go to Harvard, a national law school.

There was probably another, subconscious reason: by going to Harvard she could realize an unfulfilled ambition of her dad's. Growing up in the dust bowl of western Nebraska in the late 1920s and early 1930s, Pat's father had spent his summers painting schoolhouses and saving every penny for what he hoped would be college at Harvard. In 1931, the bank where he'd deposited all his savings went broke. He ended up at the University of Nebraska, painting schoolhouses again, working his way through.

Knowing how bitter her dad still was about losing both his money and his dream, Pat didn't tell her family that she had chosen law and applied to Harvard until she was about to leave for Cambridge.

"When I told Dad I was going to Harvard Law School, he was partially proud and partially frightened: 'What will this do to your younger brother?'" He was worried about the pressure that Pat's success would put on her brother, who also felt a responsibility to make up for the hardships their dad had experienced. Pat's mother had different concerns: "My mother said, 'Oh, my gosh! Why do you want to do this? Why don't you want to be a teacher or a nurse? Who's going to marry somebody that goes to Harvard Law School?' She had always been supportive, but she was not really sure this particular decision was so great . . . law school was bad enough, but Harvard Law School was a geek alert!"

Pat was actually a little worried about that herself, and about why she seemed so out of step with her sorority sisters at the University of Minnesota. "There was no question that my sisters were talking about 'Oh, my gosh, you gotta get married.' It was a cultural thing. So I started to go that route. I got pinned when I was in my third and last year in college. It was the scariest damn thing that ever happened during my three years at the University of Minnesota. All of a sudden I looked up and this whole fraternity was over at my sorority house serenading the house and bringing me roses. That was it! I was like 'Oh, my God! What is this about? What have I done?' It didn't last long. . . . It was the proverbial bell jar over my head. I was such a free agent, socially and personally, at the University of Minnesota. Among other things, I had been elected to the Student Senate. I was dealing with visiting politicians. I was involved in some of the huge fights we got into with the Minnesota legislature over funding the University, and over free speech at the University. So there I was—a grown-up. I was going through in three years because, since I was paying for it myself, I was really motivated to take a lot of classes and get through as fast as I could. I was flying airplanes. I had my own luxury car that I bought with my own money. I was dealing with constitutional and international issues, and nationally known politicians like Al Lowenstein and Hubert Humphrey. The University of Minnesota never had that pompous attitude I think a lot of other people in our class had to deal with at their universities. . . . My university didn't have curfews for women, or special visiting rules for men. They treated us like adults."

The change from the freewheeling, independent life Pat had lived in college, to the constrained life of rules and restrictions and requirements at law school, was a shock. Pat felt as if she had put herself in a straitjacket.

The first contact Pat had with Harvard after she was admitted was a battle over signing a surety bond, which started even before she arrived in Cambridge. The law school's finance office sent her a tuition guarantee form, which was like a bond. She signed it and sent it back. They wrote her right back: "This is not permitted. You can't sign it. It must be signed by a parent or guardian, guaranteeing your tuition, board, and room." Pat replied: "My parents aren't going to sign it. They haven't paid my tuition ever. I have always paid my tuition. What do you mean?" It became a huge issue, with letters flying back and forth for weeks. When Pat went to Cambridge for orientation before school started, she went to see the people in the finance office: "They treated me like some kind of a dummy. The tone of it was, 'How could you even be showing up for law school if you couldn't read that document accurately and realize that you weren't supposed to sign your own surety bond?' It wasn't that I didn't understand what the words said. It was that I didn't know anyone I was going to get to sign it. Harvard kept saying, 'No, no, no—don't you understand? You can't. You're only twenty. Not old enough to be bound. You are going to law school and you don't understand that? If your parents won't sign it, some other adult will have to.'"

Pat finally went to the top, Dean Griswold. He told her she couldn't start unless some "adult" signed for her. She responded directly, "You're not going to let me in? Your people know I worked my way through college. . . . I've got the money, you know. Why can't I guarantee my own tuition? No way are my parents going to sign my surety bond. If you won't take my signature, I'll not be able to come here. I'll just have to go somewhere else."

The dean finally relented. Pat signed her own bond, moved into Wyeth Hall, and donned her Bermuda shorts for registration and the first day of classes. "Everybody was dressed up and seemed out to get you. When I showed up at my first class and realized everybody had to sit in assigned seats, I was stunned. There was no such concept at Minnesota. At Harvard there were so many more restrictions, and they were much more visible, especially for young women. Harvard Law School was a real shock to me—it was uptight and in many ways it treated the students like children who needed to be threatened in order to get them to obey, and to be harshly punished if they didn't."

Aurelle Joyce Smoot (Washington State University)

Pat's suitemate our first year was Aurelle Smoot, a tall, brainy, somewhat shy girl who'd grown up in Moses Lake, Washington, and graduated with high distinction from Washington State University.

Judith Coleman Richards (Wellesley)

I had graduated from Wellesley, but I came from Defiance. I was looking for a way to follow my mother's career in public service and to avenge my preacher father, who had unfairly lost a legal battle with a Methodist bishop and ended up in ecclesiastical Siberia.

As my friend and Law School classmate Dinni (Lorenz) Gordon recalls, "You were this willowy, demure, very pretty blonde from the Middle West. When I got to know you, I realized that underneath all of that you had a will of iron."

My first-year suitemate Marge Freincle remembers another side of me: "I remember you going out on dates with all of the Harvard guys and various others as well . . . debating over which of several men you felt like going out with at a particular time. . . . And I was just kind of saying to myself, 'I can't deal with this.'"

My father, Joseph Coleman Richards, was born in 1905 in the front room of a parsonage in Mt. Victory, Ohio. His father, Joseph Joy Richards, was a fire-and-brimstone Welsh preacher; his mother, Clara Coleman Richards, an orphan who nevertheless managed to graduate from college at the close of the nineteenth century, was the first woman elected to Phi Beta Kappa at the University of Michigan. When my father was eighteen, he hitchhiked to Boston and signed up for Boston University. By the time he was nineteen, his oratorical ability and exceptional singing voice had won him a job as the winter minister in the fancy summer resort town of Dublin, New Hampshire. Although Papa eventually earned five degrees in the arts and theology from Boston University and Harvard Divinity School, he had hoped to be an opera singer. He abandoned that dream when his mother became ill, returning to Ohio to care for her and taking a job as a preacher in a rural parish. His first sermon, "The Seven Illusionistic Theories of the Origins of Religions," was definitely not well received. One farmer who had suffered through Papa's thirty-minute exegesis told him, "Reverend Richards, if you're going to get along here, you have to put the fodder where both a giraffe and a jackass can reach it."

It was a piece of down-home advice that would stick with me throughout law school and my career as a trial lawyer.

My mother, Eve, was the oldest girl in a Worcester, Massachusetts, family of eleven children. Her father owned a dairy; her mother, an orphan, cared for her children and took in sewing to help pay the bills. When Mama was sixteen, she borrowed $6,000 from a local banker and enrolled in Boston University. She promised to work for him in the summers and after graduation until the loan (with interest) was entirely repaid.

The very next year, her father's dairy business went under. He took the only job he could find, night watchman at a local factory, but it didn't provide enough money. Observing the family's troubles, the banker called in Mama's loan; she left college and went home to work for him to pay him back and to help support her nine remaining brothers and sisters. As soon as her younger siblings were old enough to go to work to help support the family, she returned to school, eventually earning her bachelor's degree, Phi Beta Kappa and summa cum laude, and, later, her master's in social work from Smith College. After she and my father were married in 1933, at the depth of the Depression, she followed him from parish to parish in Ohio, working as a psychiatric social worker and an administrator of courts of domestic relations.

I was born November 30, 1940, in Cincinnati, Ohio, my parents' only child. They gave me my father's initials, JCR, and the first name Judith, after the courageous protectress of Israel in the Old Testament. She beguiled the commander of the Assyrian forces and, when he fell asleep, cut off his head, thereby saving her nation. As I grew up, my father told me this story and its moral many times: even when evil appears to be overwhelming, the power of God, acting through a woman, will destroy the evil forces.

When I was twenty-two months old, my parents enrolled me in what was then highly experimental: the University of Cincinnati Nursery School, run by the renowned child psychologist Dr. Ada Arlitt. The school, which was on the top floor of a tall brick building, had an outdoor terrace that we used as a playground. There was a rectangular jungle gym made of iron pipes, broad at the bottom and narrowing to a single square at the very top. My sharpest memory of nursery school is that, from the very first day, I wanted to be in that top square. From the age of three on, I owned that square. I liked being at the top. I don't recall that I ever thought about whether it was lonely.

In 1945, when I was four and a half, Bishop Smith transferred my father from Cincinnati to a troubled Methodist church in Defiance, Ohio. My mother quit work to take care of me and be the proverbial good preacher's wife, teaching Sunday school and helping my dad straighten out the ecclesiastical mess he had walked into. I grew up in Defiance in more ways than one. I learned that my manners and demeanor had a direct effect on how much the congregation put into the collection plate—and therefore on how much my father earned. I learned that most people can be kind and caring and gentle, but that some people, especially those in positions of authority, can be ruthless and without conscience.

My mother taught me to knit, garden, cook, dance, and write. She was also a master dressmaker, having made the clothes for her ten brothers and sisters as well as herself. She helped me to design and make most of my own clothes with beautiful but inexpensive "mill end" yardage. The summer before I started law school, Mama spent every night after work designing and sewing a new wardrobe for her only child to wear in law school. My father taught me to sing, hunt, and when the parishioners weren't looking, to pick winners at the horse races to earn extra money, and, at the risk of losing it all back to him, to play cards very well. In the summer of 1961, when I wasn't helping Mama sew my law school wardrobe, I was at the horse races with Papa, earning the money I'd need to get through Harvard.

Both of my parents insisted that I learn to speak in public, coaching me again and again in winning area oratorical contests and giving me an essential skill that I still rely on as a trial lawyer. By the time I was twelve, I was also earning money pulling weeds, shoveling snow for neighbors, and steaming coats in the town's dry-cleaning plant. It didn't take me long to figure out that I didn't want to spend my life that way.

At about that time, my father got into a horrendous legal battle with the newly elected bishop of Ohio, and I decided to be a lawyer. Papa and his brother, Bashford, a minister and head of the Methodist hospital in Columbus, had backed the losing candidate for bishop. The victor, Hazen Werner, in his own "Christian" way, retaliated: he accused my uncle Bashford with using hospital workers to renovate his personal residence and fired him. Bashford sued the bishop for defamation, seeking reinstatement and $500,000 in damages. Bishop Werner counterclaimed for defamation, but more important, as far as my life was concerned, vowed vengeance on our whole family. Among other things, he ordered my father to move to a tiny, impoverished parish on the Kentucky border. The parishioners in Defiance wanted Papa to stay: they withdrew from the Ohio Conference, incorporated the Defiance church, and signed Papa to a five-year employment contract. The Conference immediately filed suit against the church's board, seeking to gain control over the church property (and the bank accounts, which, thanks to my dad's preaching and music, were quite substantial).

What started as a political fight over the election of a bishop became a constitutional church-versus-state confrontation played out in the Defiance County Court of Common Pleas and on the front pages of the Defiance *Crescent News* as well as newspapers throughout Ohio. Under the cover—and more to the point, the immunities—of the lawsuit, the court pleadings charged my uncle and my father with baby racketeering in connection with private adoptions they had arranged through Bashford's hospital—without any fees except for payment of the mother's hospital expenses. The lawsuit sought to have both of them not only defrocked but also indicted. An "anonymous" tip to the IRS alleging tax fraud by my parents brought federal auditors to the parsonage. Ultimately an investigation by the Ohio attorney general's office completely exonerated both my father and my uncle, but the damage to our family's reputation had been done. The local church lost; the court ruled it was under the total control of the bishop and the Ohio Conference. Papa resigned from the Ohio Methodist Conference and we moved out of the parsonage over a weekend, with all our worldly possessions heaped into a rusted-out red pickup truck. With a little money down and a mountain of debt, we bought the dry-cleaning plant where I had been working. My father, mother, and I all went to work there to rebuild our lives and our family's empty bank account.

To protect me from the nasty publicity during the height of the legal battle, my parents somehow scraped together the $500 it took to send me to the National Music Camp at Interlochen, Michigan, for eight weeks in the summer. There I honed my piano skills, sang in oratorios, acted in plays, swam competitively in the lake, and—at night—thought about how I could fight the establishment and avenge my family. That fall, I found the way.

In my eighth-grade class at Defiance Junior High, the boys were required to take shop—carpentry and auto mechanics—and the girls, home economics—cooking and sewing—all the skills the school believed we would need after graduation. To help us decide what else we might do when we grew up, the school held a Career Day every fall at which adults from the town came to describe their jobs. Afterward, we were asked to pick our future occupation, if any, and then to plan our high school courses accordingly. In my homeroom, Mr. Peters, my geography teacher, handed out two sign-up sheets: the girls' sheet offered the choices home economist, nurse, teacher, bookkeeper, secretary, beautician, receptionist, cook, and waitress. The boys' sheet offered farmer, carpenter, auto mechanic, pharmacist, policeman, fireman, engineer, doctor, lawyer, and banker.

What I saw on the girls' list didn't appeal to me, and I asked to sign up on the boys' sheet. Mr. Peters said, "It's not allowed. School policy." In what turned out to be my first successful oral argument, I was given permission to appeal the "policy" to the principal, Franklin Blue. After what seemed to me to be an interminable argument between Mr. Blue and the county superintendent of schools, Claude Hinkle, they compromised: I could choose two speakers from the boys' list. I chose the doctor and the lawyer. I was still required to pick four from the girls' list.

Karl Weaner, one of the two lawyers in town, said that law was a way to help people and to fight for what was fair and right. It sounded good: I knew firsthand that there weren't enough people fighting for fairness. That night, I told my parents, "I'm going to be a lawyer." The earth did not quake. The flowers did not wilt. They just said, "Let's talk about it at dinner, *after* you've practiced your piano." Their treating as ordinary what, in 1953, was their daughter's out-of-the-ordinary ambition was one of the luckiest things that ever happened. If they had said, "Girls can't be lawyers," I would probably have given up right then.

At dinner, both my parents said they would back me to the hilt. My dad said lawyering was a lot like cards and hunting: "Law is scholarly, tricky, competitive, intuitive . . . things you're already good at." Then he asked, as he often did, "Would you like to bet a little something on whether you'll really do it?"

"All right," I said, "how about a new car, a Ford Thunderbird, with the lift-off top and the tiny round windows on each side? Dark blue. With a red steering wheel, and white upholstery." It was the biggest thing I could think of.

"Well, for a bet that big, you'd better pick a law school, too, and your year of graduation."

"Harvard." I didn't know that the first class to include women had just graduated from Harvard Law School in June of that year. "And I'll graduate in 1964."

We shook hands. We wrote the bet down, as we always did, and signed the paper. My mother signed as the witness. It was my first contract. Later that night, my mother pulled me aside to tell me that 1964 was too soon: five years to finish high school, four years of college, and three of law school was twelve years—making the date 1965. I looked at the contract: "1964" was in ink and underlined. "What am I going to do, Mama?"

I knew, without any question, that if I didn't graduate from Harvard Law in 1964, I would have to buy my father that sports car. (Every time he beat me at canasta or gin rummy—and he generally did, and does—I always had to pay.)

She said simply, "We'll work it out." She set up a meeting at the high school with Principal Franklin Blue and asked that I be allowed to take extra courses so that I could skip my junior year and graduate in 1957. She was soft-spoken, persuasive, and determined. And she smiled a lot. Although he was generally a stickler for the rules, Blue agreed. Watching my mother charm him, I also learned how irresistible a smart woman can be, especially when she doesn't forget she's a woman.

When I left for Wellesley College at age sixteen, my mother went to work as the supervisor of the Lucas County Court of Domestic Relations in Toledo, Ohio, commuting 120 miles a day to help pay for my college. My parents had refused any financial aid for me—they thought they could "manage" the costs somehow, and they didn't want me to graduate owing a lot of money as they had. After a rugged first year, during which my highest grade was C+, I pulled up my stockings, dug in, and managed to graduate as a Durant Scholar, Wellesley's highest academic ranking. I was the first person—male or female—to go to Harvard from Defiance and the only Wellesley grad to go on to Harvard Law School in 1961.

My parents had always backed me and had been dedicated to letting me follow my own lights. My father's determination that, as he often said, I not grow up to be a "scrubwoman" came from his observations of the limited role women were too often required to play. As he looked back on how he had come to that view, he told me:

"I came to believe that every woman and particularly my own daughter should have a life where she would get the respect and the honor she deserved. Cook if she wanted, but not because of the words of a marriage ceremony, or by signing a certificate that she would have, from then on, to be a housemaid. I decided that if I ever got a chance to hit that thing, I was going to hit it hard. You were not going the route of most women who were cleaners and moppers, someone you hand a Bissell sweeper or a dust rag or cedar polish to. Nobody was going to make a typical hands-and-knees scrubber out of my little girl. I decided that I would move heaven and earth to see to it that you had every opportunity to become a distinguished, distinctive, free human being with the kind of attention that most men seemed then to get just as their natural inheritance."

The first woman I met while waiting in line at Austin Hall to register for law school was Diana "Dinni" Russell Lorenz. She was standing with a guy named Jim Lorenz. When I said how amazing I thought it was that a brother and sister were starting law school at the same time, she laughed and corrected me, "Jim and I are married." I was startled that Jim seemed so comfortable that his wife was attending law school with him, and I was even more surprised that she seemed unconcerned about what I thought would inevitably be ferocious competition with her husband. In that era, Harvard ranked every law student by grade point average, top to bottom, at the end of each year. The results were posted on the central bulletin board in Langdell Hall, and on the bulletin boards in every dorm, for all to see. Most of us still recall with precision the top students in our class, and their exact class standing. I remember thinking that Dinni was taking a big chance: outshining her husband was definitely not a recipe for a long and happy marriage.

I was relieved to learn that, like me, Jim was from Ohio. At least Ohio would be a small patch of common ground in that foreign law school environment. Jim had finished in the "senior sixteen," the top of the top of his Harvard College class, been elected to Phi Beta Kappa, and had given the English oration at commencement. Seventeen percent of our class had graduated from Harvard. Jim knew most of them and promised to introduce me around. I was grateful: other than the two of them, and my new roommates, Arlene and Marge, whom I'd just met at Wyeth Hall, I didn't know anyone in my class.

From the moment I met Dinni and Jim, I liked them for almost exactly the same reasons that they scared me. They were smart and articulate. They seemed to know exactly why they were at law school and what they wanted to do in life: they were going to use the law for nothing less than the reform of the American political system. Jim would be elected president of the United States; Dinni would craft an egalitarian political agenda, help write his speeches, and entertain the women voters at tea.

Their apparent confidence about their ability to handle Harvard Law and life afterward tied a few knots in my stomach. Even though I'd done well at Wellesley, my LSAT scores put me in the seventy-fifth percentile nationwide. In fact, when the director of admissions, Louis Toepfer, phoned me to tell me I had been admitted, he warned me about my likely performance at law school: "Congratulations. We're going to admit you. But you should know that if you manage to make it through, you'll probably end up at the very bottom of your class."

I didn't know then that he had invented the LSAT not too long before, or that he was mostly just curious to see how good a predictor LSAT scores were.

As I stood in line, chatting with Dinni and Jim while observing the well-dressed eager beavers all around me, I wondered for the first time whether I could survive even the first year. I was a preacher's kid from Defiance. My mother and I had made the madras plaid suit I was wearing, and our family had one car, an old Chevrolet with a hole in the floorboard under the clutch. After my junior high and high school stint working in the dry-cleaning plant, I had found easier and much more profitable ways to help pay my way in college: modeling fashions for department stores and New England's wholesale knitting mills, and serving as a manufacturer's representative for sterling and crystal companies wanting to tap into the huge pool of priviledged young women on the Wellesley campus who were determined to get married as soon as they graduated and furnish their new homes with the best flatware, dishes, and goblets. I was still very much a calico girl, not a velvet girl. I knew nobody at Harvard Law School, I had never been west of the Rockies or outside of the United States except to Ontario, and I had nothing to fall back on if I failed. This was the major leagues, and I was still on the farm.

Diana "Dinni" Lorenz (Mills College)

Dinni was born in Williamstown, Massachusetts, in 1938, the oldest child of a noted Shakespeare professor at Williams College and his Vassar-educated, stay-at-home wife, who had retired from music and piano teaching when Dinni was born. From her earliest years, Dinni's father encouraged her to be interested in intellectual things, support that her mother opposed and felt threat-ened by. Dinni's impression was that her mother respected her and eventually was proud of her but never really liked her.

Dinni's mother played the subordinate, supportive role in their family, and Dinni became committed to never having that happen to her: "As I was growing up and for a long time afterward, I found my mother kind of boring and not too smart, but I was wrong about that. She had to take a lot of shit as this sort of dependent partner. I grew up being really neurotically determined to be financially independent."

When Dinni was eleven years old, her dad was named dean of the humanities at Cal Tech, and the family moved to Pasadena, California. She started out at the toniest private school there, Polytechnic, or "Poly" for short, a school for the children of Pasadena's upper crust—the fabulously wealthy and socially prominent oil and real estate barons who had built Los Angeles during the first half of the twentieth century. At Poly and in Pasadena, Dinni, the academic brat, got her first political consciousness. "I was a kid from a liberal Democratic family in a sea of Republican business and oil people. This was 1949 and I was there until 1953. The voter registration in Pasadena was something like 68 percent Republican. I remember very vividly standing on the street corner about the age of fourteen, in 1952, handing out 'Stevenson for President' flyers and getting a sense of the disparity between the lives and attitudes of the Republicans who made up most of the city and my family, who were liberal Democrats and drove a clunky old Plymouth. I think that sense of politics and an interest in the politics of the little guy was part of what made me ultimately think I wanted to be a lawyer."

By the time she was a teenager, Dinni had discovered the American Civil Liberties Union (ACLU), and thought, "Boy, to be a lawyer for the ACLU would be a great thing. But I had no idea of what a lawyer did."

Dinni's father believed in the liberal ideal, liberal not in an economic sense but in a social sense, and his favorite child, Dinni, absorbed that. She remembers, for instance, President Nixon's "respectable Republican cloth coat" speech and telling her father how corny she thought it was. He thought her analysis was exactly right: "Of course, that conveyed to me approval of me and that set of political attitudes. I was close to my father, and his approval meant a lot to me."

Because she was near the top of her class at Poly, she was one of four or five of the ninth-grade graduates chosen to give a short valedictory speech. "I wrote a little speech about the right to vote. I said that, in the South, Negroes, as we called them then, are often prevented by force from voting. They are beaten and stabbed if they want to go vote. My eighth-grade English teacher was the editor for our little speeches, and he wouldn't let me use that sentence. I went home and told my father. I expected him to go down to the school and stand up for me but he didn't. He caved. . . . He was trying to protect me. He didn't want me to be the target of what he thought would happen to me if I didn't delete that sentence. It was a very important moment for separating myself from my father, for declaring my own political commitments."

After Poly, most of the students went off to boarding school in the East or to Westridge, an upper-crust private girls' school in Pasadena. Dinni rebelled, and in 1953, she entered McKinley, the local public high school. It was in the poor part of Pasadena, which had a tiny enclave of middle-class houses where Dinni's family lived. The school was about one-third Mexican—some were Mexican American—one-third black, and one-third white. "I got a great deal out of that year because I saw something, an awesome thing, about how people lived who had less than I did. My family was not wealthy by any means, but these were desperately poor urban kids."

Early on, Dinni became friends with a boy named Kennedy in her Latin class—they were the two best students in that class. At a school party, he asked Dinni to dance. "I was delighted. It wasn't any big deal; it wasn't any sexual thing. It was just a guy who I thought was nice and attractive and very good at Latin and who happened to be black. We must have been dancing ninety seconds when one of the male chaperons—he was a coach of some sort—came up and separated us. I don't remember what he said, but he was absolutely clear—he didn't say, 'You can't dance with a white girl or with a Negro boy,' but he said something, and I knew exactly what the issue was. Both of us knew. I remember we both sort of looked down and looked away and were suddenly self-conscious."

Dinni was horrified and decided to try to change the school's policy. She went home, told her father what had happened, and demanded that he do something about it. He told her that, wrong as it was, nothing could be done without making a tremendous issue of it. "For my father to have gone down to the school and said, 'Knock it off!' would have been unheard of in those days. But he was very sympathetic, very supportive. He said, 'You're right to be offended. It is a terrible injustice to both of you. I am proud that you didn't think about this when this young man asked you to dance.'"

A few months later, the United States Supreme Court struck down school segregation in *Brown vs. Board of Education*. Dinni began to understand the power of our legal system to effect changes in our society.

After finishing the tenth grade at McKinley High, Dinni went straight to Mills College, an all-girls college in Oakland, California. The summer after her junior year in college, Dinni went to Europe on the Experiment in International Living and met her future husband, Jim, on the steamship going over. "Jim was a scion of the kind of American power that went to Harvard and then went on to rule the world. He wanted to be president. When he asked me to marry him, I remember that I said to him sort of bleakly, 'Am I going to have to darn your socks?' And he said, 'Of course not. When I get a hole in my sock, I throw it away.' That had never occurred in my family. It was a symbol of the economic and social divide between us."

After they married, Dinni went back to school, earned a master of arts degree in teaching from Radcliffe, and began teaching English literature at Concord Academy, a private prep school near Boston. During her first year of teaching, she decided to study law and applied to Harvard. She was put on the waiting list. Faced with the choice of giving up her job and taking a chance that the waiting list would be tapped, or teaching another year, she decided to teach and reapply. The next year, she telephoned the Law School admissions office and asked for an interview. They turned her down, telling her they didn't grant any interviews, and that they based their decisions solely "on the numbers"—grades and LSAT scores. But Dinni didn't give up and finally got an appointment with the dean of admissions, Louis Toepfer:

"I don't remember anything about the interview except that he mentioned my LSAT scores, which I was quite proud of. I was in the ninety-second percentile and I thought that would be fine. But he said, 'Based on your LSAT score, if you were to come here, you will probably be in the bottom quartile of the class.' I was just devastated. . . . I left thinking, 'Well, I can forget about law school.'" (Dinni didn't know then that, based on my LSAT results, in the seventy-fifth percentile, the dean had predicted that I would finish at the bottom of the class.) Dinni took the LSAT again and got exactly the same score. "I was quite surprised when I was admitted. I thought, 'Well, whadda ya know? Persistence pays.'"

Ann Dudley Cronkhite (Radcliffe)

While we were standing in line, waiting to register, Dinni
introduced me to Ann Dudley Cronkhite, who was chat-
ting and laughing with a rather large number of the male
students who had gathered around her. They knew each
other from four years together at Harvard/Radcliffe.
Although Ann Dudley and Dinni had both gone to the
same junior high school in Pasadena, Polytechnic, even at
first glance they were very different: Dinni was wearing a conservative
dark skirt and blazer, a white blouse, pearls, nylons, and shoes with tiny one-
inch heels. Ann Dudley had on what could only be described as a shock-
ingly short, raspberry-pink, sleeveless Marimekko cotton shift, no stockings
on her tanned legs, and three-inch spikes.

I knew right then that, no matter how well I ultimately fared academi-
cally, I had already lost the competition for having the greatest gams in our
class.

Dinni remembers junior high with Ann Dudley: "We both went to this
private school that drew mostly from very affluent business families. I don't
know what Ann Dudley's family did, but they were part of this rich business
class, which was very different from the way that I grew up. The snobbiest
country club in Pasadena was the Valley Hunt Club. My image of her family was that they were the epitome of the kinds of people who belonged to
and went to the Valley Hunt Club."

Ann Dudley managed to escape her narrow upper-class environment
with extraordinary grace and success. As Dinni says today, "Pasadena was a
very constraining environment for a very bright little girl. For Ann Dudley
to break out of that pattern must have been really hard, much harder than
what I did."

Harvard Law Professor Charles Nesson, class of '63, remembers Ann
Dudley with awe and affection:

"Ann Dudley? Ann Dudley was and still is without any question the
brassiest babe I ever met. She had the sharpest mouth. Talk about somebody
who would stand toe-to-toe with you and just go even. She just wouldn't let
you push her around. She was—fantastic."

Ann Dudley Cronkhite was born in Pasadena, California, on October 3,
1939, "in a perfectly wonderful house" that can only be described as a mansion. It is now the main building of a well-regarded private school that two of
her great-nieces attended. Her father attended Williams College but never

graduated. He played polo, looked after his investments, and at the age of just nineteen, joined the army and went off to France to fight in World War I. When World War II began, he reenlisted and served at the front once again.

Ann Dudley's mother was a social powerhouse in Southern California, President of the Junior League, and on all the right cultural committees. She had gone to Madeira, a private boarding school in the fox-hunt country of Virginia near Washington, D.C. She herself had had an ambitious mother who had married her off at nineteen to a wealthy young man who almost certainly had ulcerative colitis and was impotent. In 1925 or 1926, after two and a half years of marriage, she went to France and got divorced. Then she and her mother went out to California to seek their fortunes in marriage. They found Gordon, Ann Dudley's father, who was recently widowed and was living with his string of polo ponies on the huge estate on Sunnyslope Drive where Ann Dudley was born.

"Although Mother would never have dreamed of going to college, her education was extremely good in Shakespeare and in the classics . . . all her quotations that I remember learning at her knee I later realized were Shakespearean or biblical. I think she probably had an informal classical education from one or another of the advanced thinkers for women at Madeira.

"My parents had a life of fun and leisure. They both read like maniacs and they both played a great deal of cards. They both drank too much, although they were never drunk. I remember, even as a child, thinking that most people probably didn't have two to three drinks before dinner and two to three afterward, but I never saw either of them any the worse for wear for alcohol—until my father was very old."

Running the Junior League was more than a full-time job for Ann Dudley's mother:

"Of course, she wasn't paid for doing it. When she was in it, it was really, really run well and did a lot of good. They sponsored pedigreed-dog shows at the Santa Anita racetrack to raise money, although I don't think they ever saw the beneficiaries of their charity."

Ann Dudley's mother was the dominant person in the family in strength of will. Gordon was the dominant parent in conversation and in taking an interest in Ann Dudley:

"He had much broader interests than my mother—he introduced me to music, he was the one who took me to concerts later. He told me all about wine and we tasted wines together. He taught me how to play bridge when I was about eleven. I remember very clearly that I had an allowance of about twenty-five cents a week, and that, for one reason or another, when people came for dinner and bridge, I would often be the fourth at the bridge table.

I would almost always play with my father. He would be my partner, with the other grown-ups playing against us. He spent time teaching me as we talked about bridge and solitaire. He also taught me about duplicate bridge. I would lose my allowance and then my father would pay for the rest of my losses. I got quite good, quite fast."

Although he didn't work at any regular job, Ann Dudley's father was smart, an excellent mathematician, and interested in almost everything. He was also good with his hands. He and his brother made scale models of trains. Eventually they found they had made the whole Santa Fe system, and donated it to Chicago's Museum of Science and History. Gordon also built miniatures of all the American ships fighting in World War II—to scale, each about four inches long with little guns that moved—and told Ann Dudley war stories, using the ships to illustrate them:

"Daddy went to Williams for two and a half years but quit to join the army and go fight in France at the end of World War One. He was excellent at all his hobbies and pastimes. But he never was much at working. As a matter of fact, he didn't work. He had kind of wacko investments every once in a while that he would take a hand in and that would never really seem to pan out. But he was a great father to me."

Ann Dudley was the youngest of four sisters, eight years younger than her next oldest sister, Cynthia. Allison was the smart one. Betsy was the nice one. Cynthia was the beautiful one. And Ann Dudley was the young one.

"Actually, all three of my sisters were very, very pretty and there were always a lot of young men around the house. Allison went away to Westover boarding school in the East—we all went there—and then to Bryn Mawr College. She stayed only one year and fell in love with some extremely unreliable person and never finished college. She was married when I was twelve. After Westover, Cynthia went to Briarcliff Junior College, where she got her ASS—her Associate in Secretary Sciences. She married when she was twenty and was married for eighteen years, separated for twenty, and is now madly in love with her husband again, whom she never divorced. Betsy went to Westover but she never wanted to go to college. She taught kindergarten for a while and married when she was twenty-two. She was married for about thirty-seven years and then was divorced. Allison had six children; Cynthia had three; and Betsy had four. All thirteen of them were born before I was married at the ripe old age of twenty-eight."

Because Ann Dudley was so much younger than her sisters, she learned to be aggressive to be heard. She ate fast. She talked a lot. She developed very definite opinions at an early age and expressed them. Nobody put her down. They might tell her that she was wrong, but they listened. The conversations around her dinner table were adult conversations. She's convinced all this helped her in tests: her vocabulary was much bigger than her friends', and her horizons much broader. Until the ninth grade, Ann Dudley attended the lab school for Cal Tech in Pasadena, Polytechnic, or "Poly," the same school Dinni attended.

"The students who went to Poly took more tests than you can imagine. We took every Stanford Binet, every this, every that—we took tests every three weeks. I loved those tests. They were much more fun than going to school. When I was there, I wasn't at all smart. First of all, I had mixed dominance because I was left-handed and right-handed. I remember when I graduated from ninth grade, there was a prize day at Poly, and luckily for me it was very close to my sister Betsy's wedding date, so I told my parents not to come. I knew I wouldn't get any prizes and I didn't—I didn't get a single prize. Not even a posture award. I was a chronic underachiever. I had no prizes and I remember thinking absolutely, clearly that I was going to go to boarding school and I was going to get lots of prizes. I was very humiliated."

Ann Dudley's three sisters married when she was twelve, thirteen, and fourteen. Just when she began to think that she might enjoy being an only child, she went away to Westover, a boarding school in Connecticut, at her own request. As she remembers:

"Westover was really supposed to be a finishing school. That meant that you went there to be prepared for marriage—to learn to be a good wife for a gentleman. You learned how to talk about the *New York Times;* how to be a good conversationalist; how to cook, sew, and drink tea; how to appreciate music. They were also very good at teaching writing. Not handwriting. I spent three years making my handwriting totally incomprehensible, which was probably a mistake. But it does look pretty. For a smart, curious young girl who wanted to learn, there was also history and literature and politics, and wonderful teachers."

After never winning anything at Poly, Ann Dudley eventually won just about everything there was to win at Westover:

"I don't know where that drive came from—neither my parents nor my sisters thought that was particularly important, nor did most of my classmates at Westover. As a finishing high school for girls, it was filled with girl talk and hockey playing. And if there're two things I don't like, it's girl talk and playing hockey in the cold."

Even though Ann Dudley won a lot of prizes, she thought she would probably go on to Briarcliff Junior College for two years, like her sister Cynthia, and then marry. But Westover's headmistress told her, "Don't go to a girls' school. It's not right for you."

Startled, Ann Dudley finally agreed: "I thought girls were boring. And they were all too soft. They didn't like to fight—they didn't like to argue. They didn't stand up for their position. They just weren't aggressive enough—except on the hockey field, which was just painful. Whack you on the shin! I wanted to be whacked in the brain."

In her last year at Westover, Ann Dudley fell in love with a senior from Yale, Calvin "Bud" Trillin. When she told him she was planning to go to Briarcliff, where her sister had gone, he stopped her: "You don't understand. Briarcliff is not appropriate for you. You should look at other places."

Bud Trillin remembers with clarity and affection the woman he still calls Ann:

"Ann had short, fluffy blond hair. She was very pretty. Lively. She was bright and she was funny and she had a sort of vivacity. She was enormous fun to be with. I met her on a weekend. She was a senior and I was a senior— it's just that I was in college and she was in high school. She had a date with somebody else in my class at Yale. I was probably three and a half years older than she was but it seemed like a lot. Especially because there were all kinds of rules about even being seen with a boy both in girls' prep schools and in her particular boarding school—lots of rules about how you could see people. I remember when I first came to Yale, I was with some guys driving somewhere. We stopped at Miss Porter's School, where they knew some girls. We started to walk with them on the street and a large man came up and said, 'You can't do this.' We learned we couldn't even walk down the street with a Miss Porter's girl without having cleared the bureaucracy there was for that at that school. So for her to go out with me was more than a little rebellious and more than a little dangerous."

Ann Dudley and Bud each were the first person in their family to graduate from college, but in different ways: Bud's father, born in Ukraine, spoke without an accent, but everybody else on both sides of Bud's family were immigrants and spoke with heavy accents. He and Ann assumed, without discussing it a lot, that her family wouldn't have found his background exactly perfect. As Bud says:

"We didn't talk a lot about it, but I think we didn't have an awful lot of debutantes in my family. I'd known a few people from Pasadena. It had this sort of enclave of well-off WASPs with connections to the East. I could picture her family: I knew her mother was active, like in a Republican-committee-woman sort of way. Her father? I didn't know he played polo until much later. I think she protected me from the polo playing. I could imagine them sitting in some very discreet porch, maybe slightly shabby in the WASP way, and discussing what really crude new rich people in West Los Angeles with entertainment money were doing and shuddering at the way some people behaved."

Bud never had any illusions: he would not have been thought of as an ideal boyfriend by the Cronkhites. Of course, Ann Dudley was a WASP and a blue blood, not exactly the nice Jewish girl the Trillins wanted their only son to marry.

Ann was very conscious of her family and of her older sisters, but by her senior year in high school she no longer swallowed their vision of what life should be: she knew she wanted challenges in everything. There was a somewhat similar expectation in the Trillin family:

"In those years and in my own family, I was expected to go to Yale; my sister was expected to go to a state university relatively close to home in the Midwest somewhere, join a sorority, and find the right guy. My parents hoped she would come back to Kansas City and raise cute children in reasonable proximity to their grandparents. And nobody questioned that at all, least of all my sister, who went to the University of Colorado for a couple of years and then got married, I think almost at the point of being an old maid. She was nineteen."

Bud persuaded Ann Dudley that the traditional model for young women of that era was totally wrong for her: "I couldn't imagine Ann seriously thinking of going to Briarcliff because she was just so obviously bright."

Ann Dudley is still grateful to Bud for expanding her horizon:

"Bud went with me to see Radcliffe, which was all girls then, with separate dorms, but all the classes were with Harvard. He was right—it looked really yummy. At that time, of course, girls couldn't go to the Ivy League schools—they were all male. So I chose Radcliffe and they chose me. My parents were quite unhappy because they thought I would end up wearing black stockings and having stringy brown hair. For heaven's sakes! I had been bleaching my hair since I was fourteen. I had never wanted to wear black stockings or have stringy hair. I had already decided that one of the ways that one got on in this world was to look well. It seemed to me that looking well, being tidy and attractively dressed helped you through a lot. I must have been a weird-looking Radcliffe freshman because I remember buying a white peignoir with little green flowers on it and painting my nails bright red. I think people thought I was kind of a flake. I remember when I got my first paper back, the teaching assistant said there was only one A and it turned out to be me. Everybody was quite surprised, not least of all me. That first indication that I wasn't out of my league pushed me ahead."

Ann Dudley thrived at Radcliffe. In June 1961 she became the first person in her family to graduate from college. Then, of course, she did the unthinkable and went on to Harvard Law School.

"Daddy and I had kind of an unwritten understanding that I was as near as he was going to get to a son. I was the fourth child. I was a surprise. He was sent out by my mother to get a vasectomy soon after my conception in the days when that was a relatively innovative procedure—which also demonstrates the power relationship between my parents. I think he was very, very pleased when I was admitted to Harvard Law School. It was kind of our ambition together. My parents might have been a little nervous: they did say they were very concerned that I would become a Communist. I also remember my mother saying, 'Oh, my God, you couldn't possibly be my child,' but she said it with great sweetness. In the end, she certainly didn't object very much, and Daddy cheered me on."

Given her family background and the ultratraditional community she had grown up in, the decision to go to law school was a stretch for Ann Dudley. As her son Jeremy says, "Everything about Harvard Law School was going against her parents."

Ann Dudley made an indelible impression on our classmates. Pat recalls, "Everybody was stunned with Ann Dudley. She was such a wonderful free spirit from California. Sexy and smart and irreverent. She was just great." As classmate Paul Dodyk put it recently: "My most powerful memory of Ann Dudley was the arresting perfume that she always wore. I can still smell it. Let's just say it focused the mind on what Ann Dudley wanted our minds focused on. Proust had his madeleine. Harvard Law School '64 has Ann Dudley.

June Freeman (Cornell)

June Freeman was Ann Dudley's Wyeth Hall roommate at the beginning of our first year. The younger of two children, June started life in the family's three-room, fifth-floor apartment in Brooklyn, New York. When she was eleven, they moved to a four-and-a-half-room apartment: "That was a big deal. The great thing about growing up in a small apartment is that you get thrilled by things. It's nice to be thrilled in life."

June was the only child she knew whose mother worked. Early in life, she began to develop an independent streak. By the time she was eight or nine years old, she was also a prodigious reader. In the third grade, she chose *Gone With the Wind* for her first book report. The teacher told her that book was not appropriate for a third-grader and made her write another report on a less adult book. She was amazed. "In my house, no one ever said I shouldn't read something. I was pretty much allowed to read and do whatever I wanted. There weren't a lot of rules. I never had a bedtime. Basically, I think I was trusted to do the right thing."

Making her own decisions from an early age, June learned to figure out life for herself. She went to high school in Coney Island, then on to Cornell, where she majored in English and graduated Phi Beta Kappa. Ever since childhood, she had pictured herself as a Clarence Darrow type. In her senior year, she decided to go to law school and applied to only one place: Harvard. "It never crossed my mind that law school was something I shouldn't do or that being a woman made any difference. I had heard you needed certain grades and certain board scores to go there and I thought I had them. I was very naive. I thought it was like going into a store and seeing a beautiful dress for two hundred dollars, and if you have two hundred dollars, you buy it. My mother told everyone I was going to Harvard before I even applied."

When June arrived in Cambridge, she looked around and decided that everyone came from a more sophisticated family than she did. When she learned that Pat was a pilot, she knew she was in a new world.

"Nobody I knew in Brooklyn was flying planes, I can assure you. They were going to the deli."

Arlene Lezberg (Radcliffe)

Arlene, twenty years old like me, had graduated fourth in her high school class and entered Radcliffe College with sophomore standing. She had majored in English history and literature while, at the same time, studying piano at a private music school in the Boston area. By the end of her senior year in college, Arlene had a "things to do" list tacked up on her wall: "get the honors thesis done, prepare  for oral examination on it, get into law school, prepare for graduation piano recital, pass swimming test." Of all of those, passing the swimming test, a Radcliffe requirement for graduation, was the hardest for her: it took her two years of swimming lessons before she succeeded.

Each of Arlene's parents had emigrated from Russia at an early age and settled in Roxbury, an ethnic Boston neighborhood of mostly Jewish people, where Arlene lived until she was ten years old. "My father was in the wholesale fruit and produce business in the market section of Boston. It was a very tough business. He was up at four in the morning, out to work, and did not get back until dinnertime."

Arlene's mother had attended Fisher Junior College, which was basically a secretarial school: "That was a way immigrants would get ahead and enjoy the good things in life and have some sort of a calling. She worked in a law office. She always told me what a good experience it was, and that law was an honorable calling."

When Arlene's sister was born, ten years before Arlene came along, her mother gave up her job. "At that time, amongst people of my background, if the wife worked, it was assumed that the husband couldn't make a living for the family. So not working was a trait to be very proud of."

Even though her parents discouraged her sister from going to medical school, their views had moderated by the time Arlene was admitted to Harvard Law School; in fact, they were enthusiastic about her decision to attend: "Most important was that Harvard was Harvard to them. It was the apex. Theirs was absolutely the immigrant mentality. Upward migration. The American dream."

Marjory "Marge" Freincle (Brooklyn College)

Marge Freincle, the youngest girl in our class, was born into a middle-class family in Brooklyn, New York, on St. Patrick's Day in 1941. Her mother was an artist; her father sold furniture wholesale. Not long after Marge was born, her brother, seventeen years older, left for the Pacific theater to fight with the U.S. Army in World War II. Marge's parents imbued her with the need to be frugal, self-sufficient, and well educated: they had endured the Depression and wanted to be sure that didn't happen to their children. "Both my parents said again and again that I should never be dependent on a husband. I should be able to take care of myself and my life."

Marge finished high school when she was sixteen, went to Brooklyn College as a day student, and graduated magna cum laude and Phi Beta Kappa. A woman professor looked at her marks and at her LSAT scores and told her, "You're going to law school." She planned to go on to Columbia or NYU until her father's boss bragged that his son was going to Harvard: "At that point, my father told him I was going to Harvard Law. I hadn't even applied."

The concept of Marge's being a lawyer was not an issue for her parents: they had already established their expectation that she would earn a good living, and law fit that bill.

Rosemary Cox (Mount Holyoke)

I met Rosemary Cox when I returned to Wyeth Hall right after registering for law school. At five feet two and a half inches, she was petite and slender with short chestnut hair and wide brown eyes that, particularly during our first year, often looked like the proverbial deer caught in the headlights—not quite sure what was going to happen next. Her usual attire, a pleated plaid skirt, a cotton blouse with a round Peter Pan collar, a blazer, and high heels, made her look very much the conservatively brought up young woman that she was. Classmate Joshua Hubbard Lane, formerly a bond portfolio manager with Salomon Smith Barney, remembers Rosemary as pretty and unspoiled, with a fresh viewpoint that was a relief from that of the typical sophisticated Ivy League girls he was used to from his days at Milton Academy and Harvard College.

Rosemary was born in Swarthmore, Pennsylvania, in 1939. Her mother, Rachel, a Texan, was a professor of educational psychology at Bryn Mawr College. Her father, Reavis, a nationally known economist, was a professor at the Wharton School at the University of Pennsylvania. In the summer of 1941, when Rosemary was two years old, the family moved to Washington, D.C.

The country wasn't yet at war, but Roosevelt and others around him knew it was coming. They had created a new government agency, the War Production Board (WPB), to figure out how to shift the country to a wartime footing—from producing automobiles and clothing and farm equipment to making tanks and planes, subs and guns. Rosemary's father, a specialist on marketing, was assigned to travel the country for the WPB, talking with different industrial leaders to find out if they could make the shift, how long it would take, and what their realistic production of necessary goods would be. He left his family behind in Washington.

Just before they moved, Rosemary's mother had been finishing her Ph.D. at the University of Pennsylvania. But Rosemary's father, with no consultation and little advance notice, had uprooted the family so that he could join the government. Rosemary's mother tried for a while to commute between Washington and Philadelphia, but found it virtually impossible. Transportation was uncertain, and with the war effort in full swing, she couldn't find anyone to help care for her two small children. She gave up, turning her extra energies to working for the Red Cross as a social worker at Walter Reed Army Hospital. The strain of work, family, and unfulfilled ambition soon became too much for her, and she suffered a breakdown. As Rosemary recalls her mother: "One of my very earliest memories [was] her taking us to the Jefferson Memorial again and again. She would read to us the writing on the walls of the memorial. It was her way of trying to explain to us why there was a war and why it was important—why my father was away so much. That the war was about human rights, human dignity. Democracy. There was this belief that the Nazis were going to take over the world unless we stopped them, and the men had to go away and the women had to cope with everything else. Of course, at some level those principles got internalized very powerfully in me. When I got older and realized that women were oppressed, that African Americans were oppressed, that Jews couldn't buy property or live in certain communities, I determined to do whatever I could to change that."

When the war ended, the Cox family moved back to Swarthmore, where Rosemary eventually finished high school. "In high school, I was not one of the popular girls. I did not get invited to the parties with the cheerleaders and football players, and it hurt terribly. Yet my father loved smart women. He loved my mother. He loved me. So, again, it was this complex situation for me—and I developed a kind of outrage. I was smart, I was reasonably pretty. Why wasn't I one of the popular kids? No matter how hard I tried, I was still one of the brainy kids. If the devil had come and said, 'I'll make you popular, but you'll lose some of your brains,' I would have taken the deal in a flash. I did manage to pull off one particularly big social coup in high school. A boy who came to our school in junior year was incredibly handsome, an intellectual, not an athlete. I made up my mind in my dogged little way that I was going to get him to date me and so I did. But it was not particularly sexual. . . . The societal messages were 'Stay a virgin until you marry, and what you do after that we're not going to give you information on. Whatever that is. To be desired you have to be pretty and a little on the brainless side.'"

Rosemary just kept thinking to herself, "I'm darned if I'm going to be marginalized, or on the social sidelines. I'm going to fight this." So she did, and for that, her mother became supportive: she helped Rosemary organize the brainy kids so that they developed an active social life. Rosemary gave parties to which she invited only the nerds: they would get together every weekend, usually on a Friday night, and just hang out together to talk all night about politics and books. "I lived in an academic community, so the brainy kids were the children of the college professors—and once we found each other, we had great fun. Once in a while, I'd even be very cheerful about my lack of popularity. My mother told me, 'One day, men will appreciate you. Just wait until you grow up. You'll see.' And I think I believed her—a little bit anyway. I had the advantage of my parents' marriage, where my father, who was an accomplished, intelligent, good person, loved my mother, who was a professional. I knew that she was unusual in her day—most of the professors at the women's colleges were single in those days. And even though my mother was clearly an exception, I was also aware that, from her perspective, she felt she· paid a very high price for being a professional. It is odd: on one level, she often talked about her mother's disapproval of her in that she didn't spend enough time on her clothes or her house or entertaining. She also told me that other women disapproved of her for not being home enough with my brother and me. On another level, she didn't seem very interested in my spending time on clothes, and yet she exerted this enormous pressure on me to marry, to have children, to keep my family's home. How was I going to attract the right sort of man if I didn't have the right sort of clothes?"

By the time Rosemary got to high school, there was an even more jarring disconnect. The academics in the quiet Quaker town of Swarthmore, who claimed to be purveyors of tolerance, at the same time excluded minorities and Jews from their schools and neighborhoods. Rosemary has a sharp memory of the first time she experienced the discrimination there: "I thought my entire high school class was always invited to what were called the junior assemblies—the girls would go in floor-length, strapless gowns, and the boys would be in suits and ties and you would have dancing lessons. In my senior year, a boy in my class, Jim McCorkel, said, 'Do you realize that the Negro kids are not invited to the dances?' I knew they never came, but most of them lived in the adjoining community, so I thought it was just too far—I didn't think about it. Well, Jim got a petition up to ask that the Negro kids be invited. And my mother, who had taken me to the Jefferson Memorial all those times and read me all his words about democracy and equality, was furious: 'Jim is a troublemaker. What is he doing?' Jim is also the one who told me that if you were Jewish, it was virtually impossible to buy a house in Swarthmore. Although the Jewish professors were provided housing by the college, many people in the town didn't want them there as permanent residents."

Rosemary's uncle in Houston, Texas, had the same kind of prejudices. She remembers visiting him in the late fifties and sitting in his backyard— listening to him talking about why black people should sit in the back of the bus. "It makes sense, you know, they've been working hard in the fields and they often smell bad." And Rosemary said, "Why not just ask all the people who smell bad to sit in the back of the bus? Even though my parents were not Southern, redneck racists, they were what we would think of today as racist—polite Southern racists. Meaning that they thought lynching was unacceptable and what happened to blacks when they stepped out of line was regrettable, but still somehow understandable. In Swarthmore! The town that had been a stop on the underground railroad for slaves escaping from the South, where the grandparents and great-grandparents of my friends would have helped them and kept them safe. Yet the black kids in my class couldn't come to our dances. And the disconnect, the dissonance went to what kind of profession I would want to go into. I am very clear that one of the things that drew me to law was that it was about power—I did not want to be Florence Nightingale binding up the wounded—or a teacher—all those nice things women did. I wanted to be a part of funda- mental shifts in power. In the United States of America, the route to that goal was the law. I really wanted to be at Harvard . . . because I felt people at Harvard were more likely to end up in places with power—power to change some of the things that weren't right."

When Rosemary went to Mount Holyoke after high school, it was, in many ways, like entering a convent: dating or even meeting boys was diffi- cult in an all-girls school located in the small New England town of South Hadley in the middle of Massachusetts, and Rosemary had neither the time nor the money to travel.

After four years of achievement—and isolation—in college, Rosemary applied to law school at Harvard. There was absolutely no opposition from her family: both parents assured her that she could do whatever she wanted. If anything, they expected her to get a graduate degree. Rosemary's conflicts and tensions came from a different direction: her mother wanted her to have the same values as she did, particularly where sexual abstinence was concerned. For Rosemary, her parents' insistence that she remain a chaste, innocent virgin until marriage clashed with their expectation that she should be a confident, independent professional woman who knew her own mind. As far as Rosemary was concerned, "The two images of wom- anhood just could not be reconciled."

Judith "Judy" Ann Wilson (Radcliffe)

Judy Wilson, born in July 1939, came into her adoptive parents' lives in December of that year. She was a Christmas present—the best one they ever had. Her father, John Lewis Wilson Jr., was a prize-winning architect, a graduate of the Columbia University School of Architecture, who devoted a part of his professional life to developing affordable housing for Manhattan's disadvantaged. Early in his career he was one of the architects who designed the Harlem River Houses, one of the first projects dedicated to the concept that public housing should be humane and nurturing. Judy often went with him to see the progress—and the people—in his buildings. Her mother, Hazel Thomas Wilson, was a graduate of the Juilliard School of Music who retired from the concert stage to become a full-time mother when they adopted Judy.

By the time she was three, Judy was attending nursery school at Dalton, a private school in Manhattan where she stayed through high school. She had no brothers or sisters, but her friends from Dalton filled the gap and remain friends to this day. Like many only children, she grew up close to her parents and involved with their lives and their causes. They were devoted to her, and at least as far as the outside world was concerned, she was the perfect child. They took her everywhere with them, even to the golf course, where her father, an avid golfer, would wait patiently while she took three or four strokes for every one of his.

After graduating from Dalton, Judy went on to Radcliffe College, where she majored in American history and graduated with honors. Her parents' dedication to helping the less fortunate in society, and Judy's own interest in improving the lives of children, particularly those who got involved with the juvenile justice system, led her to Harvard Law School. Judy was one of only three black Americans in our entering class, the other two being Sheila Rush from Buffalo, New York, and Chatham College, and Fred Wallace from Toledo, Ohio, by way of Amherst College. Law school was a new, strange experience for her: "I did not come from a family that sat around the dinner table talking about law and the origins of law. It was a complete new world for me." She remembers the first reception the Sunday before classes began—where the men seemed to have their lives all planned out: many wanted to end up with Wall Street law firms, others, inspired by the Kennedy rhetoric, wanted to serve in the federal government. One man told her that he would be governor of Missouri one day. When classes began, Judy observed many of the boys taking notes in bound leather notebooks: they told her they wanted to make a permanent record of the beginning of their successful careers.

Alice Pasachoff (Cornell)

Alice Pasachoff was born in the Bronx, New York, the oldest of two daughters in her family. Her father was a dedicated pediatrician who had graduated second in his class at "P&S," Columbia College for Physicians and Surgeons. Her mother, a Hunter College graduate, gave up her job as an elementary school teacher when Alice arrived, but sought intellectual stimulation by auditing courses at Hunter until she was in her midnineties. Alice's family placed a heavy emphasis on getting an education: "It is very common among the first and second generations of American children born to Jewish families who emigrated to the United States. Three out of four of my grandparents were born in Eastern Europe. My parents and all of their siblings were born in the U.S., and there was a strong cultural emphasis on higher education as the way up the ladder. Not so much on athletics or physical accomplishment. Jewish boys of my generation were not pushed out the door by their fathers to join sports teams."

By the third grade, Alice was reading voraciously, scaring the wits out of her mother by crossing the Grand Concourse, a six-lane street in front of their apartment building, with her nose in a book. She taught herself to knit from the *Book of Knowledge* encyclopedia (with a little help from her best friend's grandmother) and started to knit her own sweaters and mittens, an interest she still retains. Alice was bored with school. Her teacher called her mother and asked her to send an extra book with Alice every day so she could read while the other children were struggling with their assignments. The next year, Alice's parents transferred her to P.S. 114 in the Bronx, a pubic school with a class for gifted children. Alice remembers how much she loved P.S. 114: "I feel as if my intellectual life actually began there in the fourth grade in three respects: I had a stimulating intellectual life; a stimulating peer group; and a highly charged, intellectually competitive environment. I was exposed to a fierce degree of academic competition at age nine, and by the time I reached Harvard it was nothing new."

Alice went on to attend the selective Bronx High School of Science, which was only one-third female at that time, and Cornell University, where she graduated with honors in English literature and served as the women's editor of the *Cornell Daily Sun*. As women's editor of a college daily newspaper that proudly called itself "Ithaca's only morning newspaper," Alice reported on major campus events and had the responsibility, one night each week, for laying out the front page and putting the paper "to bed." At that time, Cornell had a strong commitment both to academic excellence and to "gracious living," a term used to describe the evening meal in the women's dorms, which was served by students employed to wait on the tables. (All female students wore skirts or dresses not only to dinner but all the time at Cornell in that era: no slacks were allowed except for blizzards.) Alice wrote an article for the *Sun* about the end of "gracious living"—and the beginning of cafeteria service—headlined "University Considers Fate of Gracious Living," in which she quoted Janet Reno, president of the Cornell Women's Student Government Association and Alice's soon-to-be colleague at Harvard Law School: "I don't think there is such a term as gracious living. What has existed will continue to exist, and it will end a hypocrisy that has long existed . . . the bad taste created when women sit in strained silence, awaiting their release from the dining room."[5] (Janet, of course, went on to be the first woman Attorney General of the United States, and a candidate for governor of Florida.) The next year, Cornell abolished "gracious living," switching to cafeteria-style service and less formal attire for all meals.

In Alice's senior year, she applied to Harvard, Yale, and Columbia Law Schools and was admitted to all three. She wanted to sharpen her mind and expand her options for whatever came next. "Getting married and having a family was very important to me, but it was also important to me to maintain an active intellectual life." Although Walter Burns's constitutional law course had sparked her interest in studying law, her first love was journalism. "Going to law school didn't, from my viewpoint, require me to make any choices. I was going on to an experience that would expand my possibilities and expand the group of people that I was meeting. There wouldn't have been any reason in that context to think about long-term goals."

Alice decided on Harvard, primarily because she thought she would come into contact with more women law students there: Yale's entering class had only six women out of about two hundred students: "Six women seemed like a very small group of people to embark on a three-year experience with."

Her parents encouraged her, particularly her father: "He, more than anyone else, was the person who was most instrumental in my deciding to go on to professional school."

Barbara Margulies (Mount Holyoke)

Barbara Margulies, born February 28, 1940, grew up in Cliffside Park, New Jersey. She was beautiful, precocious, and strongly encouraged by her prominent parents to work hard, strive to be the best, and grow up to be whatever she wanted. After high school, she attended Mount Holyoke, where she graduated magna cum laude and Phi Beta Kappa, before entering Harvard Law School in the fall of 1961.

Grace Weiner (Mount Holyoke and Michigan)

Grace Weiner was born December 18, 1939, in Englewood, New Jersey, the oldest child of her father, a public health statistician who had emigrated from Russia at age ten, and her mother, who remained a homemaker until the early 1950s, when she became a real estate saleswoman. They brought her up to believe that there were no limits on what she could achieve in life. In Grace's high
school senior year, she met Barbara Margulies, her future law school classmate, when both competed for a countywide scholarship. (It was close, but Grace won.) They ran into each other again at Mount Holyoke, and later, at Harvard Law School.

Grace stayed at Mount Holyoke for only a year; the sense of total isolation and detachment from the world that she felt there was not to her liking. She transferred to the University of Michigan, graduating in 1961 without a clear idea of what she wanted to do professionally. Going to law school was a way to keep her options open. All she knew for sure was that she was committed to the burgeoning movement for civil rights, and that training in constitutional law would be essential to joining that effort. The only place she applied was Harvard.

Grace shared an apartment with a college friend her first year at law school. Wanting more time for study and a more convenient location, she moved into Wyeth Hall for her last two years. She regrets missing the camaraderie of Wyeth our first year, but we came to know her anyway. As classmate Nancy Kuhn Kirkpatrick remembers, Grace was outgoing, peppy, and a lot of fun. It was impossible not to like her.

Eleanor Rosenthal (Michigan)

Eleanor Rosenthal, classmate Alice Pasachoff's first cousin, was born in New York City. Her mother died when she was six, and she was brought up by her father, a CPA who worked for the city. Like Alice, she attended the selective Bronx High School of Science, graduating in the groundbreaking first coed class at what had previously been an all-boys school. She did her undergraduate work at the University of Michigan, again demonstrating a willingness to make nonmainstream choices by transferring from the popular English Department, with over three hundred undergraduates, to the Philosophy Department, where there were twenty undergraduates, ten of them in her honors program.

After graduation, Eleanor returned to New York, planning to get an "English major's editorial job." When those proved hard to come by, she enrolled at the Speedwriting Institute and, after a summer spent studying shorthand and typing, took a job as a secretary at the National Broadcasting Company. She worked her way up to the sought-after position of manuscript reader, helping to select scripts for such television shows as *Matinee Theatre* and the *U.S. Steel Hour*. When she began working at NBC, during the "golden age of television," there were nine dramatic anthology shows, and each needed manuscript readers and editors to select and edit outside submissions. By 1960, however, television had changed. Most shows were assigned to staff writers, and manuscript readers were no longer required. The only show that needed them was the *U.S. Steel Hour*, and she was already working for it. What's more, readers and editors from the eight shows that had folded were lined up waiting for jobs like hers.

Seeing few prospects for advancement in television and looking for new challenges, Eleanor decided to apply to law school. The Harvard Law School catalog used philosophy as an example of the kinds of majors that were suitable preparation for law. That seemed to be a good omen: she had never before come across a nonacademic occupation that welcomed philosophy majors.

When she was applying to law schools, her lawyer friends advised her that if she didn't get into Harvard, Yale, or Columbia, she should give up the whole idea. "As a woman without a top credential, they said, I would end up spending three years in law school only to earn the same one hundred dollars a week I was already making in television. I was not discouraged by the fact that a small percentage of practicing lawyers were women, nor by the advice I had been given that the field itself was not woman-friendly."

When she took the LSAT, she scored just under the 99.4th percentile, a ranking, she computed, that placed her approximately seventieth in the country. "I figured that if only half of those seventy went to Harvard, I would be statistically in line for law review. However, I also knew that I usually tested considerably better than I performed. Nevertheless, I thought I had a good chance of turning in a respectable performance at the Law School, and when I was accepted, I decided to go."

Elizabeth "Liz" Daldy (Radcliffe)

Liz Daldy was born in St. Louis, Missouri, on November 23, 1939. Her parents were well educated, and although they didn't get along with each other, they were united behind Liz. When Liz was four, they moved to Philadelphia, where Liz eventually attended Friends' Central High School. In 1953, she came under the tutelage of a ninth-grade English teacher who changed her life. A Quaker with a brilliant mind and a strong social conscience, he spotted Liz's talent and encouraged her to become involved in politics and government. He became her mentor and her hero: "Whatever I did in life, I wanted more than anything else to please my ninth-grade English teacher."

After Friends', Liz went on to Radcliffe College and graduated with honors in 1961. Her senior thesis on *New York Times* coverage of the Cuban revolution helped her firm up her decision to go to law school; she hoped to become involved in politics and to work for Latin American land reform. Harvard was the only place that she applied.

The summer between college and law school, Liz worked as a waitress at Cronin's Restaurant in Harvard Square to earn money for books and tuition. Her second week on the job, one of her regular customers, Richard Dyson, asked her out. He was a third-year law student, tall, handsome, and an editor of the prestigious *Harvard Law Review*. Although Liz had never expected to marry, she and Richard became engaged seventeen days later. In accepting Richard's proposal, she wavered only a little: "I'm starting law school in the fall and who knows what it will do to my head. Let's get married sometime in the middle of my first year if we're still in love." Liz and her Radcliffe classmate Judy Wilson had planned to share a Cambridge apartment for their first year of law school, but Richard changed all that. Liz told Judy that her plans had changed: she and Richard would probably be getting married in November. Richard and Liz didn't live together—Richard lived across the street until they married in November: "Probably the biggest reason we got married was sheer physical attraction."

Nancy Kuhn (Trinity College)

Nancy Kuhn was born June 4, 1939, in Philadelphia, Pennsylvania, the third of five children. Her father worked as an editor and creative marketer for the Sun Oil Company; her mother was a public grade school teacher. Education was important in their family: her parents kept reminding her that during the Great Depression you needed a college degree even to get a job in a five-and-dime store. Eventually, all five of the Kuhn children would work their way through college and graduate school.

Nancy attended Catholic schools in the Philadelphia area for nine months of the year and spent her summers at her grandmother's cottage at the Jersey Shore. Her grandmother, a teacher, had been widowed early, yet she found ways to support herself and her two young children throughout the Depression. She was a powerful role model for Nancy: confident, independent, and strong. Nancy, a curious child who tried and succeeded at everything, didn't like dolls, preferring her brothers' train sets, toy soldiers, and friends: "I wanted to do everything my brothers could do, as well as they could or better. I would try to run around with my brothers and be part of their 'gang.' They would all say, 'Well, you're a girl. You can't do what we're doing.' I became determined to show them that they were wrong. I really didn't like being told I couldn't do things. The song from *Annie Get Your Gun* became my theme song: 'Anything you can do I can do better.' "

Nancy graduated first in her class of 356 from Notre Dame Catholic Girls' High School of Moylan Rose Valley on the outskirts of Philadelphia. Her parents, with two sons already in college, and two children still at home, told Nancy they couldn't help with her college education costs. But, if she went to the local teachers college, they told her she could continue to live at home for free.

Teaching wasn't what Nancy had in mind. At her father's suggestion, she had taken an aptitude test during her junior year in high school. A psychological testing company that tested executives for head-hunting agencies summarized the results for her: "You think like a man. You should go to Vassar" (which, at that time, was an all-girls college). "Thinking like a man" was the classic subtle put-down in those days—no female was expected to be logical. And Vassar was as far away from the life she knew as the moon: "Where I came from, Vassar was not something that was within the realm of possibility."

With help from the nuns at her high school, Nancy won a full scholarship to Trinity, a small, exclusive Catholic women's college in Washington, D.C., run by the Sisters of Notre Dame and populated with the daughters of senators, governors, and ambassadors. She majored in English literature, did well, and set about trying to figure out where she would go next.

The boy she was dating from Georgetown was taking the LSAT, and suggested that she take it with him. She scored in the ninety-eighth percentile, much higher than he did. He handed her his Harvard Law application form, told her that he couldn't get in but she could, and offered to lend her the $10 application fee. Although she had planned to try for night law school at Georgetown, so she could work during the day, the Harvard application appealed to her: "It was a simple three-by-five card, name, address, college, grades, test score. Georgetown's wanted to know three lawyers I'd know for ten years . . . which was out of the question: I'd never met a lawyer. So I sent in the Harvard application."

She was accepted three weeks later. When she called home to tell her parents she was going to Harvard Law School, they were astounded: they didn't even know she had applied. Her father's first response was "Well, you're not thinking of going, are you?" She answered, "Yes, I am. If I can figure out a way to do it, I would like to go." He replied, "Well, do you mean you've decided never to get married?" He told her that he knew of only two female lawyers and that they were brusque, aggressive, and "manly."

But Nancy plowed ahead: she had already been making her own way, and her own decisions, for four years.

In August 1961, less than a month before law school was to begin, the scholarship Nancy had been promised from a Trinity College alumna fell through. Undeterred, she left for Cambridge anyway. "When I finally heard in the middle of August that the woman was not going to help me out, I went to my folks' bank and asked for a student loan. They refused because I wasn't going to law school in Pennsylvania. I hitched a ride with a friend who was going to college in New York and applied to banks there for a loan, but they weren't interested either: I had no credit, no job, and wasn't planning to attend law school in New York. So I caught a ride to Massachusetts and applied for a loan there when I arrived. The banker's first question was 'How much money are you making?' Of course, I was unemployed. They said, 'No way.' So I walked over to Harvard Law School and found my way to Dean Toepfer's office. I knew his name because he'd signed my letter of acceptance. He was in his office in shorts with his feet up on the desk. I said, 'Dean Toepfer, I've been admitted to the class that starts in two weeks, and unfortunately, I haven't been able to find the money to come, so is it all right if I go to your night school?' He laughed at my naïveté: 'Sorry, we don't have a night school.' I said, 'Well, then, may I go to your four-year program, so I can work and study law at the same time?' He answered, 'Sorry. We don't have a four-year program.' So I said, 'Well, would you hold my acceptance for a year?' My acceptance letter had said that they didn't hold places from one year to the next, but it was worth a try. He finally relented: 'Look, it's much easier to pay us back after graduation. How much do you think you'll need? A thousand dollars? Two thousand dollars? Three thousand dollars?' I thought he was going to reach in his pocket, pull out a wad of bills, and start counting it out for me. He told me, 'Just come, and we'll take care of it.'"

As soon as she had registered, Nancy began looking for a job. A woman in the Harvard Financial Aid Office mentioned that a law professor, Arthur Sutherland, and his wife were looking for a cook–nurse's aide to live in, cook for parties twice a week ("She mentioned that they liked pies for dessert"), and help out with the wife's mother, who was bedridden, and with his daughter, who had muscular dystrophy and was confined to a wheelchair.

"I could wing a lot of things, but not having spent a lot of my time nursing, cooking, or making pies, I decided I would be more nervous about my job than law school. I turned the job down."

Eventually she found a job at the Law School Placement Office. Working there, she observed firsthand the de facto discrimination practiced by many law firms not only against female law students but also against minorities and law students from the lower end of the socioeconomic ladder. The head of the Placement Office, Eleanor Appel, was a nice, efficient woman, but she didn't buck the big firms. Instead, she viewed her job as explaining the way things actually worked so students wouldn't waste their time. "It wasn't fair, and I had started from the assumption that things were not fair. I was very angry as a young girl that there were distinctions. I went to Harvard Law School assuming that the world was very unfair and that for a woman to get ahead, she had to be as bright and work twice as hard as the men. That's the way you had to do it. It was a fact of life."

The first day of classes, and for quite a while thereafter, Nancy would walk on the east side of the street from her tiny apartment at 39 Lee Street to the Law School, clutching an armload of heavy books to her chest. Three male classmates, who lived nearby, generally headed out about the same time, but walked on the west side of the street. Several years older than Nancy, they were all either married or engaged and had all completed their tours of duty in the military. "I was quiet and shy, but I was determined to walk as fast on my side of the street as they did on theirs. Underneath, I was competitive at everything. Eventually, they noticed me and we all became good friends. We would eat lunch and have coffee and sometimes even a beer or two on Friday nights. They came to treat me as one of the boys, which was what I wanted. They and their wives were my main support during my first year, along with the other female students."

I bumped into Nancy—literally—sometime during the first couple of weeks of law school. She was heading up Massachusetts Avenue to classes with her heavy load of books. I was running down the same avenue in my high heels, carrying an equally heavy load of books, and slammed into her. Nancy remembers me from that day, and from the many conversations we had after that: "I remember you were very goal-oriented. Clear-minded. Sort of clear-thinking on what you wanted to do, to accomplish. . . . My image of you is in heels all the time. You were always in a hurry. You always walked very quickly, spoke very quickly, and did everything very quickly. You had a clear identity, a clear picture of yourself. You always seemed to be well groomed and well dressed. You always looked smashing. You really did."

Thanks to Mama!

Katherine Huff (Stanford University)

Katherine Huff, the older of two children, was born September 10, 1938, in New Orleans, Louisiana. She was the first of her family to grow up in the city. Katherine's mother, the third of seven children, had moved from a dairy farm in Missouri to a farm within commuting distance of Louisiana State University in Baton Rouge, where she eventually matriculated. Katherine's mother  was a brilliant woman who had an aptitude for chemistry and physics but, at LSU, majored in home economics on the advice of her mother and went on to teach home economics and English at a rural high school, before going to work for the Works Progress Administration (WPA) in the 1930s, screening welfare cases.

Katherine's father grew up near Natchez, Mississippi, on a cotton plantation, which his family had operated since 1773. The family was active in politics (a grandfather was state senator for decades) and, rare for that time, provided educational opportunities for all families, black and white, that lived on the plantation. His family was one of many who left the cotton plantations after the boll weevil reached that part of Mississippi. He frequently reminded Katherine when she was a child, "The South did not lose the Civil War. The South lost Reconstruction, because the men were dead and the women couldn't hold it together. I don't want to have a daughter who can't be in charge."

It made a lasting impression. Katherine wasn't raised to be a flower of the South. Among other things, her dad taught her to be proficient in rifles and handguns.

Though he came from a long line of college-educated forebears, Katherine's father dropped out of school after eighth grade, over the objections of his own father, to help support his family. (His sister, Katherine's aunt, had continued in school and obtained a law degree from LSU, in the early 1930s.) Working hard initially by himself and, eventually, with Katherine's mother, he moved to New Orleans and established a series of successful businesses: trucking, storage warehouses, natural gas, and real estate. But he imbued Katherine with his Depression mentality: no amount of success would ever sap her initiative.

Katherine grew up in a large old house in the Garden District of New Orleans. Her aunt and uncle on her father's side lived with them, and visitors from both sides of the family were frequent. Katherine says that key to her development as an individual distinct from the essentially frivolous young belles of New Orleans who were her close friends was the support of this gifted and (on her father's side) eccentric extended family, active involvement in Prytania Street Presbyterian Church, and her attendance at Miss McGehee's, the small private girls' school across the street from her home. "The hardest academics I encountered in all my school years were at Miss McGehee's. Those teachers, all very intelligent women, denied other careers of course, were determined that we'd be equipped to excel in college and have more options than they had."

Katherine notes that she was "part of one of the last generations to benefit from the kind attentions of African Americans who, being denied access to both jobs and good education, worked as cooks, household workers, and gardeners. Our wonderful cook, Lily Mae Boles, was with us for decades. She was smart as a whip and thoroughly devoted to my brother and me. We'd write letters for her and also read mail that came for her and her neighbors."

After high school, Katherine decided to head west to Stanford to college. "I was determined to get the hell out of the South. I found it oppressive and limiting, and I didn't like the roles that women had in the South. I also was sick to death of the way black people were being treated—it just made me crazy."

After graduating from Stanford in March 1960 summa cum laude and Phi Beta Kappa, she took the best job she could get, a secretarial position with the Republican National Committee in Washington, D.C. Within a few months, she was de facto running the Young Republican Division: "People up and down the East Coast and in the Midwest didn't realize that I had a boss. They thought I was it." Then her boss, later treasurer of the state of Kansas, would put in an appearance. "The way he treated me was denigrating. He excluded me from meetings with people coming to work on projects that I had initiated—he'd just have me bring the coffee. Then after the meeting, I would be told to execute whatever had been decided."

If Nixon had won in 1960, Katherine would have gone to work in the White House, but his loss meant there was a surplus of young Republican staffers looking for jobs. Katherine decided to change course and apply to Harvard for both a law degree and a Ph.D. "I knew it was the only way I could keep from being a secretary for the rest of my life and earning a secretary's wages." Although the odds were against a woman being admitted to either Harvard program in 1961, Katherine was accepted into both and chose law school.

Katherine also knew that the chances of a woman, even a graduate of Harvard Law School, getting a job as a lawyer were slim, but fortunately: "I had my first law job pretty well lined up before I started: Judge John Minor Wisdom [of the Fifth Circuit Court of Appeals] was a backdoor neighbor of my family's in New Orleans. He told me to come talk to him after I graduated."

When Katherine arrived in Cambridge, she decided to work to help pay her expenses. She took the job Nancy Kuhn had turned down, earning her room and board living in the home of Professor Arthur Sutherland, helping care for his elderly mother-in-law, cooking, making pies, and generally "being present."

In December 1961, she married another first-year law student, Michael D. O'Neil, whom she'd known at Stanford. "Looking back on the times, people got married. It was just the way it was, a natural, socially correct way to proceed."

Sheila Rush (Chatham College)

There were no Asians or Hispanics in our class and, as noted earlier, only three blacks, of whom Sheila was one. Sheila was talented and beautiful and she came to Harvard with enthusiasm and optimism: "I've always been kind of a trailblazer. That's been my experience most of my life." Nancy Kuhn played bridge with Sheila and others after the law library had closed and, looking back, reflects  that "life must not have been easy for her, but you never knew it being with her. There wasn't a hint of bitterness or antagonism."

Sheila Rush was born and grew up in Buffalo, New York, one of three children of a well-respected family involved in business, politics, and the community. Sheila had what she describes as "a pretty solid middle-class upbringing. When I was six, we moved to a predominately white neighborhood, probably about one-third Jewish, maybe one-fourth Catholic. It was the fifties, so of course it was something of a problem to be a black family in a white neighborhood in those days. It was not the easiest situation to cope with, but I can't say I was scarred permanently by it, and I always went to good schools."

Sheila's mother stayed at home until Sheila and her older brother were in college, then took a job for several years as an administrator for a Head Start center, helping minority children from some of the poorer neighborhoods in Buffalo get off to a good beginning in life. Her third child, a son, was born at the end of Sheila's first year of college.

Sheila's father was a self-made man. Soon after he and Sheila's mother married, he somehow scraped together the down payment for a small hotel in a mostly black neighborhood in Buffalo and also started a restaurant there. As the hotel and restaurant prospered, he purchased rental properties and a Laundromat. Eventually, he went into local politics as well, receiving a number of political appointments. "Financially," Sheila says, "we never had a lot of money, but my dad was a good provider. We were comfortable. We had a nice three-bedroom house. I always had enough."

Sheila attended Bennett High School in Buffalo, where she excelled: she was always in the honors class, the only black there. In her senior year, she was elected president of the Latin Honorary Society and followed the society's tradition of having the closing party at the home of the president. "The high school principal came, as did all the society's members. He mentioned what a nice house we had. Probably none of them had ever been in the home of a black person before. It was all very pleasant, but that was the only time they were ever at my house. And the only time I was ever in anybody else's house was for something similar."

Chatham College, a small, excellent women's college in Pittsburgh, Pennsylvania, recruited Sheila. She entered in September 1957. According to Sheila, the school had about four hundred students and was very conservative. She was one of three blacks in her freshman class of eighty students, and the only black student living on campus during three of her four years at Chatham. Although Chatham had only a few single rooms, Sheila was assigned to one of them: "It just shows you that they weren't going to impose this interracial situation on anyone. I developed a lot of friends in college, but it was like they were consciously breaking out of some restriction or other when they befriended me. Eventually, I had a roommate. She told me that her mother asked her, 'What are you trying to prove by rooming with Sheila?'"

In her senior year, Sheila, a political science major, learned that her roommate's mother had studied law for a while. Somehow Sheila instantly knew that she wanted to go to law school: "It was really intuitive, an inner sense that this was what I was meant to do. No one in my family had been to law school—I didn't know any lawyers well. But from that moment on, I knew that I would be a lawyer. I applied to Harvard, Yale, and Columbia and got into all of them. I decided to go to Harvard because it was the best. It was also the Kennedy era, and I was very much a supporter of Kennedy. The fact that he had graduated from Harvard and that so many Harvard Law School professors had joined his administration gave Harvard a certain mystique that the other schools didn't have. I wasn't thinking that I would practice law. Instead, I thought it was a very good degree to have, a very flexible credential. I was interested in international affairs and I thought I could probably get a job at the United Nations doing something interesting."

Sheila graduated first in her class from Chatham in 1961 and, after a summer at home in Buffalo, entered Harvard Law School in September: "I was scared. Really scared. All those men! It was nothing I was accustomed to. Law felt like a foreign language to me initially. The concepts were just so alien to my experience. They were not the subject of dinner-table conversation in my home, I assure you. Law school was just incredible for me."

Rosemary remembers meeting and befriending Sheila early in our first year of law school:

"Sheila was reserved. I had never really met a middle-class black person before. The black kids in Swarthmore, where I grew up, were working-class kids and their parents were janitors or maids. Sheila and I spent a lot of time talking about books and ideas. She was the first friend I had who was, along with Judy Wilson Rogers, a part of the New York white world as well as the black world. That was one of the eye-opening experiences at law school—for the first time being as good friends as I had with people who I'd been taught to believe were from a totally different background. She was smart, bright, and cultivated. And wary."

Sonia Faust (University of Hawaii)

As mentioned earlier, Sonia Faust was born in 1936 in Honolulu, the daughter of a motion-picture engineer employed as a civilian by the U.S. Army, and a school-teacher. After being evacuated from Hawaii with her mother and brother just before the battle of Midway began, she lived with her grandmother in Indiana near the Illinois border, entered first grade in Chicago, and even-  tually returned to the islands when the battle was over. She finished high school in Maui and had just started college at the University of Hawaii when her dad, the sole support of their family, became seriously ill. Sonia dropped out of college and went to work to support her family and to try to save a little money for a time when she hoped she could return to college. Sonia's father died when she was twenty. Three years later, she had saved enough to return to the university, where she graduated with highest honors in 1960. She had aced the LSAT, and a friend told her she could go to Harvard. All Sonia said was "Girls go to Harvard?" She spent the next year in a training program on public policy in San Francisco, saving money for law school.

Sonia entered Harvard Law School with our class, arriving in September 1961 in a beautiful Hawaiian muumuu and sandals. She found the school much bigger than she'd expected, and much more competitive. "I loved the substance of what we learned and the way we learned it. But it didn't take very long for me to get caught up in the anxiety of being a law student. There was the sense that you were never quite caught up with things. It was always moving a little faster than you were. Still, there were a whole lot of beautiful people there. And I thought they were all multimillionaires."

The Cambridge climate was hard on Sonia—she missed the warmth and the more relaxed life of the islands. Sometimes even in the coldest months, she would wear her muumuu and sandals when she worked at the front desk answering the phones in Wyeth Hall. Moving from a tight little island to an urban, crowded world was a rough adjustment for a brilliant, sensitive islander, but she managed it with grace. As her second-year roommate, Marge Freincle, remembers:

"The Harvard Law School atmosphere was tough for her. But she finished. She finished. She had a tremendous amount of grit and a lot of courage."

Susan Wall (Radcliffe)

Susan Wall, a petite, serious blue-eyed blonde, arrived at Harvard Law School from Minneapolis, Minnesota, by way of Radcliffe. We hardly had the chance to say hello before she disappeared. Rumor had it that she was intimidated by one or more of the professors and a number of her male classmates the first week of classes. She packed her bags and headed home before the end of September.

CHAPTER 8

Necessities: Food and Toilets

Harkness Commons was where we would eat for the next three years, but its role in our lives was much more important than just providing food: there we had a chance to discuss informally the cases we were studying, figuring things out collaboratively, not competitively.

Eric Fox

Eric Fox remembers sitting with fellow classmates Steve Breyer and Paul Dodyk at lunch going over the cases they had studied that morning: "It was just give-and-take, and they were as open as they could be." Breyer and Dodyk finished at the very top of our class, and Eric was close behind. Their approach was entirely different from the dog-eat-dog manner of the guy who finished first, Paul Posner. To this day, Eric Fox remembers Posner's response to his question about a case we were all struggling with: "He said he really couldn't discuss it with me because it might give me an unfair advantage in the exam over him. That's the only guy that ever pulled that stunt with me." I had virtually the same experience with Posner at the end of our first year. After the torts exam, I asked him how he had analyzed a particularly thorny exam question: "I shouldn't really talk about that; you might copy me." "For heaven's sakes, Paul," I replied, "the exam's over." But he still refused.

If Wyeth Hall was where the women got together in our first year, the cafeteria and eating hall on the second floor of Harkness Commons was where we crossed paths informally with most of the other students and even with the Law School faculty and came to know a group of people who would remain friends for the rest of our lives. Harkness, designed by Walter Gropius in the 1950s and decorated by artists of the Bauhaus school, including Joan Miró, Josef Albers, and Jean Arp, was and is a large, clinical-looking, two-story, beige-brick-and-concrete building with a slightly curved facade of plain, round concrete pillars facing the Law School yard, and Langdell, the Law School's main classroom and library building. The first floor contains meeting rooms, rest rooms, student mailboxes, and a long corridor lined with bulletin boards; the second floor features stainless-steel-clad cafeteria lines with a series of steam tables, and several dining rooms that can accommodate upward of a thousand people, all eating and jabbering at once. In the early 1960s, the food wasn't particularly good, but it was the only food on campus, and it was plentiful and cheap: every night there was a ninety-nine-cent special for dinner, generally something enticing like meat loaf, mashed potatoes and gravy, canned green beans, Jell-O, and coffee, tea, or milk. The saving grace, in addition to the bargain prices, was that there were always fascinating people to talk to; over a week, we would generally run into most of the people we knew at the Law School.

Early in the first year, a number of us started sitting together at breakfast and lunch at one of the long Formica-topped tables in Harkness Commons. The breakfasts were wretched: powdered scrambled eggs (before we realized eggs were bad for us), soggy toast, or lumpy Cream of Wheat. Whatever was cheapest that day. But, even at seven in the morning, the conversation was quick and fascinating, and Ann Dudley was among the quickest. One morning classmate George Bullwinkle, a tall, large-boned, pale-skinned redhead from Chicago, came over, sat down, and opened the day's conversation with "You know, women really don't belong in law school. They're not tough enough. They'll never stick with it." The table became electrically silent. Ever so slowly, Ann Dudley looked up over the edge of the *Daily Racing Form* that she'd been studying, fixed George with a steely look from her navy blue eyes, and uttered the perfect response: "Balls, Bullwinkle!" The table erupted in laughter, and "Balls, Bullwinkle!" became a rallying cry for the women in my class. I also decided right then that if I could ever afford to move out of Wyeth Hall, I wanted to share an apartment with Ann Dudley. As for George Bullwinkle, he mostly had breakfast with others after that.

Steve Breyer was part of our informal eating club and remembers it with great fondness: "Parts of law school were a lot of fun. We used to eat together at a long table in Harkness Commons—David Stone called it Harkness Monster, and the name stuck. We had a regular group. It was great. Ann Dudley was part of that group. She had a certain glamour. She had a good sense of humor and didn't appear to take law school too seriously, although, of course, she actually worked hard and did well

Steve Breyer

in the end. Was that the short-skirt period? If it wasn't, no one stopped her from wearing them. I think she always had gorgeous blouses. That's about all I remember. I really didn't notice too much." Marge Freincle (Haskell) has a slightly different recollection: "Steve was smart, likable, and very funny.

Although he was superbright, he didn't flaunt it all over the place. He also liked women. I don't know whether he had a crush on Ann Dudley, but he certainly noticed when she was around. I remember I was having breakfast in Harkness Commons one day, with a group that included Steve. My back was to the door but I noticed that Steve's head suddenly picked up and his eyes just kind of glowed. It was just kind of like, Ohoooooooooooooh! I just looked at him and said, 'Did Ann just come in?' And he said, 'What are you talking about?' But sure enough, there she was and she came over and sat down with us. Ann had a body that literally would stop every male around in his tracks. It was unreal. It was like Whoa! Steve definitely noticed her."

Most but not all of our male classmates were as open and welcoming as Steve Breyer. At times that first year, when classmate Nancy Kuhn took an empty seat at a lunch table in Harkness Commons, male classmates would get up and move: "Usually they would not say anything. They would just get up and go sit at another table. If they didn't leave, they would eat very quickly and often start shaking or trembling. I decided that Harvard Law was the achievement of their lives, an end in itself. And somehow to have a woman there was messing that up." Nancy also remembers regular encounters with male classmates on the stairs going up to the second-floor library reading room in Langdell Hall: "I can't tell you the number of times boys stopped me and said things like, 'How dare you come here? We have to support a family. You don't!' Of course, I'd pretty much been supporting myself since I was eighteen."

Harkness played another extraordinarily important role in the lives of the female law students: it housed one of the two ladies' rooms on the Harvard Law School campus during our time there. Bathroom facilities for Law School women had been a problem from the beginning: "The Dean mentioned the administrative problems concerned with opening the School to a substantial number of women students, and pointed out that [admitting women] had cost the [Harvard] Medical School $80,000 in internal changes [for ladies' toilets]. This, he said, was a real and practical consideration."[6]

In 1949, after the Corporation approved the admission of women to Harvard Law School, Dean Griswold asked Louis Toepfer, the Law School's vice dean and director of admissions, to take charge of the ladies' toilet problem, and to keep an eye on costs in coming up with a solution. Toepfer got estimates of what it would cost to redo the facilities in Langdell Hall "for the goodly accommodation of women." The price was, in his judgment, "astronomical, and for Griswold, who was a very frugal dean, it seemed even more wasteful." In addition, Dean Griswold was adamant that he did not want to take away any of Langdell library's book space for a ladies' toilet if space could be found elsewhere. Toepfer finally proposed that the school convert a janitor's closet in the basement of Austin Hall, which already had cold running water, into the ladies' bathroom for the Law School. It was—and still is—a fair distance down a low-ceilinged, cement-paved passageway under a thicket of overhead, asbestos-wrapped heating pipes, a little less than a block south of Langdell, the main classroom and library building. As Dean Toepfer recalled to me decades later, "It was awkward, it was inconvenient, it was certainly not very desirable—not right—but that is what we decided we would do. Make do for a while."

Toepfer's solution was duly noted in the 1949 faculty report recommending that women be admitted to Harvard Law School:

> With respect to housing, medical and other similar problems which the admission of women to the Law School would present, the Committee, appreciating their seriousness, is persuaded that their dimensions are not such as to justify the continuation of our policy of exclusion. One of the minor problems is capable of easy solution: The Building and Grounds Department has advised the Committee that toilet and rest room facilities can be installed in the basement of Austin Hall for an estimated cost of $11,000.[7]

When we arrived twelve years later, in 1961, and even when we graduated in 1964, there were just two ladies' rooms on campus: the original one in the Austin Hall basement at the south end of campus, and the one in the newly constructed Harkness Commons, at the north end. For three years, it was quite a sprint for us, especially during exams, when every minute counted. I remember racing out of the middle of the property exam in Langdell at the end of my first year and sprinting across to the Harkness ladies' room: it was the wrong time of the month, and by the time I arrived, the back of my skirt was bloodstained. I was followed almost into the stall by a male exam proctor, who was certain that I had secreted crib sheets somewhere in there; he was bound and determined not to let me get my hands on them.

Marge remembers the problems we had coping with the lack of facilities: "We had to go way, way down the tunnels between the buildings, then down the halls, all the way to the basement of Austin Hall when it was too cold to go outside in the dead of winter."

Ann Dudley sometimes tried a different tactic: "We used to sneak into the men's in Langdell if we possibly could, but otherwise we had to go all the way over to the Harkness Commons, or to the basement of Austin Hall, which was even farther."

Off the second-floor library and reading room, there was just one bath-

room, forcefully marked FACULTY. There was no confusion as to who was entitled to use it, as Professor Charles Nesson recalls: "'FACULTY' described the
entire place in the early sixties, and the entire place was male. It was a totally
aggressively male institution."

The faculty's secretaries, like the women law students, were relegated to
sprinting to the Austin or Harkness toilet.

There was one advantage to having only two ladies' rooms on campus: all
the women law students crossed paths at least once a day, stopping to
exchange information, triumphs and horror stories, not to mention gossip,
with no men around to overhear or comment. But we never forgot the
inconvenience and, at times, the embarrassment of not having facilities
closer at hand. As Nancy says, "The first time I went back to Harvard Law
School after graduation was in 1989, for our twenty-fifth reunion. The
first thing I did was use the ladies' room in Langdell Hall. I went in and had
a celebratory flush. When we were there, you had to leave the whole huge

building to go to another
building . . . even in the
middle of six-hour exams.
Which, looking back, was
blatant discrimination,
although we didn't think
that way then. Nor, of
course, did the school. We
didn't complain—about
that or anything else. We
thought we were lucky to
be there, and we didn't
want to upset anything."

Austin Hall: Ladies' room (1950–2001)

CHAPTER 9

Classes Begin

Harvard Law School has no glee club. The next three years are
mine.

— Welcoming remarks, Dean Erwin Griswold,
September 1961

On a Sunday afternoon in September 1961, the day before classes were to
begin, our class, nearly six hundred strong, gathered in the august, dark-
paneled James Barr Ames Courtroom in Austin Hall to receive Dean Griswold's greetings: "My name is Griswold. I am the dean of this place." The
dean, originally from Ohio, was short and stocky with a penetrating gaze that
always seemed to be questioning whether we were doing our best. He was a
renowned scholar in the field of tax law, a civil rights advocate before that
was popular, and a brilliant administrator. By the time we arrived, he was in
the fourteenth year of his deanship, a tenure noted for the recruitment of an
outstanding faculty and for the construction of the Law School dormitories
and Harkness Commons, as well as the enormous expansion of scholarship
funds. As noted at the time: "Scholarship and loan
funds to help complete a legal education are available to any student after his first year and many
scholarships are even available to first year men
[sic]. [Dean Griswold] contrasts this with the situation at the School before his administration
when scholarships were only available to the top
twenty percent of the student body."[8]

Dean Griswold told us that our class came from
46 states and 117 colleges and universities and
ticked off the number of Rhodes, Marshall, Fulbright, Rotary, and Woodrow Wilson scholars we
had, as well as the number of Phi Beta Kappa

Dean Griswold

members, magna and summa cum laude graduates, and student body presidents. He mentioned that we had an Olympic gold medalist in swimming, two former Harvard football captains, a father of three children, and the past proprietor of a San Francisco espresso shop. He stressed the seriousness of our purpose over the next three years and talked briefly about legal ethics. He recalled a former law dean's warning: "Look at the person to your right, and the person on your left, because one of the three of you won't be here at the end of first year," and told us that was no longer true. He cautioned us, however, that what was often referred to as an excessively competitive atmosphere at the Law School was rather just the school's tradition of excellence. When he finished, we went to a huge reception on the lawn in front of Harkness Commons, the building where the meeting rooms and the Law School cafeteria were—and still are—located.

The next day, we would start our first year of law school, known then and now as 1-L: "The first year is a year devoted to learning the ways of the law. . . . Through the practice rounds of the Ames Competition, [students] are introduced to case research and brief writing. The work is hard; the load is heavy; but Harvard is not for those whose dedication to the Law is dilatory."[9]

Our class was divided into 4 sections of approximately 140 students, each including 5 women. Each section would spend the first year together in every class, learning how to "think like lawyers" by studying the infrastructure of

First-year reception: Professor John "Black Jack" Dawson, center,
talking with first-year classmate Dinni Lorenz

the law: contracts (how and when the bargains people make with each other are binding and are enforced), civil procedure (the rules governing the litigation of noncriminal disputes), torts (the law relating to civil wrongs, such things as personal injuries, assaults, and batteries), property (ownership rights in real and personal property), criminal law (the rules relating to crimes, including felonies and misdemeanors), and agency (the law of whether and when someone acting for another can bind the other). The concepts were new to most of us, and simultaneously difficult and tedious. To open our minds to this massive amount of complex information, and to keep us alert and on the edges of our chairs in fear of being called on to recite, our professors had perfected the Socratic method of teaching law, a methodology first developed at Harvard Law School late in the nineteenth century during the tenure of Dean Christopher Columbus Langdell, for whom the Law School's main library and classroom building is named. They never told us what the answers were, and except for Professor Charles Fried, most implied that there weren't any answers: "The law is not as precise as you might think," they told us. "The point will be to train your judgment to deal with multifaceted problems." In class, the professors assumed that we had done the reading and politely but insistently battered us with complicated hypothetical questions about its implications and the merits and flaws in the assigned cases. They called on one student after another to respond, pitting us courteously but also devastatingly against each other. Classes could, on the same day, be terrifying, mystifying, hilarious, and embarrassing. But because of the teachers and even because of the tension they cultivated, classes were never dull.

On the first day of classes, the professors offered brief introductions to each course, then pushed us directly into the hard and fascinating work of studying law. In a real sense, we were learning a foreign language, and Harvard's law school methodology was "total immersion." It took us months to realize that up to 75 percent of the cases in our textbooks had been selected precisely because they were wrong, and that our task was to figure out how they were wrong, and what a better result would be.

As classmate Fred Hitz, who had graduated at the top of his class from Princeton University (and later became the first Statutory Inspector General of the CIA and, thereafter, a professor at Princeton University), told me: "I'll never forget my first day of classes at Harvard Law School. I had done very well in college and thought I could handle anything, but the professors totally melted my Phi Beta Kappa key with their blowtorch questions."

Fred Hitz

The second class of my first day was Civil Procedure with Professor Benjamin Kaplan (now Justice Kaplan of the Supreme Judicial Court of Massachusetts). Kaplan was one of the era's most brilliant legal scholars, a former staff member for Justice Jackson at the Nuremberg war crime trials following World War II, and the Reporter to the Advisory Committee on Civil Rules of the Judicial Conference of the United States. The first case he assigned us was the United States Supreme Court case *Sibbach vs. Wilson & Co.* "State the case of *Sibbach vs. Wilson*, Mr. Jones." "How does that strike you, Mr. Jackson? Did Mr. Jones leave out anything you think was essential?" "Well, Mr. Jones, what do you have to say for yourself? Is Mr. Jackson right?" "And tell us, Mr. Futterman, what crucial point did both of them miss?"

As Tom Jackson (now Judge Thomas Penfield Jackson of the United States District Court for the District of Columbia Circuit) recalls, when he was stumped and floundering, Professor Kaplan would often turn to Mr. Boudin (now Chief Judge Michael Boudin of the United States Court of Appeals for the First Circuit): "Mr. Boudin, could you help Mr. Jackson out and explain for us how this case should have been decided?" We struggled for a month with that case and still didn't get it quite right.

Thomas Penfield Jackson

Forty years later, Justice Kaplan told me that he started his textbook and his class with the *Sibbach* case precisely because it was the most difficult case in all of civil procedure, and he wanted to expose us to the vast complexities of the law right from the start.

Classmate Joe Wheelock tried to figure out why they didn't give us at least some clue about where we were going: "I thought civil procedure was some kind of methodology by which people were supposed to be polite with each other."

Michael Boudin

We were given assigned seats in every class so that the professors, using huge seating charts with our passport-size photos pasted on them, could call on and question us individually. In most sections, including mine, the five women students were all assigned seats in the front row.

Pat Scott (Schroeder) was astonished: "I had thought we all got to sit where we wanted. . . . And then in two of my classes the guys on either side of me wanted to have their seats changed because they had never sat next to a

Joseph Wheelock

girl in their entire educational lives. And I thought, 'Well, isn't this inter-esting.' I think they must have wanted to make us feel particularly welcome! Having come from the University of Minnesota, where, when you have class, if you are smart enough, you are going to come, and if you're too dumb to come, you're gonna fail, Harvard Law was a shock. And to suddenly have seats assigned *and* to sit in the front seat if you're a girl, *and then* to have these bozos say they are going to change their seats because they've never sat next to a girl? Like they're getting estrogen contamination?"

Marge Freincle (Haskell) has similar memories: "Most of the men in our classes didn't know what to make of us. They didn't get it. If they had come from one of the all-male Ivy League schools, they were used to being let out on occasional weekends to chase around a bunch of chicks down at some girls' school. Princeton was like that. They didn't know whether to flirt or be serious or how to treat us. The fellows who had gone to the coed schools didn't seem to have the same kind of problems."

As Dinni Lorenz (Gordon) told me: "I remember many things about my gender that shaped my law school experience. I remember walking into the library in Langdell Hall, through those vast echoing spaces, and my heels would make a clicking sound on the hard, polished cork floors. A hundred pairs of eyes would look up and heads would swing. People would stare. It seemed that every male in the library would turn and look because they knew this was the sound of a woman's step. I would feel a clenching of my stom-ach. For me, it was excruciating, just excruciating. I felt exposed in a way that was really very painful for me. There was constantly the sense of being such a tiny minority that stuck out and was the object of curiosity."

Before school started, a number of the men in our class who had studied in England on Marshall, Rhodes, and Fulbright scholarships successfully lob-bied the administration to assign them to the same section, angling to get what they'd heard was the best overall collection of professors. As it turned out, four of the top ten in our class, and eight of the top twenty-five, came from that section, the one with Casner for Property, Dawson for Contracts, Sacks for Civil Procedure, and Fried for Criminal Law. I was not in that sec-tion—I didn't know one professor from another when I started and had no idea that you could—or should—lobby for section placement. I had fabulous teachers nonetheless.

On the first day of classes, that "preferred" section began at 8 A.M. with A. James Casner's Property course. Casner's approach was "to make the stu-dent carry the ball and teach himself. . . . [There] isn't just one answer—it is the process of thinking that a student puts behind the answers that he gives [that's important.]"[10] A. James Casner was probably the nation's most erudite property law scholar of his day—a conclusion he found a way to mention to his section that first day. He zeroed in on Peter Berle for his opening gambit. Peter, a former lieutenant in the U.S. Air Force (who went on to be New York state's Commissioner of Environmental Conservation and then became President of the National Audubon Society), looked like central casting's version of

the parachutist and military intelligence officer he had become: tall, muscular, with wavy blond hair and electric

Professor A.
James Casner

blue eyes. Peter was also the son of A. A. Berle, the world-famous economics professor from Columbia University. Though Peter was smart, charming, and handsome, he was no match for Professor Casner, who led him through a series of questions calculated to stump him—and entertain the rest of the class—by having him distinguish between when you can own property in animals and when you can't. "Can you have property in

bees? Can you have property in wild birds? Can you have property in wild geese? Why? Why not? What is the basis

Peter A. A. Berle

for your distinction? What should be?" Casner kept boring down. Peter was reeling. Just as the class was about to end, Casner delivered the coup de grâce: "Son, can't you advance our understanding even a little bit this first day of class? Can't you at least tell us the difference between the birds and the bees?" The room exploded with laughter. Lieutenant Berle laughed, too, but also turned scarlet and slid down in his chair.

It wasn't long before Professor Casner called on Paul Posner for a complicated analysis of a question of personal property. Before entering Harvard Law, Posner had studied law at Oxford for two years and had received Oxford's highest ranking, a First, for his achievements there. He had been offered second-year status at Harvard Law School but had turned it down: he told me he wanted to try to finish first in the class and thought he'd have a better chance if he started over as a first-year student. Paul answered Professor Casner's questions coolly, comprehensively, and, it seemed, brilliantly, but Casner apparently wanted to show him who was boss. Classmate Eric Fox remembers "as if it were yesterday" how Casner cut Posner down to size while simultaneously egging him on to do his best, giving him his highest backhanded compliment: "Mr. Posner, I can't believe how stupid you are. But one day, if you work very hard, you may be as brilliant as I am."

Eric was just glad he hadn't opened his mouth. (As it turned out, Paul Posner finished first in our class all three years.)

The next day Casner questioned Paul Dodyk, an Amherst Phi Beta Kappa graduate and Rhodes Scholar who had grown up in Hamtramck, Michigan, where his dad was a steel-press operator at the Dodge Motor Company. Casner pursued Paul slowly and relentlessly for nearly an hour. Near the end of the period, he sprang the final question. "Mr. Dodyk, suppose you gave me your watch, I gave you a claim ticket, and when you came back for your watch, I refused to give it back to you. What are you going to do?"

Paul Dodyk

Paul rose to the occasion: "I'm going to tell myself that I ought to figure out never to give anything to you again." The class erupted with laughter and Professor Casner joined in. The test seemed to be not how right you were, but how resilient, how quick-witted. Dodyk had passed that test with flying colors.

Marge Freincle (Haskell) remembers how she felt when classes began: "I was shaking, scared, and miserable. A. James Casner just picked you out when he felt like killing you. Actually, he just killed you generally. Because there were so few of us chicks, I felt that if I was wrong, every other female there afterwards was going to be considered wrong by everybody in the whole darn class. It's bad enough to carry your own water, but to have to carry it for every other woman in the class if you screwed up was not fun. Being called on in that atmosphere is something I could have done without. But, twenty-twenty hindsight, it may have made a better person of me. Somehow I survived."

The women in my section weren't singled out any more—or any less—than the men. But the kinds of questions we got often seemed designed to amuse the men— and embarrass us. In her section, Ann Dudley Cronkhite (Goldblatt) remembers that the only teacher who called on her early in our first year was Professor Charles Fried in Criminal Law. Fried, the son of Czech refugees and a graduate of Princeton, Oxford, and Columbia Law School who had clerked for Justice Harlan, was six feet three, lanky, and patrician. He always wore impeccable three-piece suits to class. (Ann Dudley wondered whether he wore three-piece pajamas to bed, too.) What she didn't realize was that, at twenty-six years old, Charles Fried was hardly older than we were. He was the youngest tenured professor in history at Harvard Law School, Criminal Law was the first class he had ever taught, and the first case assigned in that class was the

Professor
Charles Fried

nineteenth-century British case *Regina vs. Dudley & Stephens,* about men on a life raft who'd been adrift for many days. They were starving, and eventually, they ate the cabin boy. Because of the "Dudley" in her name, Ann Dudley was the first person Professor Fried called on the first day of classes to discuss whether eating the cabin boy was murder. "There were five women and over one hundred men and he calls on me. I was nervous. My mouth was dry. I said something that wasn't altogether wrong, but I was framing it in a funny way. I was trying to protect myself. And he said, 'Miss Cronkhite, do you know what a negative pregnant is?' and I thought, 'Oh, shit!' Fortunately Steve Breyer was sitting next to me and he whispered, 'That's the worst kind.' So I said, in my best little-girl voice, 'Oh, Professor Fried, that's the very worst kind.' Everybody laughed, including Fried, and I was saved. In fact, it probably made my reputation for the whole first year."

Charles Fried was never a proponent of Harvard Law School's unadulterated Socratic method. His conception of being a teacher of law, then and now, was first to master a field and then to find the best way of communicating that mastery: "I thought there were answers. You figure them out and then you try to put that before the students."

The boys in our class who had studied together in England on scholarships before beginning law school, and who had lobbied their way into the section that included Professor Fried, hoped to have some fun at his expense:

"Steve Breyer, Paul Dodyk, Bert Rein, Hugh Jones—they were all in my first Criminal Law class and they were out to get me. Not in a terribly unfriendly way, but they were out to get me and they worked hard at it. They were only a couple of years younger than I was. They were out to see if they could run circles around me, and they couldn't. I had already studied criminal law with the great master, Professor Herbert Wechsler, when I was at Columbia Law School. I was using his textbook, and I had thought my way through to the end of the course. So it worked out all right."

By comparison, one of our first-year Contracts professors, Clark Byse, was a strong proponent of the Socratic system, in which the answers seem to be much less important than the questions or the methodology of thinking about the answers. Classmates in his section soon came to realize that whatever it was that they thought they had just grasped was going to slip through their fingers by the end of each class hour.

Professor Robert Braucher, a former air force pilot and later a Justice of the Massachusetts Supreme Judicial Court, taught Contracts to the section I was in. He was also serving as the Reporter for the Second Restatement

Professor
Robert Braucher

of Contracts and as the coordinator for the revision of the Uniform Commercial Code and was teaching at the Harvard Business School as well as at the Law School, all at the same time. To amuse us and make us think, Braucher condensed purported principles of law into "great sayings," which we still remember:

- The purpose of the law of evidence is to hide the truth.
- The purpose of the law of consumer protection is to raise the price of goods and services.
- The purpose of the criminal law is to free the guilty and to convict the innocent.

Braucher used the same tongue-in-cheek approach to force us to analyze the ethical responsibilities of lawyers, in light of Dean Griswold's determination to insert ethics from the very beginning of our study of law: "I have a memo here from the dean, who tells me I'm supposed to teach ethics. Very well. I'll tell you a story about ethics. Once there was a lawyer. His client gave him one hundred thousand dollars for safekeeping and left for Europe. The lawyer took the hundred thousand dollars and invested it in the stock market on the theory that if the stock went up, as it was bound to do, he would split the profit, giving half to the client and keeping the other half. Well, he invested, it, the stock went up, he gave half the profit to the client. Nobody ever found out. Now that's the end of the story."

To liven up the classes and relieve the intense pressures we were under in our first year of law school, our professors tried to have some fun with us, and also with each other. Contracts was the first class of the day in my section. We began at 8 A.M. and were supposed to end at 8:50, but Professor Braucher often kept us longer. That made us late for our 9 A.M. Civil Procedure class with Professor Kaplan. Kaplan finally got fed up. One day, when Braucher was still going strong at 9 A.M., we heard a deep male voice roaring "Braucher! Braucher!" from the

Professor
Benjamin Kaplan

back of the classroom. We spun around in our chairs. There was Professor Kaplan. With his thick shock of white hair and massive shoulders, Benjamin Kaplan already looked like Moses, but that day the image was inescapable. He was standing on a chair in the middle of the last row, arms outstretched: "Braucher! Braucher!" he repeated. "I've warned you again and again. Now, I command you. Let my people go!"

We loved it! And Professor Braucher never kept us late again.

The professors in my section seem to have collaborated on how to keep us interested in the difficult subject matter. One way, they apparently decided, was to have some fun at my expense. Day after day, classmates all around me were called on to recite, after which each professor made a point of putting a check mark beside their names. After a few weeks, everyone in my section had been called on in every class. Everyone, that is, except me: I had not been called on in a single class. As the days and then the weeks passed, the teachers began calling on students for a second time, but still no one called on me. I couldn't understand why I was being skipped over, and the pressure to be ready when the fateful day came increased exponentially. Then one day in early November, nearly two months after classes had begun, I was called on in every class on the same day. And in most classes, the theme was the same: sex. In Contracts, Professor Braucher asked me whether, in a "breach of promise to marry" case, the girl has to give the diamond ring back. My answer was "No, because the ring should be considered a gift, not consideration for completing the marriage contract." Braucher dismissed what I thought was a pretty good answer under the circumstances: "A nice girl gives the ring back, Miss Richards." The men in the class applauded. In Criminal Law, Professor Paul Bator, who later became a great friend of mine, called on me to state a rape case. By the time that class was over, we had been through all the grisly details, including whether the man could claim that the woman's provocative clothing meant that she had consented to his advances. I survived and hope I had the wit to understand that I was being trained to keep my emotions in check in analyzing a legal case in order to come to a clearheaded conclusion.

In Torts, Professor Jaffe called on me to discuss a "harmful touching" case. Jaffe had studied under Professor (later Justice) Frankfurter, clerked for Justice Brandeis, and served as dean of the University of Buffalo Law School before joining the Harvard Law faculty. His questions to me focused on a case involving what, today, the law would view as egregious sexual harassment in the workplace, actions for which, in 1961, remedies were much less available. Professor Jaffe extrapolated hypothetical situations from the case, pushing me to come up with some legal solution, some line beyond which an employer's conduct would constitute a "tort" against his female secretary sufficient to give her a viable claim in court. When he told her he liked her dress? When he mentioned that he liked her in tight sweaters? When he said that it would be easier to work if she sat on his lap? When he fondled her as she was taking dictation? When he suggested that they have dinner? When he said that unless she went to bed with him, she was fired? For me and some of the other women in my section, who'd already experienced similar behavior in summer jobs, the fact that most of the hypotheticals were not then actionable in court only proved the proverb that "the law is an ass." In desperation, I finally suggested that the secretary should "waive the tort and sue in assumpsit," essentially acknowledging that, since the law of torts didn't seem to supply a remedy, she could rest her case on an implied contract of employment, which was breached by the boss's actions. The class loved it and Professor Jaffe did, too. I was—at last—off the hook for the day, and even proud of myself that I'd made it through without buckling.

Classmate (now federal Judge) Thomas Penfield Jackson, an ex–navy officer, was in my section, and he still remembers that day, almost as clearly as I do: "The first six months at Harvard Law School was one of the worst periods of my life. It was an exercise in intellectual humiliation. The professors were very astute in leading students out on a limb and then lopping it off. For me, it was a terrifying experience. And I really remember when Louis Jaffe went after you. It was the first really salacious case we studied in Torts. He picked on you to state that case. He beat you up. I didn't think it was funny. I thought he should have been ashamed of himself. I thought it was a cruel thing for him to do."

I hadn't thought it was cruel, and even today, when I think back, I still believe Louis meant his questions only as a challenge, a test of wit and quickness under fire, as well as a way to lighten the heavy slogging of the first year of law school. Although I didn't know it then, it would prove to be much like innuendos I would regularly face in the practice of law. A few days after my "big" day, Professor Jaffe and his wife invited me to dinner at their beautiful Cambridge home filled with French Impressionist paintings, right down to a Renoir above the mantel in the living room. Whether the invitation came because I had acquitted myself well on "harmful touchings," or because he was sorry he had pushed me so hard, I'll never know. What I do know is that he and his wife became close friends and advisers, not only on legal theory but also on art, the good theater in town, and how to live well and honorably in the law. Professor Louis Leventhal Jaffe was a brilliant teacher and a Renaissance man, who, without doubt, indelibly taught me the law relating to "harmful touchings" in a single hour.

Professor
Louis Jaffe

Rosemary Cox (Masters) blossomed in law school. On October 19, 1961, she wrote her parents that the conflicts and issues she was addressing were fascinating, and that she was finding her true self: "I am beginning to slough off the sweet and simple girlish Mount Holyoke image which was never really me at all. I never want to become hardened or insensitive to the needs of those around me; yet how silly to pretend to be sillier and more naïve than I really am. The nice thing about the law school is that so far the boys seem to like and respect the direct and unadulterated me more than the simple sweet disguise which I laboured under during high school and college. I believe I feel freer in these five weeks of law school than I have felt in my entire life."[11]

We were launched. Despite the difficulties, most of us were having a great time at law school—the teachers were extraordinary, the material challenging, and most of our fellow students brilliant and engaging.

CHAPTER 10

Ladies' Day

Professor W. Barton "Pappy" Leach, selectman of Weston, Massachusetts, and a former air force general who had led a fighter wing in World War II, taught the law of property to section one of our class, the section that included Pat Scott, Judy Wilson, Rosemary Cox, Nancy Kuhn, and Alice Pasachoff. Pappy was tall and muscular, and he would pace back and forth on the podium while he lectured with few, if any, notes. Like most of our professors, he exuded self-confidence. He was thought to be one of the Law School's "most valuable and most legendary professors. . . . Satirical and/or bawdy poetry, Ladies' Days, and anecdotes augment Professor Leach's considerable teaching skills."[12]

Professor
W. Barton Leach

Leach's stated philosophy of teaching was simple: "If you can toss a laugh in and keep it fairly relevant, so much the better. Start off a lecture with a laugh. It gets oxygen in their lungs."[13] While Leach delivered what he, and even his students, thought were a lot of laughs, many of them were at the expense of the women in his classes. He was reputed to be quite a ladies' man, but that didn't extend to welcoming ladies into his classes—we cramped his raunchy "just us guys" approach to teaching. Besides, what kind of woman went to law school anyway? In 1949, he had been one of the two members of the faculty who voted against admitting women to Harvard Law School.

Pat Scott (Schroeder) remembers that Leach started off his first lecture by stating that he was still mostly opposed to having women at Harvard Law, and that he would not call on us to recite except for the few days a year set aside as "ladies' days." Charles Buffon, a Dartmouth alumnus and now a top litigator at Covington & Burling in Washington, D.C., recalls that Leach "made the point very forcefully on the first day that he was a military figure as well as a law school teacher, and that he was the boss in the classroom."

Nancy Kuhn (Kirkpatrick) remembers that ladies' days were nerve-racking, and that when the classroom discussion slowed down, Leach, as well as some of our other professors, would say, "Well, I have a good story I would tell to illustrate this, but now that we have to have women in the class, I can't tell it." According to Nancy, "Leach believed he was courtly and courteous to women, but in fact he enjoyed putting us on the spot very publicly." Nancy didn't complain, but she didn't like it: she was quiet, shy, and deferential, but she was also very determined to get through law school and make a success in the law.

Marie Driscoll, in the class ahead of us (now a top intellectual-property litigator in Manhattan), says that, deep down, Leach was a shy man where women were concerned. "He was afraid if he called on us out of the blue and we didn't do well or couldn't answer or hadn't read the case, he would embarrass us. He was reluctant to do what he did to the men, which was to push them to the wall with questions—he could be terribly cutting and sarcastic in questioning the male students. He didn't want to do that to a woman. I don't think he did it to be malicious. That's what I think now, but it didn't seem that way at the time."

Leach's actions and motivations were confusing to us and probably to him: he seemed to be trying to be entertaining, patronizing, and perhaps even kind, all at the same time. Looking back, it was odd that neither the women in Leach's section nor the rest of the women in our class took offense at ladies' days: we thought they were just another aspect of the hazing that everyone, male and female, was subjected to that first year. We were determined to get through whatever they threw at us and join the fraternity, and if this was part of the admission ritual, so be it.

According to Harvard Law School Professor Charles Nesson, who studied Property with Leach the year before we arrived and eventually became his colleague on the Law School faculty, "W. Barton Leach was this fearsome character who drank too much and would often come to class kind of red. He had a vein that stuck out in his forehead when he was feeling a little hungover, and it sort of went from his nose straight up. It sort of bulged; you could see that this guy had rage very close to the surface. Bart had the rationale that women couldn't be heard in

Charles Nesson
(Harvard Law
class of 1963)

class—he said they couldn't speak as loudly as the men, so they should go up on the stage to be questioned. But, of course, that was just an excuse. He wanted to tease them, entertain the men—and maybe the women, too— and relieve the tension which was evident, particularly in the first few weeks of first year. Ladies' day wasn't meant to put people down. And yet, at the same time, it was awful. It was built on sexist assumptions which, when revealed years later, just blew me away. It's hard for me to imagine that I didn't notice then that something was wrong."

Alice Pasachoff (Wegman) recalls her first Property class with Professor Leach: "He said, in a tongue-in-cheek fashion, that it was unchivalrous to call on a lady without advance notice. Therefore, he told us he would only be calling on the women in the class on ladies' days, and that he would announce the day and the case to be analyzed forty-eight hours in advance. He may have intended humor, but it was also his intention to put the women down. But from the perspective of the women, who had received a lot of positive feedback from our families and our friends in connection with deciding to come to Harvard Law School, I can't say that we didn't enjoy the attention on some level. So it was a little of both: a big put-down but also a way of singling us out, giving us an edge, which was not altogether negative from our viewpoint."

The presumption that the women students had a special advantage because they had advance notice of the cases they'd be questioned on was, of course, absurd: every student always had the assignments in advance in every class, but it didn't do us much good. Our edge was the old-girl network: the upper-class women who knew what Pappy was up to.

The first ladies' day arrived in late October, six or seven weeks into the semester, when Leach assigned the women a case involving personal property, specifically the fraudulent sale of dozens of pairs of woolen underwear to an unsuspecting buyer, known in the law as a bona fide purchase, or a BFP. Presumably, in those uptight times, an hour-long discussion of "unmentionables" would embarrass the women and amuse the men. The women in Leach's section found out from the second-year women in Wyeth Hall that Leach had chosen the same case the year before. One of them, Marie Driscoll, offered to coach them the night before the first ladies' day.

On Monday, October 30, 1961, Alice wrote in her diary: "We met to review for Ladies' Day tonight, with Marie presiding. . . . We wrote a poem and will recite it tomorrow. I am nervous about tomorrow's poem. I hope it works smoothly. I suppose it will be taken in fun."

Marie Driscoll recalls, "I sat down with the 1-L women and rehearsed them on what to expect. I had saved my notes from the prior year: I gave them all the questions and all the answers."

On Halloween 1961, like trained seals doing tricks for an eager audience, the five women in Leach's section, dressed in high heels, skirts, blazers, and pearls, were ready. They left their seats in the front row of the large, fan-shaped classroom seating, mounted the steps to the dais, sat down on the five folding chairs that had been arranged in a line facing the rest of the class, crossed their ankles, and waited calmly for the first question they already knew was coming. Leach left the dais and went to the middle of the classroom, where he stood to interrogate them, surrounded by 140 or so male students, who hooted and laughed and sometimes stomped their feet, thinking it was marvelous fun. Actually, most of the women thought it was fun, too. It seemed totally normal for Harvard Law School then. Nancy remembers, "It was sort of like Picnic at the Zoo Day—and we were the animals in the cages."

Alice recalls what happened on the first ladies' day for our class: "He questioned us for the solid hour. We felt very confident sitting there because we had been very well prepared by Marie. We all had typed pages of notes and our answers were fluent and correct. If we had been called on without notice, in the early weeks of law school, we would likely have felt intimidated. But because we had been prepared, it was more of a performance. Afterwards, we heard from some of our male classmates that our performance made them very nervous because we had more of the answers than they would have had at that point in law school."

For Judy Wilson (Rogers), Professor Leach was a "powder puff," and she worked for him during the summer after her first year. For her, ladies' day was

Professor W. Barton Leach, left, sits among his students conducting ladies' day

not cruel but "like an entertainment. Because we had been warned—and coached by upper-class women—we all knew the answers. There were no trick questions or anything like that. But those were the only times we were called on in his class all year."

Looking back on the experience, Alice commented, "Ladies' day actually did us an unanticipated disservice. For me, Property was the subject I studied least, since I knew I wouldn't be called on—and my final grade reflected that."

At the end of that first ladies' day the women in Leach's class delivered the poem they had written celebrating the purloined-underwear case, *Higgins vs. Lodge*. Their ditty was a parody on "Tom Dooley." That night, Rosemary wrote her parents with the first few lines:

> Hang down your head, John Higgins
> Hang down your head and cry
> Hang down your head, John Higgins,
> This action's going to lie.[14]

Alice's diary contains the rest of the poem:

> You met him in the basement,
> Selling underwear.
> You should have been more cautious.
> The buyer must beware.
>
> His actions were peculiar,
> His money running low.
> His motives were deceitful;
> Were you suspicious—NO!
>
> The judge said to the jury
> If a man is notified,
> He'd better make inquiry,
> Or he ain't bona fide.
>
> That court saw just one issue
> And muddled up the law,
> Thought August was September;
> That was their fatal flaw.

Bring writs of error and review
The judges to impeach,
This time you'll surely win your case
With counsel Barton Leach.

Rosemary commented in a letter home: "At the end of the class the boys all gave us a tremendous ovation, while Leach himself seemed quite delighted with our ballad of a B.F.P. (Bone [sic] Fide Purchaser.)"[15]

Ladies' days continued to occur from time to time in Leach's class throughout our first year. Each time, the 1-L women were coached by the upper-class women, they came to class fully prepared, sat calmly on the dais, and gave all the right answers. Sometimes, they all went out for coffee or a beer with Leach after the class ended. Leach seemed to think they enjoyed the hazing, and that he had made friends with the female students in his classes. He invited them to his house just before the Christmas break. Pat remembers standing around the piano singing carols with Leach, his wife, and the other women in the section. When Rosemary and classmate Jon Masters decided to marry at the end of first year, Leach sought an invitation to the wedding:

6 June 1962

Dear Rosemary:

Before I put in the final grade on Property I, I want to know WHY I HAVE NOT BEEN INVITED TO THE WEDDING! [emphasis in original] Am I or am I not a friend? I don't promise to attend, but I hate not to be invited! If I attend, shall I sit on the Bride's side or the Groom's side of the church? Please advise me.

Sincerely,
W. Barton Leach
Story Professor of Law

(Rosemary, WBL has taken a preliminary look at your examination and is holding up the final determination of grade until his letter is answered. But there is no *significant* risk of failure.) h.a.s. [WBL's secretary][16]

Rosemary believes that while Pappy Leach could be an intimidating teacher, he was essentially a kind man who simultaneously feared women law students and yet wanted them to succeed.

Pat's recollection of Leach's hazing is that it was absurd, something to be endured and then ignored: "I really don't remember any particular questions I was asked. It's kind of funny because my attitude was just 'Eh! So this is how they get their jollies. I'll play. Ask me a question and I'll answer it.' I didn't have a lot of patience with it and I just didn't obsess about it. I just thought it was all silly."

Charles Buffon has one particularly vivid recollection of ladies' day: "The unfortunate fact is that the one indelible thing that I remember about ladies' day our first year is when one of the women started crying. The professor, Barton Leach, just went nuts. He started yelling something like 'What area of the law? Don't tell me if you're arguing before the Supreme Court and you've got a tough question to which you don't know the answer, you're going to start to cry?' That was the one occasion that I remember that, finally, the male students in the class began to hiss the professor."

Charles Buffon

Eventually, when Derek Bok was Dean of Harvard Law School, it fell to him to tell W. Barton Leach he could not teach anymore. According to Bok, "He was quite arrogant, quite willing to cut corners, to run over people to achieve what he thought the right result was or what his result was. He was terribly opinionated. He was not one of the people I looked up to in the Harvard Law School faculty. Some people would laugh at what he was doing, but I had to stay out of his way—I just didn't take to the man. And then of course I had to go and tell him he couldn't teach anymore."

Vice Dean Louis Toepfer knew Leach well, both as a student and a colleague, and became increasingly concerned about him. "Bart Leach was very, very smart. I had him as a student in 1940. None of the oddness was evident then. But he was different after he came back from the war, after he had been blessed as a general. . . . Bart was really gifted, a very good teacher. . . . But one of his peculiarities was that he called on all the ladies in the class on ladies' day, and that was the only day he called on them. The rest of the time, he dismissed them. I thought it was a terrible thing for him to do. But he had tenure, and at least in those days, you didn't interfere with a man with tenure. Bart was a smart smart-aleck. He was also, I think, somewhat disturbed by then. He was peculiar and getting more so. I don't hold it against him that he had ladies' days—he was losing his marbles, so to speak—I think he was under great pressure of some kind. . . . Then, one day, he called me on the telephone and he complained to me about the wastebaskets that were in the corridor, saying that they shouldn't be there because there might be a fire, and telling me I had to do something about them immediately. He ordered me to get them out of there. . . . That was the day he committed suicide."

Alice believes we didn't rebel against the system and Pappy Leach's approach for two reasons: "Society, and therefore we, had no external voices that were urging us to defend the rights of women, rebel on behalf of women, and since we were not being asked, or incited, and the actual recitation of the information made us look good rather than bad, we didn't have a need to rebel on our own personal behalf. The second, wholly separate issue was that during this time period, there was unquestioned respect on the part of students for the authority of a professor, wholly apart from the issue of being female students. It was only some number of years later that there was a change on campuses and students started to question the authority of faculty, and that there were student rebellions, protests, and uprisings. Nobody would have dared to do anything like that at the time we were at law school.

"As for ladies' day, there was no self-doubt on our part as to whether we should have behaved any differently. Essentially it was an exaggerated version of our everyday experience: we were in an unusual position in an unusual place for women to be. It's only looking back by hindsight that it raises a lot more questions as to what this experience says in a broader context."

CHAPTER 11

Dinner at the Dean's

Dean Griswold invited all of the girls in each class (and none of the boys) to his house once a year for dinner, along with a few members of the faculty and their wives. He generally asked one of the female students to handle the invitations. Pat Scott (Schroeder) got that honor our first year. Just after she had successfully negotiated with the dean over whether she would be permitted to sign her own surety bond guaranteeing her tuition, he invited her to the dinner that he and Mrs. Griswold would be hosting for the first-year female students. When she accepted, he also asked her to send out the invitations for the event. It was, without question, a mark of his respect for how well she had handled the surety bond negotiation, but Pat remembers thinking, "I'm not the social secretary around here." Nevertheless, she handwrote invitations to the first-year women as well as several members of the faculty, put them in the mail, and with the rest of us, showed up on the appointed night, October 17, 1961. An invitation to dinner at the dean's was like an invitation to a state dinner at the White House: an honor and a command performance.

The Griswolds lived in a large clapboard house, full of antiques, in Belmont, Massachusetts. Among the Law School faculty, the house was known as Dry Hill, because alcohol was never served at the Griswolds'. Rosemary Cox described the Griswolds' dinner to her parents: "This evening is famous among the older women law students as being horribly awkward and stilted. Dean Griswold is extremely gruff and reserved. He is a short stocky man with a stern puritanical expression. I managed to make some conversation with him about the Quakers in Swarthmore, and he managed to show a little interest. . . . His wife, who is crippled with polio, is very well meaning."[17]

We dressed up for the occasion. Rosemary wore the new outfit her parents had given her to start law school. "The silk dress has been simply marvelous for dress up occasions like the Griswold's party. It is exactly the restrained yet femine [sic] sort of thing I have needed."[18]

Professor John Mansfield, who was a former clerk to Justice Frankfurter and who would teach us the law of evidence our second year, attended that first dinner. Although Dean Griswold knew Mansfield was single, he greeted the professor at the front door by asking how he was and then loudly inquiring, "And how is Mrs. Mansfield?" Equally loudly, Mansfield reminded the dean that he wasn't married: "I was probably invited to meet my prospective wife. That was not unthinkable in those days. Professors frequently married students."

Professor
John Mansfield

The menu was always the same: sparkling Catawba grape juice for cocktails, stewed chicken and lima beans for dinner, and interrogation for dessert. We ate at card tables set up in the dining room. After dinner, we moved our gray metal folding chairs to the living room, arranged them in a circle, and took our assigned seats to await the dean's inquiry: "Why are you at Harvard Law School, taking the place of a man?" It was virtually the identical question he had raised in 1949 during the debate on whether to admit women to Harvard Law School.

Ruth Bader Ginsburg (now Associate Justice Ginsburg of the United Sates Supreme Court) told me about her own stumbling response in 1956: "It was one of life's most embarrassing moments. I stood up to answer, forgetting that I had a full ashtray in my lap. I watched in horror as butts and ashes cascaded onto the Griswolds' carpet. The dean appeared not to notice. Being married with a fourteen-month-old baby, I managed to mumble that my husband was a Harvard 2-L and it was important for a woman to understand her husband's work."

Professor Mansfield recalls that the dean reacted to some of our stuttering replies with an abrupt "Ha! Ha! That's not a very good reason," a response that, at least at the time, was more than a little intimidating. Mansfield has a different view: "It was characteristic of Dean Griswold . . . he meant to show you that he was paying attention, that your answers were important to him."

Janet Murphy, Dean Griswold's longtime secretary, knows that, without any question, the man who was her boss for over a decade had enormous vision, intellect, and kindness. Although she admits that he could be gruff and brusque, she says that underneath he was actually shy. He cared deeply about issues, particularly civil rights, about maintaining the excellence of the Law School, and about demanding the best performance from the professors and from the students who had won the privilege of studying there. She says the Griswolds invited the women to dinner "to make you aware that you really were part of the student body, even though you were a very small minority. They certainly didn't invite the men."[19]

Former Vice Dean Louis Toepfer agrees: "Erwin and Harriet [Griswold] wanted to give the women a sense of belonging. They couldn't possibly have all of the men, but because of the small numbers, they could have all of the women. They intended to help you. But I have an impression that the women students found it painful. If so, it was not intentional on Erwin's part. He was the kindest man I ever met and he would not do a thing like that . . . but he was probably curious about why you were at Harvard Law."

For Pat Scott (Schroeder), "Those dinners were not particularly fun, special evenings. I remember when Dean Griswold asked everybody why we were there, everybody's knuckles got white on the sides of the chairs. We were trying to think of something profound to say. My view was that he didn't want us there. What he told us at that dinner was that Harvard Law School let us in equally. . . . He wanted to know whether any of us were really gonna use the education we were getting, whether we were serious—that kind of stuff. Actually, though, we weren't taking up any male spaces because the Law School let in that many more men to make up for us." Dean Toepfer told me later that, in fact, the Admissions Office had not done that, but in our class, more people, both men and women, than they expected—or wanted—had accepted the Law School's invitation to study there starting in 1961.

Nancy Kuhn (Kirkpatrick) recalls the first thing she said to Dean Griswold when she arrived at his home: "I remember standing in the reception line. The first thing I said when I shook his hand was 'Dean Griswold, why do you have a quota on girls here?' It never dawned on me not to ask: he was curious as to why we were there, and I was curious as to why there weren't more of us."

The dean forcefully denied the existence of any quota, an assertion later confirmed to me by Dean Toepfer, and asked Nancy how she had developed such a wrongheaded notion. She replied, 'Well, for eleven years, there have been almost exactly the same number of women admitted in each class—in 1950, the first class with girls had fifteen; eleven years later, there are twenty of us starting in our class."[20] (In fact, twenty-seven of the forty-eight women who applied to Harvard Law School in 1961 were admitted, but only twenty decided to attend, and only fifteen of us finished at Harvard in 1964.)

Marge Freincle (Haskell) remembers that the whole evening at the Griswolds' was uncomfortable: "There we were balancing teacups trying to be polite, sitting in a circle answering questions. I felt like it was one of those rites of passage, which you had to do. Get it behind you and move on."

By the time it was Ann Dudley's turn to recite, she was irritated and rebellious: "They would never say 'account for yourself' to the men in such a way." She announced that she came to Harvard because she was turned down by Yale.

Pat loved Ann Dudley's response but remembers that the dean got furious: "I remember him just going crazy, flaming crazy, saying, 'That's not true, Yale always lets more women in than we do,' and so forth, the implication being that Yale had much lower standards than Harvard."

June Freeman (Berkowitz) attended only that first dinner at the dean's. It was just before she confirmed his worst fears by quitting Harvard Law School to marry a dashing young doctor who was shipping out in the public health service: "He and his wife, Harriet, were curious to know why we were all there. I was really taken aback because I didn't think about it much when I made the decision to go to law school. I was just twenty-one. When he asked that question, it was the first time I knew that being there was a really, really big deal. . . . Seriously, how many guys in the class could answer a question like that?"

Grace Weiner (Wolf) responded that she came to law school because she didn't want to be either a secretary or a teacher. When my turn came, I told the story of the bishop victimizing my father in Defiance, Ohio, and said I came to law school to right that wrong.

At the end of the evening, Mrs. Griswold made a special effort to see us to the door in her wheelchair. As we left, she mentioned that we should be sure to write her a thank-you note, and to be sure to call ourselves to her attention over the next three years. At the last dinner in our third year, I finally screwed up my courage and asked her why, with a group of obviously polite and well-brought-up young women, she felt she had to remind us each year about writing our bread-and-butter notes. She laughed: "Bread and butter is exactly the reason. I put your notes in the law school yearbook by your picture. When hiring partners call me up to ask if I know you and can recommend you, I go to the yearbook, remember your face, and reread your letters. It gives me something definite to say other than just 'Oh, yes. She's been here for dinner a few times.'"

Rosemary wrote her parents: "At length, the evening came to a close, and although I had found things quite a strain, I was nevertheless quite pleased to have attended such an affair. . . . Once again I found myself pleased by the high caliber of my fellow women law students. They are a marvelously attractive and intelligent lot, on the whole a thoroughly feminine yet quite urbane group of girls with varied backgrounds of study and work experience that make them tremendously exciting people."[21]

Intended or not, dinner at the dean's also prepared us for the blunt questions we would be asked by prospective employers and clients. Again and again, they asked us, "Why should we hire you when we can hire a man who will stick with us, not quit to get married and have children?"

As Professor Mansfield told me later, he enjoyed the Griswolds' dinners and believed they were beneficial for both the women students and the faculty: "Having the women over for dinner was Dean Griswold's way of taking you seriously. The women's annual dinner may have been somewhat uncomfortable, but the dean knew who you were, he was there, he was totally engaged, he wanted you to use the privilege of a Harvard Law education to make the profession and the nation better."

In his 1992 personal memoir, *Ould Fields, New Corne*, Dean Griswold reflected on his annual women students' dinner:

> My wife and I . . . were afraid [the women students] might feel some pressure from the fact that they were so greatly outnumbered by the men. We thought that it would be useful for them to get to know each other better, thus helping to develop solidarity and support among them. After dinner . . . I used to ask the women what it was that had led them to choose to come to law school. . . . I said on a number of these occasions that one of the things that had been considered in connection with the admission of women was whether they would really practice law, or, in some way, would use their legal training effectively for the benefit of the community. I said, among other things, that there was concern that there might be a number of women students who did not use their legal training to any considerable extent, and that they might be taking the places of men students who would devote their careers to the active practice of law. I was assured that this was not the case. . . .
>
> To my regret, I now find that these questions—though purely factual in intent—were resented, and that they are now recalled by some women graduates as examples of sexism on my part. That was really far from my intention. I was trying, if anything, to encourage the women to make full use of their legal training, in practice or in service, of varying kinds, to the public. Now it is more than forty years [since Harvard Law started admitting women] and I am enthusiastic about them. It is obvious, though, that they have a very difficult assignment, particularly in the childbearing years. They face this, and meet it with great determination, and very effectively. And they receive, in most cases, great help and cooperation from their husbands. I am proud of them.[22]

We came away from each of Dean and Mrs. Griswold's dinners with the strong impression that what we did would affect the opportunities for women law students and women lawyers in the future. We realized we had an obligation to work hard for more than ourselves: we felt obliged to make it easier for those who came after us. Nancy Kuhn (Kirkpatrick) believes the real purpose of the dean's dinner was to convey to us that we were the ultimate test: "We were role models, and the school's decisions on women in the future would be based in great part on how we performed."

CHAPTER 12

Men in Our Lives

I flip when a fellow sends me flowers,
I drool over dresses made of lace,
I talk on the telephone for hours,
With a pound and a half of cream upon my face!
I'm strictly a female female.
And my future I hope will be—
In the home of a brave and free male,
Who'll enjoy being a guy, having a girl like me.
—"I Enjoy Being a Girl"
from *Flower Drum Song,*
Rogers and Hammerstein, 1958

The images of our growing up, including the popular songs we sang, assumed and reinforced the view that a woman was a somewhat giddy, boy-crazy being whose ultimate goal and only fulfillment in life was marriage. The "real man" we were supposed to be looking for was portrayed equally simplistically—a guy who believed that "there ain't a thing that's wrong with any man here, that can't be cured by puttin' him near, a girly, womanly, female, feminine dame!"[23] At the same time the women in my class were breaking with these traditional notions, we were also embracing them: we wanted careers and husbands, rewarding work at the office and fulfilling families at home, and all at the same time. Harvard Law School was the place where we could—and mostly did—lay the foundation for realizing both objectives.

When we entered law school in September 1961, Dinni Lorenz (Gordon) was the only one of us who was married. A year later, five more had added "Mrs." to their pedigrees, and one, Katherine Huff O'Neil, had given birth to her first child. Except for Susan Wall, who had left before the end of the first month, none of us had given up our notion that somehow we could have it all, and eventually almost everyone tried to, with varying degrees of success.

Alice Pasachoff (Wegman)'s diary entry for Thursday, October 5, 1961, reflects that we weren't spending all our time trying to figure out the difference between replevin and assumpsit:

> Marge Freincle was talking to me last night about advice she received on techniques of being a girl in law school. 1. Isolate your victim. 2. Make him see you as a person, not a law student. 3. Make him see you as a woman person. She added that one should assume that 80% of the boys in your class have thought of asking you out but don't know how to go about it. It works. I have a date with X for Saturday night.

The boys who asked us out didn't know what to make of us, as Alice noted in her diary on Saturday, February 24, 1962: "The last words [my date said to me] last night [were]: 'It was interesting talking to a lawyeress.' I had wanted just to be a girl."

Dan Emmett

The women in my class weren't the only ones taking advantage of the extraordinary opportunities there were to socialize at law school in Cambridge. Dan Emmett, an irreverent Californian whose dad was a cattle rancher, didn't buy into the stuffiness of the East Coast. His wardrobe for law school was three pairs of Levi jeans, T-shirts, one Pendleton shirt, a sweater, and three pairs of cowboy boots—work boots, riding boots, and dress boots for Sunday. His friend Frank Morgan, class of '63, had persuaded Dan to come to Harvard rather than attend his first choice, the Law School at the University of California at Berkeley, Boalt Hall, but not because of the superb professors, unequaled law library, or future professional contacts he would make. "Look," Frank told him, "there are eighty girls' schools within fifty miles, and they're all here to marry some guy from Harvard—Law School, Business School, or Medical School. So you're going to have a good time. Don't make the mistake these East Coast guys do. They study all the time."

Dan spent most of his first year getting to know the local girls, but, except for Aurelle Smoot, left the law school girls alone: "It was too much trouble. So many guys chasing too few goods is a bad supply/demand situation. It wasn't worth the time for the girls in law school."

Even though we were graduate students, there were strict parietal hours in the dorms: men were only allowed in Wyeth Hall rooms on Sunday afternoons between 2 and 5 P.M. Women were permitted in the men's dorms every day but only until 10 P.M. Dan didn't let that stop him. One night just before finals, somebody in Dan's dorm ratted on him, probably hoping to gain some sort of an edge in the exams coming up. Dan had a girl from the Boston Museum School in his room—actually, in his bed. There was a knock on the door. It was the dorm committee.

Dan opened the door: "What's up?"

"You know the rules, Emmett. No girls in the room after ten. We've heard reports that there's a girl in your room."

Dan threw open the door wide. "You fucking guys are nuts. Don't you have anything better to do? Do you see a girl in my room?"

They looked over at the very comely girl now sitting up in bed.

"See? There's nothing and nobody here, you guys. Go back to something more constructive. See you later."

Dan pushed the dorm committee out of the room, slammed the door, and went back to bed. No action was ever taken against him. He got an A on the exam, finishing around seventieth in our class at the end of first year.

Ann Dudley Meets Stan

Stan Goldblatt

Ann Dudley Cronkhite caused quite a stir when she showed up in Harkness Commons on the first day of classes. With her short, bouncy blond hair, deep blue eyes, spike heels, and a great figure enhanced by the couturier clothes she collected, she wasn't what anybody expected a first-year female Harvard Law School student to look like. A lot of our male colleagues noticed, including Stan Goldblatt, a brilliant and handsome second-year law student from Chicago, who'd graduated at the top of his class from Harvard College. Stan was a member of the Board of Student Advisors, the group of students who ranked from twenty-sixth to fortieth in the second-year class. Their duties included advising first-year students on our required Ames moot court competition. Stan took one look at Ann Dudley eating breakfast in Harkness Commons and made sure he was assigned to advise her. His parents, owners of Goldblatt's Department Store chain in Chicago, had been encouraging him to get together with his brainy and beautiful law school classmate Wendy Marcus, the apple of the eye of her father, Stanley Marcus. The senior Goldblatts envisioned a whirlwind romance, and a great merger: Neiman-Marcus-

Goldblatt's. When Stan saw Ann Dudley, the only merger he was interested in was with her.

Ann Dudley dressed carefully for her first meeting with her adviser. "I remember exactly what I was wearing that day—a straight skirt, alligator high-heeled shoes which matched my handbag, and a silk blouse which, among other things, may have been a little too tight—I think several of you mentioned that all of my clothes were too tight, a statement to which I took great exception. I thought they were—just exactly right."

Stan started their meeting being businesslike and ended it by asking her out. He was "very cute and persuasive." Ann Dudley accepted: "I didn't see any reason not to mix business and pleasure—nor did he." They went to an Italian restaurant, had a great time, and started seeing each other regularly.

Stan had lots of competition, though, including a motion picture producer who met Ann Dudley in New York when he blew in from Hollywood, a proper Bostonian investment banker who lived in an oceanfront "cottage" in Beverly Farms, Massachusetts, and drove her around in his British racing-green Buick Riviera, and a number of law students.

Ann Dudley was a free spirit who played as hard as she studied and excelled at both. Despite her mother's early admonition that "abstinence makes the heart grow fonder," Ann Dudley rejected that advice: it was prudish and too constraining for a gal who had already jettisoned more than a few of her prominent family's conservative traditions. In an era when "nice girls don't do it" and when it was a felony in Massachusetts for doctors to provide birth-control devices to single women or to prescribe the recently discovered birth control pill at all, Ann Dudley bucked that norm. With courage and determination she found her way to a leading obstetrics and gynecology practitioner at Boston's Brigham & Women's Hospital. "I remember thinking very seriously, 'I don't want to get married yet, but I certainly don't want to live like a monk.' So I asked around and found a doctor to help me. When I got there, I discovered he had the biggest office in the hospital because he had all the diaphragms. In 1960, he had learned about the pill—a year before it was commercially available—and he had a supply of those, too, which he would prescribe whether you were married or not. He was very brave. He broke the law every day to help his patients."

Rosemary Marries Jon (June 1962)

Rosemary Cox and Jon Masters started dating the
Wednesday before Thanksgiving in 1961, just after classmate Judy Wilson, who was in the same first-year section,
introduced them. Jon, from a prosperous Park Avenue,
aggressively WASP family, had graduated from Princeton
and already traveled the world. His sports jackets carried
a London tailor's label, and, perhaps best of all, he drove
a silver Porsche. It never crossed Jon's mind not to ask
Rosemary for a date, even though she was a law student:
in the culture he grew up in, "dumb was bad, smart was good." And, of
course, it didn't hurt that Rosemary was also pretty.

Jon Masters

Rosemary thought Jon was dashing and sophisticated, nothing like the
boys from her Quaker community in Pennsylvania nor the uptight, boring
boys she'd met when trying to escape her monasterylike existence at
Mount Holyoke. He was smart and handsome, an ex–navy man, and that
he was attracted to her was a validation that she could have a career, like
her old maid professors at Mount Holyoke, and also be involved with an
exciting man.

Rosemary was struggling to find time to study. After four years in an isolated all-girls college, she had a lot of social life to catch up on and didn't
want to miss any of it. On January 19, 1962, she wrote her parents: "Practice exams are two weeks from tomorrow, and we should find out then how
much I really know. . . . Life in the social sphere has been quite gay this past
week." After describing several different dates, she wrote:

> But I suppose Jon Masters has probably occupied the bulk of may [sic] giddy
> life, since I went out with him last Saturday . . . and am going out to dinner
> with him tonight. I still don't really understand him any better now that [sic]
> I did at first. . . . He has a lovely gift for making me feel most "womanly"—in
> the middle of a heated political discussion, he will break off [and] say "I like
> your hair that way," and continue with an analysis of Kennedy's foreign pol-
> icy. Quite calculated to set a girl a-flutter, I assure you.[24]

Jon and Rosemary started having sex later that month. "I was in love, he
was in love. I told him, 'I can't have sex until I marry.' And he said, 'Why
not?' I told him I was afraid of getting pregnant. And he said, 'Well, I can
wear a condom.' With that, I couldn't think of a single other valid reason not
to. In that moment, it wasn't just passion, it was . . . 'What's the big deal?'

Then I got terrified—that I was a bad girl, that my parents would find out, that I would get pregnant."

Rosemary needed advice fast and sought out classmate Dinni Lorenz (Gordon), who, being married, was sort of a house mother to all of us even though she was only a year or so older than we were. Dinni told Rosemary about Enovid, and Rosemary thought, "Holy smoke! It's a new world." Enovid was, of course, *the pill.* Rosemary didn't realize it at the time, but the pill was not only the start of her own liberation but also of the sexual revolution.

Rosemary soon discovered, however, that she couldn't get a prescription for the pill in Massachusetts, and the Harvard University Health Service was not about to break the law. Jon continued to use condoms, and Rosemary continued to be terrified—of her parents, of pregnancy, of managing a career and a baby born out of wedlock. In February, Jon proposed and Rosemary accepted. Jon's mother was upset but thought the marriage was inevitable. Jon's father was dead set against it. According to Jon, "He was absolutely opposed to the whole thing. He told me that Rosemary was too smart, that he wanted me to marry someone like the Rockefeller girl I'd gone out with a few times. They told me that a lady lawyer was not what was expected of me."

On Sunday, March 11, 1962, Rosemary wrote her mother and father:

> What I have to say reduces itself to three sentences—I love Jon; I will marry him; I want to marry him in June. I have weighed as carefully as I could the alternatives and risks in what I am undertaking. I gave up independence and the freedom of choice only when I became convinced that the only life I want—the only way I can ever fulfill my desires and my ideals is by joining my life with Jon's.
>
> I know you also need to know of the practicalities. . . . Although I know he is hoping that you will continue to pay for my tuition, he plans to take care of everything [else]; and he is able to. Jon is firmly determined that I should complete law school, for he is convinced that I should be able to have a professional life of my own if I should want to or need to. We recognize there is a chance I may have a baby, but we have the security and maturity to deal with this possibility.[25]

On March 18, Rosemary's father replied, but to Jon, not Rosemary:

> Mrs. Cox and I must ask your indulgence and Rosemary's if we wince a bit when you tell us that you want to take her away. . . . It hurts a little to come up against the stark fact that she is ready to go. . . . What we can do and

have done . . . is to ask you to hold back and make sure that you know what you are doing. . . . All that we can ask for is evidence that the responsibilities are understood and accepted. . . . Whoever marries [Rosemary] is going to be a fortunate man. Be sure if you are that man to do everything in such a way that she gets to be all that she is really capable of becoming.[26]

Jon and Rosemary were married on June 16, in the Swarthmore, Pennsylvania, Presbyterian Church, with the President of the Union Theological Seminary of New York officiating. Rosemary was twenty-two years old; Jon, a few days shy of twenty-five. Rosemary was happy to be married and relieved that, finally, she could stop worrying about pregnancy: "I was married and I could, at last, get the pill legally." Today she thinks that, but for all of the guilt and uncertainties about sex, they wouldn't have married so quickly.

Three years later, the United States Supreme Court decided the law suit by the executive director of the Planned Parenthood League of Connecticut against the state of Connecticut on behalf of the league and its medical adviser, a Yale Medical School professor, who Connecticut had charged with violations of the Connecticut statute that prohibited any person from using "any drug, medicinal article or instrument for the purpose of preventing conception." In *Griswold vs. Connecticut*,[27] Justice William O. Douglas, writing for a majority of the United States Supreme Court, found the law unconstitutional and opened the door to what became not only the sexual revolution but also a foundation for the women's liberation movement. *Griswold* also contains the seeds of the abortion dispute that continues to divide our society and the justices of the United States Supreme Court today:

> The present case . . . concerns a relationship lying within the zone of privacy created by several fundamental constitutional guarantees. And it concerns a law which, in forbidding the use of contraceptives . . . seeks to achieve its goals by means having a maximum destructive impact upon that relationship. Such a law cannot stand. . . . Would we allow the police to search the sacred precincts of marital bedrooms for telltale signs of the use of contraceptives? The very idea is repulsive to the notions of privacy surrounding the marriage relationship.[28]

Justices Stewart and Black dissented:

> This is an uncommonly silly law. But we are not asked in this case to say whether this law is unwise, or even asinine. We are asked to hold that it violates the United States Constitution. And that [we] cannot do.[29]

Pat Marries Jim (August 1962)

Before entering Harvard Law School in September 1961, James W. "Jim" Schroeder attended Princeton University on an ROTC scholarship and served three years in the U.S. Navy as assistant navigator on a cruiser. He was one of the cadre of military men in our class, many of whom were married, and some of whom had children. They were a distinct subculture in our relatively young law school class, older and more self-sufficient than the rest of us. They also seemed more relaxed: most of the other men

Jim Schroeder

were stressed out not only about the rigors of studying law but also about being drafted into the armed forces. Pat Scott understood those military men immediately—they were a lot like her. Whether former soldiers, sailors, or pilots, they were self-confident and had a much broader perspective than just the walls of Harvard Law School:

"These guys were really serious. They had been there. They had seen people die. Even though we weren't officially fighting in Vietnam, they knew we were in up to our eyeballs. So they had a view of law school from ten thousand feet, rather than all the hysteria of the moment."

Frank Blatz, a former U.S Air Force pilot, and Kevin Conwick, an ex–navy helicopter pilot, kept telling Pat about Jim: "He's like us. He's even nice." Jim had already noticed Pat at a class mixer: "She stood out. She was very pretty but she was wearing this awful, crazy sweater. Her clothes were really out of it."

A couple of months into first year, as Pat tells it, Jim approached her, while she was studying in Langdell library, with a tongue-in-cheek opening: "I see you really love this place, too." (His version is that she approached him and asked him to get a book for her from a high shelf, "one of the oldest tricks around.") At the time, Jim was "not into coeducation," having been part of two then all-male institutions: Princeton and the U.S. Navy. He had been devoting most of his free time to chasing the Wellesley girls, and hitchhiking on Kevin Conwick's reserve-duty helicopter flights, taking detours to buzz the Wellesley campus. But Jim recalls that by the end of that casual library conversation with Pat, he was surprised to find that he had asked her out to dinner, and she was surprised that she'd accepted. One dinner led to the next, and before long, Jim was not only spending less time at Wellesley, he was getting over his long-held belief that marriage would be "boring." For Pat, Jim was smart, good-looking, and a grown-up, a guy who gave law school a more human scale: "I kept thinking these military guys are all having lives while going to Harvard Law School. . . . This is possible. This is what I want to do here."

Jim went home to Illinois for Thanksgiving, and Pat stayed in Cambridge. Some of the men who were also far from home asked Pat to cook a turkey for them during the Thanksgiving break. Pat asked, "What are you guys going to do? Why am I supposed to cook the turkey?" They told her their reason: they were too busy studying. She told them she was busy, too, but she did the cooking anyway. Jim heard about it when he came back and liked what he heard. (It must have been another rite of passage for women law students far from home: that first Thanksgiving in law school I made a turkey dinner with all the trimmings—including pies and cranberry sauce from scratch—for some of the fellows who'd studied together at Oxford, including Hugh Jones and Steve Breyer.)

Jim Schroeder was a member of the Kaplan Club, one of a group of small clubs established to organize the Law School's moot court process, the Ames Competition. Professor Benjamin Kaplan, patron saint of the Kaplan Club, hosted a celebrated dinner at his home each May to which club members and their wives or fiancées, but not their girlfriends, were invited. As spring approached, Jim knew that if he didn't bring Pat, she'd never let him forget it. The only way to include her was to propose marriage.

In April 1962, Pat and Jim announced their engagement at a seder dinner prepared by classmate Jeff Vail and his wife at Kevin Conwick's apartment. Having decided that their gentile friends were insufficiently acquainted with the rituals of Judaism, the Vails prepared the food, brought the wine, explained the traditions, and led the prayers. The Scott-Schroeder engagement announcement was the highlight of the evening. As Kevin remembers it, "It was a marvelous experience, one of the best of my law school days. It has stuck with me all these years."

In contrast to her terrifying and short-lived "pinning" experience at the University of Minnesota, Pat was happy about her decision to marry Jim. Like her dad, he was sure of himself, and he actually liked being with a strong woman. Besides, he wasn't overwhelmed by Harvard Law School. With him, she knew she could make it through the last two years of law school.

Pat and Jim were married in Des Moines in August 1962. Jim was twenty-six; Pat had just turned twenty-two. For their honeymoon, Jim found a marvelous lodge in Rocky Mountain National Park in Colorado owned by a man who formerly ran safaris in Africa. They thought it would be great: "We'll pretend we're in Kenya." On the first night of their honeymoon, they checked into their small cabin, walked up to the lodge for dinner, and were just sitting down in the bar for a before-dinner drink when in walked ladies' day's own Professor W. Barton Leach with his wife. Jim hadn't been in his class, but knew him by reputation: "He was the guy who wrote a will for a family guaranteeing no one could break it. Then, when he was hired by the heirs, he succeeded in breaking it. He almost got disbarred. It took the entire Harvard Corporation, the university, and everyone else to save his butt." Pat was horrified: "Oh, shit! Can you believe we could find the one place on the planet where W. Barton Leach was spending his August? It was like our worst nightmare." And Leach screamed, "Oh, my God! Finally we've got a third and a fourth for bridge!"

They spent their first night of marriage playing bridge with the man who had tormented Pat during ladies' days. Fortunately, Pat was a lousy bridge player: "That's the only time when not playing bridge was a great advantage." At the end of the evening, they told Leach they'd be leaving soon. He didn't seem disappointed.

CHAPTER 13

Exams

Five months after we started studying law, all 1-L students took a practice exam covering everything we were supposed to have learned in the first four months of law school. It was intended to give us something of a read on how we were doing, but what it accomplished was to scare most of us into working even harder.

Most of us had taken our books and class notes home over the Christmas holidays to start preparing. By the time we returned on January 3, 1962, we knew we hadn't worked nearly hard enough. The professors continued to assign heavy reading for classes while, at the same time, we were trying to cope with reviewing the voluminous material covered since September. As Alice's diary entries reflect, we were pushing hard and doing little else but studying:

> Tuesday, January 9, 1962: The tension begins to increase. I have begun to outline in earnest and to increase my work hours but the prospect of continuous study until June depresses me. Wednesday, Jan. 24, 1962: It is impossible to avoid the competitive atmosphere. I see more and more people using pills to fall asleep, pills to keep awake, tranquilizers to stay somewhere between the two. I have unanswered mail, unwashed stockings, unread novels, undone assignments—and yet I am never without the pressure of work. The pressure seems to come from the cumulative nature of the work—it can't be digested, stored away, spewed forth and forgotten, but is continually being relearned.

We took the practice exam for eight hours on Saturday, February 3. Alice recorded that it was "exhausting and overwhelmingly comprehensive." Our classmate Dick Denney wore his tuxedo: his wedding was that night, and the exam schedule left him no time to change before the ceremony. Other men in our class grabbed a quick dinner after the exam ended and headed straight back to the library to start outlining for the June finals. We were worn-out and scared that we might not make it through. As Alice wrote on February 22: "Never before have I so jealously hoarded and rationed the hours." Steve Breyer thought he might have flunked. In fact, he was in the middle of the pack. Then.

Although we knew we needed to start getting ready for the June finals, most of the girls in our class wanted a few nights out on the town before settling in to the relentless pressure of finishing the year's work. We were already having fun together, fun that—as much as the hard yet heady work of studying law—was cementing our friendship. One cold, wintry afternoon in February 1962, Rosemary wrote a long letter home about the latest events in the social lives of three of the women students in our class:

> All sorts of nice things have happened this week. Judy Richards has arranged the party for the Wellesley Benefit dance, and it promises to be a great deal of fun. It is to be held at one of the very elegant Boston Clubs—the building is a handsome old Victorian mansion that has been converted into a social club. . . . There will be six of us going to the dance—Dinnie [*sic*] and Jim Lorenz, Judy and her beau at the medical school, and Jon and I. Dinnie is going to give a dinner party before the dance—she is an elegant cook, so we should enjoy ourselves immensely.
>
> Coming up next week is the Lincoln's Inn formal. We have arranged another party for that. By the combined machinations of Jim, Jon, Dinnie and me, we have gotten a very nice date for Judy Richards . . . Josh Lane. He is a sophisticated and charming young man—tall and blond with blue eyes—he should be very much to Judy's taste. A fourth couple for the Lincoln's Inn dance will be Pat Scott and a friend of Jon's from Princeton [*sic*] [Jim Schroeder].[30]

I don't remember much about the dance except that Rosemary was absolutely right: Joshua Hubbard Lane was indeed very much to my taste. Over the next five years he became my closest friend and, in many ways, my soul mate. He taught me to play pool and backgammon, took me sailing and dancing and offered steady encouragement not only in law school but after graduation, when the realities of breaking into the legal profession hit home.

Joshua Lane

Spring arrived. The days sped by. The pace of work quickened—the assignments became longer and the pressure even greater. By March, a rather large number of the men in our class had abandoned their suits and ties for faded jeans or khakis and baggy sweaters. They were often unshaven, and the scent about them suggested it had been a while since they'd seen the inside of a shower. The women in my class didn't allow themselves to fall into the gray and grungy category, but we were digging into the books a lot more intensely than in the fall. I found a quiet desk in the fourth basement of the International Law Library where I hid out for twelve to fourteen hours most days, except for Saturdays, when I tried to take a break after morning classes. Fortunately, a former all-Ivy football star whom I'd also been going out with occasionally found the same hide-away, so there were a few opportunities for a quick break in the stacks. But mostly everybody studied. The dating and cultural events we'd enjoyed in the fall were abandoned: we thought our very futures depended on how we did on the six upcoming exams. Our small study groups were meeting weekly, or even more often, exchanging course outlines and talking over what might be asked on the finals. By May, all of us were looking and feeling exhausted and apprehensive.

Classmate Charles Buffon asked me for a date around that time: "You were an attractive person. At some time or other, it occurred to me that I had never had the guts to invite any female in our class out. I didn't know you, but finally I screwed up my courage and called you up. I invited you out for a beer. You turned me down because you had study group. It was probably genuine, but I didn't give you a second chance. Turned down for study group! That was about as bad an insult as a guy could get back then."

The dreaded exams began on Monday, the fourth of June, six four-hour sessions, one per subject, to be administered over one and a half weeks. Except for the February practice exam, we had taken no tests, written no papers, and received no evaluations on how we were doing. We would rise or fall on those six exams: they determined not only our entire grade for each course, but, we feared, our entire professional future—job opportunities, promotions, ultimate success or failure in the world of the law. For most of us, it was terrifying. We took Hershey bars with almonds and thermos bottles of orange juice to exams for energy, earmuffs to block out the noise of 140 people typing furiously, and alarm clocks so we wouldn't run out of time for each question.

There were only a few distractions, but at least one of them was on purpose. The Law School classrooms where we wrote our exams were not air-conditioned, and even when the windows were pushed up, they were hot and airless. We sat side by side at the long, curved wooden tables, sweating. Ann Dudley chose her exam wardrobe carefully. Although she says today that, contrary to class folklore, she never stripped down to her bikini during finals, she does admit to dressing not only to be comfortable and cool, but also distracting. In a system where everyone in the class was ranked top to bottom, any marginally legitimate tactic that gave you an edge could be—and often was—used.

"I had this dress which was a little shift," Ann Dudley recalls, "only it landed about halfway between my knees and my waist. This was before miniskirts, which were, what, four years later? Underneath it I wore a pair of white tennis shorts, because we didn't have panty hose then, we had stockings and garter belts or girdles. People were outraged. But I did better than most of the men in my section on those exams."

Alice wrote in her diary on Wednesday, June 6, 1962: "I count the days until exams are over. The tension here is very apparent—our conversations are sharp, our tempers quick, our movements short. I feel as if I have been tossed and turned by a tornado this past week."

On June 13, the first year was over—the excitement of intense learning in a high-powered, electrifying environment, the joy of making new friends who, as it turned out, would stick with us for life, the long conversations over meals and between classes, and the extraordinary pressure and tension and competition. We had learned more than any of us thought possible. Regardless of the grades we received, the women had proved themselves: fifteen of the twenty who had started ten months earlier would be back at Harvard Law in the fall, and all but one of the other five would eventually finish law school, either at Harvard or somewhere else. We were elated we had survived and also exhausted by the arduous year behind us. As Sheila

First-year exams

Rush remembers, "I just limped home to Buffalo and became a camp coun-selor to cool out."

We left for home to start our summer jobs and to wait for the grades to arrive. The entire class would be ranked on a thirteen-point scale: out of a possible, or actually an impossible, score of 100 on an exam, 75 was an A; 72–74, a B+ and honors; 68–71, a B and respectable; and 62–67, a C to D and passing. Extraordinary examinations would be awarded grades above 75, with anything above 80 being ranked summa cum laude.

Based on their grades on these exams alone, the students who ranked one to twenty-five would be elected to serve on the prestigious *Harvard Law Review*, those ranking from twenty-six to forty would join the Board of Student Advisors, and those from forty-one to fifty would serve on the Harvard Legal Aid Society. As it turned out, four of the top ten in the class were those who had gamed their way into the section that had the reputation for the largest number of great professors. Paul Posner finished first, with an 82.8 average, confirming Professor Casner's early prediction that if Paul worked very hard, he might one day be as smart as his teacher. Steve Breyer, with a 79.7 average, and Paul Dodyk, with 78.9, ranked in the top five. None of the women in our class ranked in the top fifty at the end of our first year. My own average was 71.4, one-tenth of a point short of "honors," which began at 71.5. That put me somewhere near the bottom of the top 20 percent of the class—respectable, certainly much better than Dean Toepfer had pre-dicted, but not extraordinary.

The 1962 *Harvard Law School Yearbook*, published at the end of our first year, reflected our grand view of our teachers, and indirectly, of ourselves:

> The greatest legal educators in the world are found on the Harvard Law School faculty. Brought here by the challenge of teaching top students in an atmosphere of academic freedom, these men have been an inspiration and a guide to thousands of lawyers. Theirs are the names affixed to the definitive texts and treatises on all fields of Law. From the Gluecks on Juvenile Delin-quency to Professor Loss on the Blue Sky Laws, their research is granted world-wide recognition. The faculty is what makes the Harvard Law School truly outstanding.[31]

In the summer of 1962, these conclusions rang totally true to us. We didn't notice how arrogant they might have sounded to anyone outside of Cambridge. We were just intensely proud to be at Harvard Law, and to have survived 1-L.

CHAPTER 14

Dropouts, Departures, and Deferrals

Against all predictions, nineteen of the twenty women who started at Harvard Law School in 1961 eventually earned their law degree, either at Harvard or another top school. Fifteen of us graduated from Harvard in June 1964. Two of us who transferred to other law schools also finished in 1964, Eleanor Rosenthal at Columbia and Liz Daldy Dyson at the University of Kansas. Mary Elizabeth "Liddy" Hanford (Dole), who spent our first year working in the law school library evaluating whether to enter Harvard Law School, finally began in the fall of 1962, graduating with the Harvard Law Class of 1965. The two women who married early in our first year each took more than a decade to start their families before reentering law school and earning their law degrees, June Freeman Berkowitz from Harvard in 1975, and Katherine Huff O'Neil from Northwestern School of Law at Lewis and Clark College in Portland, Oregon, in 1977. Given the obstacles we faced in those days, it is an extraordinary record. We were, as Admissions Dean Louis Toepfer predicted, a special breed—organized, focused, persistent, and brave.

June Freeman Marries Mordecai Berkowitz and Drops Out
(but only for eleven years)

Buried in the stack of information we had received when we registered for classes in September 1961 was a sign-up form to volunteer in the surrounding community. Being interested in both medicine and law, I had signed up to work with infants at Boston City Hospital, the area's community hospital for patients who couldn't afford to go anywhere else. Starting in October, I spent one afternoon a week caring for infants diagnosed with "failure to thrive," a malady that can afflict newborns when they are not held enough, not cuddled. June also signed up to work with children at Boston City, but it took her in an unexpected direction. The first day June showed up, the child psychiatrist who was to be her supervisor was unavailable, and they sent her to orientation in the emergency room instead.

June walked in, sat down, and almost immediately found herself listening with awe to a speaker describing the miraculous rebuilding of the body of a patient whose lower extremities had been crushed. June took one look at the side-by-side X rays, one showing bones fractured in a million pieces, the second showing them completely mended, and fell in love with whatever doctor had performed that miracle. "This is what Dr. Berkowitz did," the speaker said.

Dr. Mordecai Berkowitz was the co-chief orthopedic resident at Boston City. After taking the volunteers to visit the wards, he asked June to work with a man who had just lost both legs in an accident. June was in shock: she thought she was going to be working with children under a psychiatrist's supervision, and there she was talking to a double amputee.

A few days later, Mort called "Miss Freeman" at Wyeth Hall: "This is Dr. Berkowitz. I know you're probably too busy, but would you like to have dinner with me?" June abandoned her usual rule of playing hard to get. She simply said, "No, I'm not, I'm not too busy." As soon as she hung up, June called her mother and told her she was getting married.

Neither June nor Mort remembers whether the food was any good, or even whether they ate it. Mort asked her if she was busy for the weekend. June responded, "When you call, I'll never be busy." They were engaged within a couple of weeks. Mort had volunteered to join the U.S. Public Health Service and was scheduled to leave for San Francisco on January 1. He asked June to marry him right away, and June accepted: "I knew he was leaving and that if I didn't marry him, he'd be gone. And I knew the Law School would still be there, and if I wanted to do it later, I still could."

When she notified the Law School that she was leaving, they wrote that they were sorry, and that they hoped she would come back. Mort scraped together $1,000 to repay her scholarship. Because she had taken no exams, she received no credits for the semester she was there.

June and Mort were married January 1, 1962. She was twenty-one, he was thirty-one. After the ceremony, they got in Mort's car and drove to San Francisco. Their first child was born nine months and eighteen days after the wedding: "I really wanted to have a baby, and it happened right away." Their second child was born sixteen months later: "It didn't occur to me to work or to go to school. In fact, it wouldn't occur to me now, because my mother worked, and I didn't want to do that with small children." Ten years later, in 1972, with three young children and a busy professional husband, June reentered Harvard Law, graduating with honors three years later.

Liz Daldy Dyson Transfers to the University of Kansas Law School

At the end of Liz's first year in law school, her husband, Richard, graduated from the Law School and accepted a job teaching law at the University of Kansas Law School. Liz decided to forgo a Harvard degree and, instead, followed her husband to Kansas. "It would have been nice to have a Harvard Law School degree, but, hey! I wasn't not going to Kansas with my husband. I trotted out after him."

Liz enrolled at Kansas Law School and graduated near the top of her class. For her, it was one of the best things she ever did. "I think I got a much better education at KU than I would have at Harvard. The classes were smaller, there was less intimidation for me personally. I had some good professors, including my husband—I had two courses from him. I got on law review, which I don't think would have happened at Harvard. The amazing thing was that, having had one year at Harvard, it was as though I had graduated from there. Later, when I interviewed at Arnold & Porter [in Washington, D.C.], they didn't say, 'Well, gee, you only went to Harvard for a year.' They were impressed that I went for a year. It was like having a Harvard degree, but with none of the pressure or baggage."

Eleanor Rosenthal Transfers to Columbia

While Eleanor made good friends at Harvard, she was twenty-seven when she entered law school and soon began to feel that her age set her apart from most of her classmates. She missed her former social life and her friends and contemporaries in New York, so she transferred to Columbia.

Contrary to the folklore that Harvard Law School's faculty was cold and uncaring, Eleanor's contracts professor, the great "Black Jack" Dawson, whose wife had befriended Eleanor when she was an undergraduate at the University of Michigan, took the time to write her about her decision to transfer:

Law School of Harvard University
Cambridge 38, Mass.
Aug. 7 [1964]
Dear Elly:
  . . . It has been a great pleasure for me to get to know you so well this last year. I certainly wish you the very best and hope we can meet

again. If there is anything I can do by way of testimony or otherwise to give an assist, do let me know. My best regards.

Yours sincerely,
John Dawson

Katherine Huff O'Neil Drops Out (for thirteen years)

Katherine continued as a first-year law student at Harvard after she married Michael D. O'Neil in December 1961.

A particularly vivid memory is a law school reception she attended after her marriage: "In a cluster of students and faculty, Dean Toepfer lit into me about taking a man's place in the class when I had chosen to marry and so should be at home raising children. His words were unprovoked. I think that I had just said hello. What response can you make to one of the powers who controls the paperwork and your career? Since then, I've wondered if Dean Toepfer would have similarly attacked a male student who married during the first year."

There is probably a simple explanation for Dean Toepfer's strong reaction to the early marriage of a female law student. Unbeknownst to us at that time, he had invested a lot of personal capital in each woman admitted to Harvard Law School in those early days. He had fought hard to persuade

Katherine Huff O'Neil (*second row, third from left*), from member of the Class of '64 to Recording Secretary of the Harvard Law Wives Organization. Mrs. Erwin Griswald is to her immediate right.

the other members of the Admissions Committee that we would value the then rare opportunity being offered us, that we would have the fortitude to stick it out for three years, and that we would use our education for the benefit of the legal community and our society. Even his predictions about how well—or how poorly—we would perform were meant to challenge us to work hard, do well, and never quit. In a real sense, he was our Pygmalion, spurring us on not only to prove the accuracy of his predictions but to pave the way for other women who would follow us.

Katherine recalls another aspect of life for the woman law student at Harvard that was particularly annoying to her: the attitude of some of the single, young, and beautiful women behind the reception desk at the library in Langdell. "They'd come to Harvard Law to find a husband. They would not respond to any female if there was an eligible male anywhere around who might want to ask them a question. I found that even some of the women employees of the law school were chauvinist."

Thoroughly disheartened by her Harvard experience and ambivalent about a legal career, Katherine nevertheless finished her first year and took the exams, ending up in the middle of the class although she quit reading the casebooks shortly after the first few months of class. That summer she took a job as a secretary running the import/export desk for a New England manufacturing company: "I did typing. I finished my job by ten-thirty or so in the morning and took the rest of the day to reorganize their entire filing system and learn about import/export regulations. You can't get through life without typing—at least you couldn't back then."

When Katherine's first son was born in September 1962, she decided not to return for her second year at Harvard Law School. Instead, she stayed home in a tiny Cambridge apartment with her new baby and joined the Harvard Law Wives organization for an outlet, serving as the recording secretary, once again using her typing and organizational skills: "It was a wonderful group of women, often much superior to their husbands. Welcoming. Smart. Confident. Focused. It was a privileged group. They all seemed to come from parents with money. As did I. We were very supportive of each other. The law wives seemed to have the vision for the family—where their husbands' careers were going, where they would live."

At that time, Harvard Law Wives was the only women's organization at Harvard Law School. Professor Arthur Sutherland's history of Harvard Law School, *The Law at Harvard: A History of Men and Ideas*, published in 1967, devotes over three pages to the wives' organization but only two and one-half paragraphs to the admission and matriculation of women law students.

The Harvard Law Wives had monthly social activities, often with excellent speakers. It was a kind of support group before anyone really understood that concept. The wives lunched at each others' homes, held regular bake sales at Harkness Commons, and wrote a cookbook. "By offering an intellectual and entertaining program of events, the Harvard Law Wives organization provides a unique opportunity to make the years at Harvard rich, eventful and rewarding ones. Bi-weekly meetings featured guest lecturers on such varied and thought-provoking topics as the undercover activities of the FBI, strange and wonderful things about Boston, concepts of corporate control, and preservation of historic works of art in Egypt. In addition, the meetings served to introduce the members both to distinguished outside lecturers and to several of their husbands' outstanding professors."[32]

Derek Bok, then a young professor and later Dean of the Law School and President of Harvard University, spoke to the Law Wives in 1960. His speech caused an uproar:

"It was a pretty male chauvinist period in American life. I agreed to give a speech to the Harvard Law Wives, and I decided to talk about the need to

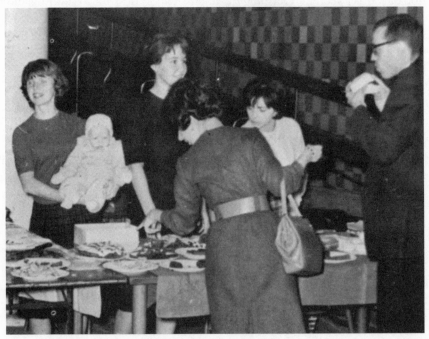

One of the regular Harvard Law Wives' bake sales in Harkness Commons

think about having, for some significant portion of your life, a career of your own. Not a very radical notion, but one that seemed to me a little provocative. I quoted various statistics about overprotective mothers who had nothing else in life but their children, and that that was thought to be a significant cause of their mental breakdowns at the time of the Korean War. I quoted various sources like [Oliver Wendell] Holmes's old statement 'Washington is full of interesting men and the women they married when they were young' and explained that one of the reasons for that kind of statement was the lack of any kind of stimulation for many women who stayed home. I mentioned that having a career was not for making money necessarily, but for having some engaging occupation. I was very careful to say that 'I am not a woman and a mother, I understand the demands of motherhood,' but I pointed out how many decades of your life go on after your kids are spending a full day in school, and what happens during those decades if you don't start thinking about that eventuality and preparing for it.

"Well, I got through it and found I had been totally mistaken about what I thought would be their response. The women in the audience—it looked like a fertility cult, they were all in the advanced stages of pregnancy as far as I could tell—said, 'This is subversive. You are telling us we should abandon our babies and give up our roles.' It was the whole ethos after World War Two—life in the suburbs, the man in the gray flannel suit. There was an active resistance to the idea of careers for women or even thinking about them, and even to making women think that anything that wasn't a lifetime of wife and motherhood could be questioned. I was kind of shocked: when people get very hostile and put words in your mouth, you know you've touched a sensitive nerve. I found it remarkable. And that mind-set was certainly very much in evidence at the Harvard Law School and in the Harvard Law Wives group at the time."

One of the highlights of the Law Wives' events was the spring fashion show and luncheon. The models for the clothes were always the Law School faculty wives. Derek Bok remembers watching with pride as his wife, Sissela, a brilliant and beautiful Swedish blonde, sashayed down the runway every spring, sporting the latest fashions: "Sissela, who by all odds was the finest of the lot, was always invited and then participated very dutifully. I remember her sort of mincing down the aisle and getting a big round of applause."

One of the things Katherine O'Neil and the other law wives didn't realize at the time was the terrible work habits their husbands were getting into: "The work habits they developed in law school were the ones they would maintain for their whole careers after graduation. I remember the wives saying, 'It'll be good to have time again with our husbands after graduation.' Of course, there wasn't time with husbands if they went to the big firms in D.C. or New York City." Most of the women who stuck with law as a career adopted the same overcommitted pace, both in law school and after graduation. It was a recipe—perhaps a requirement—for the success that was expected of us and that we expected of ourselves. But it was not the best plan for a well-rounded life.

Katherine remembers what she thought at the time was a humorous incident at the spring luncheon of the Harvard Law Wives in 1964: "The wife of a younger faculty member was the keynote speaker. She urged us to carve our own identities and not submerge our personalities into the career of our husbands. Revolutionary talk in those days! So revolutionary that Mrs. Griswold spoke up. She basically told us that, if our husbands were to be successful, we would have to forsake our personal ambitions in order to support our husbands' careers. Mrs. Griswold's remarks resonated with us. I think that's how we all had been living and intended to keep on living."

By the time Mike O'Neil graduated with the class of 1964, Katherine had given birth to their second son, Charles. The O'Neils moved to Portland, Oregon, where Mike went to work for the largest law firm in the state. With her Depression "always stay on the payroll" mentality, Katherine did freelance writing for the Portland newspaper *The Oregonian*. Ten years later, when her boys entered junior high school, Katherine returned to law school at Northwestern School of Law at Lewis and Clark College in Portland, finishing her law degree in 1977. "With the boys as old as they were, they didn't require as much attention from me. I needed something to occupy my mind and my time."

Katherine served on the law review and finished among the top students, even more remarkable because, by then, she was a single mom with a pair of middle-school sons.

In 1986, Katherine and her second husband, John Paul "Toby" Graff, Yale '57, opened their own boutique law firm specializing in civil appeals.

Mary Elizabeth "Liddy" Hanford Decides to Enter Harvard Law
in the Fall of 1962

With the help of Earle Borgeson, the Law School's head librarian, Mary Elizabeth Alexander "Liddy" Hanford, the Duke University May Queen who had considered starting with our class, had secured a job in the Harvard Law School library. She wanted to "try the place out" while she was simul-

taneously getting her master's degree in teaching at Radcliffe.[33] She was working behind the reserve-book desk in
Langdell library when I met her during my first week of
law classes. She helped me find and hang on to some of
the limited copies of articles and books the professors
assigned that first week. I was grateful for the help: I had
heard the rumors about students secreting assigned read-
ing and cutting pages out of books to try to disadvantage
their fellow students, and I needed an ally behind the library desk to make
sure I didn't fall victim to those practices.

Liddy and I talked mostly about whether and how a woman could strad-
dle what seemed then to be the huge chasm between the traditional career
world, which was overwhelmingly male, and the traditional world of home
and family, which was, at that time, almost totally female. She quizzed me
on how being a law student had affected my personal life. She wondered
whether my social life had dried up, whether I sensed that I was suddenly
being perceived as masculine, how I could simultaneously become an
"invulnerable" lawyer while being a vulnerable woman, whether I planned
to marry, and how I thought I could juggle a husband, a family, and a legal
career. I didn't have answers for most of her questions. I just thought that,
somehow, things would probably work out.

Liddy was glamorous, funny, smart, and generous, a gal with great
warmth and almost equally great anxiety as to whether she could combine
the roles of gracious Southern woman and hard-charging professional. She
had an extraordinary drive to achieve big things in her life. Even then,
she was thinking about the highest public service—becoming first lady
was what she talked about most, but once in a while there was a hint that
she thought she might try to become president of the United States herself.
Liddy was a quintessential Southern belle, the proverbial velvet glove over
an iron hand.

Liddy also seemed destined to marry a prominent and powerful man.
She had a bevy of beaux both around the Law School and at some of the
other Harvard graduate schools. She was clearly focused on finding the
path to a future that was even more ambitious than those most of us saw
for ourselves. And that was saying a lot.

Pat Schroeder recalls meeting Liddy early in our first year: "She was thinking about being in our class and then she panicked. They gave her a year to
think about whether she was actually gonna do it. I met her early on. I
remember having these conversations with her about how she just didn't
know if she could be a lawyer and a *laaady*. And I was kinda 'Ahhhhhhh!

Didn't you figure this out before you sent in all those papers?' Earl Borgeson, the librarian, and Dean Louis Toepfer told Liddy to continue to work in the library to determine whether law school was for her. That's when I was so glad I had not been raised in the South. I was like 'What are your issues?' I think she talked to every woman who came to the library about the same things."

Harvard Law School Professor Charles Nesson asked me later, "Do you suppose anybody takes a year to think of whether they can be a man and a lawyer?"

Yet in that era of "all man" and "all woman" stereotypes, Liddy's trepidation was typical of young women in the early sixties, if, in fact, they thought they had any options at all. It would be quite a challenge for a gently raised Southern woman of that time to be comfortable admitting to the world that beneath her grace and soft Southern drawl lay a brilliant mind and a killer instinct. Even her mother was puzzled that Liddy wanted to go to law school: "Don't you want to be a wife, and a mother, and a hostess for your husband?"[34]

As Cynthia Fuchs Epstein points out in *Woman's Place:*

The image of woman includes as well some noncharacteristics: lack of aggressiveness, lack of personal involvement and egotism, lack of persistence (unless it be for the benefit of a family member), and lack of ambitious drive. . . . Conflict faces the would-be career woman, for the core of attributes found in most professional and occupational roles is considered to be masculine: persistence and drive, personal dedication, aggressiveness, emotional detachment, and a kind of sexless matter-of-factness equated with intellectual performance. Women who work in the male-dominated occupations in particular are often thought to be sexless. The woman who takes her work seriously—the career woman—traditionally has been viewed as the antithesis of the feminine woman. . . . Many accepted the notion that the traits required of a professional woman and those required of a feminine woman were mutually exclusive. Women who did attempt to demonstrate both sets of traits . . . risked surprising or confusing their role-partners. The colleagues, friends, and others with whom they came in contact often did not know how to react to them; should one, for example, assume an easy familiarity with or a protective distance from one's female co-worker?[35]

Throughout our first year, Liddy did her homework on how women reacted to and were changed by law school. She had a front-row seat in the library to observe how, if at all, being a "lady law student" affected men's attitudes toward us. Liddy eventually enrolled at Harvard Law in September

1962, graduating three years later with the class of 1965. During her second and our last year at Harvard Law, she roomed with our classmate Nancy Kuhn: "Liddy was a lady. At the time I lived with her, she was dating someone who was clerking for Justice Brennan. She knew many of the professors, and a lot of different people all over Cambridge and Boston. Liddy lived her own life. We shared the apartment, but we didn't socialize together—she was already socializing with this group of professors, people at Harvard Business School, and others who weren't in the realm of the Law School. She was already heading for the big world."

Classmate Jim Schroeder remembers talking with Liddy in the library about her concerns: "I think that she wouldn't have stayed there and continued doing that job if she hadn't wanted to see what was going on. I think by talking to people like Pat and you and others and seeing that you weren't one-dimensional or sexless, she decided that she could do it. I think it's to her credit that she took the time to figure it out."

CHAPTER 15

The Last Two Years of Law School

The second and third years of law school brought a heavier workload than the first year. Now that we had the basics down, the professors were pushing us hard into the substantive thickets of the law—corporations, commercial transactions, constitutional law, evidence, federal courts, taxation of the corporation and shareholder. We were working even harder than our first year, but at least most of us were more relaxed about it: we hadn't flunked out, and we now understood that much of the professors' bluster was not meant to humiliate us but was simply a way to keep us riveted to the massive amount of substantive material, which, without their well-honed theatrics, could have been excruciating and dull.

By second year, Kevin Conwick, captain in the U.S. Marines Corps Reserves, was taking the place in stride. He had Dean Griswold for tax and, on occasion, just ignored the dean's strict rule that nobody was to enter the classroom after class had begun. One morning, Kevin showed up twenty minutes late, ambled down the aisle to his seat in the front, opened his tax textbook, and looked up at the dean, who was obviously annoyed.

Kevin Conwick

"Well, well! Good morning, Mr. Conwick," the dean growled.

"Good morning, Dean Griswold."

"Now, Mr. Conwick. You know my rule about not interrupting class discussions by coming in late?"

"Sure do, Dean Griswold."

"And, Mr. Conwick, aren't you a military man, a helicopter pilot in the U. S. Marine Corps reserves?"

"That's me, Dean."

"Now, Mr. Conwick, in the Marines, what do they say to you when you come in late?"

"Well, Dean Griswold, they generally say, 'Good morning, *sir!*'"

The class broke up, and even the dean laughed. It was the last time he tried to discipline Kevin Conwick.

Professor Derek Bok was one of our star teachers during our second and third years. He had graduated from Harvard Law School in 1954, then served for three years in the Army Judge Advocate General's Corps, before joining the Harvard Law School faculty. By the time we arrived he was teaching Labor Law, Antitrust, and a new course, which he had developed with Professor Donald Turner: Economic Regulation of Business. He recalls that era, as well as the time when he was a student a few years earlier, as a time when the professors wanted their students to do well, both in school and in the profession, and pushed everyone to the limit to achieve that objective:

Professor
Derek Bok

"We all felt that we had gained a lot by being pushed, and that, although in my case I did not look back on my first year of law school with much pleasure—it was a difficult grinding thing, where I really thought for a while I was likely to flunk out—I don't think I ever doubted that it was the single most valuable educational experience I have ever had. It really trained my mind, and I use it to this day, it's in everything I do."

Faculty who had offices near Bok's at the Law School remember that he sometimes became so upset when students missed the point of his lectures or his exam questions that he would kick the wastebasket across his office. Although Bok has no recollection of kicking wastebaskets, he clearly remembers his frustration that many law students didn't seem to understand the course work. He blamed himself for "my own obvious lack of ability to communicate as well as I would have liked." Early in his career he had served on the Harvard Law School Admissions Committee. He knew the quality of the students coming in and couldn't understand why more of them didn't do better, or why they didn't understand the material better:

"I would read the exams and certainly the top ten or fifteen percent were really very good indeed, and the top one-third were competent though with significant problems. By the time you got down to the bottom third, it was a pretty dreary performance. Putting those poor exams together with what I knew about the quality of the class, I was frustrated and disappointed. I decided to depart from a very common practice in the law school, which was to select people into your seminar who were at the very top of their class. Seminars were generally oversubscribed and the practice was to take the best students and let the other ones find some other place where they could fit in. I decided not to do that. Instead, I took the students with the lowest grades because what I really wanted to do was to bring them closer to their potential. I cut the seminar from thirty to fifteen or sixteen, assigned very short papers every week, and I went over them, edited them, worked with the students and asked them to write their papers over. I don't know how many people I helped. The results were not dramatic. It really made me feel that the problem of communicating to people whose minds didn't work logically and clearly was infinitely more difficult than I had thought. I can't say I was successful with a whole lot of them, and there was obviously a deeper frustration than I had experienced up to that time. But kicking wastebaskets? I wouldn't put it past me, but I don't recall. My feet don't hurt."

Our professors were still tough in the classroom—where A. James Casner had often used a bludgeon in property class, John Mansfield, who taught us evidence, used a rapier. Ann Dudley remembers precisely how subtle Professor Mansfield could be. He led off an early evidence class by holding up a mason jar with a large cockroach in it and turned to Ann Dudley for an analysis of the jar and its contents: "Miss Cronkhite, what is in the jar?" Ann Dudley responded immediately, "There's a bug in the jar." Without any comment, Mansfield turned to Steve Breyer: "Mr. Breyer, what is in the jar?" and Steve answered, "There *appears* to be a bug in the jar." Both Mansfield's question and Steve's answer were perfect illustrations of a basic rule of evidence: never assume anything.

Classmate Tony Bloom remembers his first lecture with Professor Louis Loss, at that time the preeminent American authority on securities regulation: "He started off our class, which had about one hundred and eighty third-year students in it, by telling us, 'If you can find six people you can beat in this class, you'll pass.'"

One way or another we were challenged and kept on the edges of our chairs almost every day. The professors' unrelenting demands for clear thinking and quick responses meant we had to be prepared every day and to focus intently, exactly the same discipline we would need in the rough-and-tumble of law practice. Outside of class, it was different: our professors reached out to many of us, inviting us to dinner and the theater, joining us over lunch at Harkness Commons, and competing with us at sports. Pat and Jim Schroeder even continued to socialize occasionally with Professor Pappy Leach, going to his home each Christmas to sing carols around the piano. Ann Dudley Cronkhite played tennis regularly with Phil Areeda, the antitrust guru. Eric Fox, a gifted natural athlete, played squash with Professors Areeda, Vorenburg (later Dean of Harvard Law School), Braucher, and Westfall; tennis with Professor Loss; and basketball with Derek Bok, who was as forceful on the basketball court as he was in the classroom and, later, as President of Harvard. Eric remembers Bok's athletic style: "He was a big guy, very strong, very fast, and he did not like to be pushed around. He was brilliant in the classroom. But on the basketball court, it was just physical. He was forever smashing into people. Talk about a competitive guy— *that* was one competitive guy."

Athletics was yet another way to distinguish yourself at law school—a way to let off steam and demonstrate your competitiveness and agility outside of class.

Our criminal law professor, Paul Bator, was almost the same age as his students; he and his wife, Allie, often socialized with us. They had been married his last year at Harvard Law School, a time when he was an editor of the *Harvard Law Review*. It was an intense period, just as it was a few years later when we arrived. Paul did not want to be distracted from his work and asked that Allie not disturb him during the week. Almost every day Allie drove into Cambridge from their small apartment on the outskirts of town, parked her car on the street, and watched him walk from the *Law Review* office across the Law School yard to lunch at Harkness Commons. She didn't speak to him and he didn't see her. Professor Bator expected no less concentration, no less dedication, from his students.

By the beginning of our third year in law school, the civil rights movement was gaining strength. Many members of the class of '64, including Dinni Lorenz, Sheila Rush, Fred Wallace, and Hap Dunning and his wife, who was a high-powered executive in Boston, went to the organizing meetings for those who wanted to be involved in civil rights demonstrations and were prepared *not* to disperse immediately. They learned how to fall, how to go limp, how to protect their kidneys in case the cops kicked them, how to be arrested, and what their rights were when that happened. Several of the law wives volunteered for the front lines, but most of the law students didn't: we were nervous about getting through the state bar committees and worried that an arrest would block our admission into the practice of law. I remember I was concerned about that. I had sat in for desegregation at the Woolworth's counter in Cambridge while I was still in college, but for years I told no one, fearing that such an act of civil disobedience, if known, would be held against me when I applied to join the bar.

Classmate Fred Wallace's return to law school for the beginning of third year was delayed by what he described as a "legal lynching."[36] A Prince Edward County, Virginia, grand jury had indicted him for felonious assault on a Virginia policeman, even though the only person

Fred Wallace

who had been beaten was Fred. Seven members of our class, including Richard Klein, Peter Berle, and Jim Lorenz, established an ad hoc committee to raise funds for Fred's defense. Dean Griswold became personally involved, working with the Lawyers Committee on Civil Rights to obtain counsel for Fred, and appearing as a character witness at his trial.

Dinni Lorenz was studying, and demonstrating, but she also made sure to fulfill her duties as a traditional wife to Jim in their first-floor apartment at 64 Frost Street, the same house where Ann Dudley and I lived in the attic. Like the rest of us, she was a child of the fifties and felt guilty when she failed to do all the things a woman of that era was expected to do. She had negotiated with Jim early on that she was not going to darn his socks or iron his shirts, but she did everything else. Besides, Dinni's mother never let her forget her responsibilities, always ending their long-distance phone conversations with "How can you be a good wife and be studying so hard? I hope you remember that the role of wife comes first." With the help of a "cleaner" who came for four hours each week, Dinni kept their tiny apartment immaculate; she also hauled their laundry to the Laundromat and Jim's shirts to the dry cleaner, did the marketing, cooked, and threw great dinner parties for friends and teachers alike. She would often leave the law library and bicycle like mad up Massachusetts Avenue to the apartment, watch Julia Child cook on WGBH, then bike like mad back to the library and head to her carrel to study. It was an exhausting pace, emotionally as well as physically. Yet, with all that, Dinni still thought she was a fraud: she didn't have confidence in her ability to be a lawyer; all she knew for sure was that she could cook and keep house. Jim took Dinni's housewifery for granted. He studied hard. He competed successfully in the moot court competition, eventually winning the final round as a member of the Griswold Club team, along with teammates Joe Wheelock and Ann Dudley Cronkhite. And he took out the garbage. Period.

One night, when Professor Jack Dawson and his wife came to dinner, Dinni made Julia Child's new recipe for cherry cheesecake. Then, at the end of dinner, when she tried to unmold the cake, the bottom fell out of the springform pan, and the cake dropped into the plastic dish drainer beside the sink. It was the last straw: Dinni burst into tears. Jim, to his eternal credit, picked up the dish drainer together with the rubber mat under it, dripping with cherries and cheesecake, and carried it like a presentation out to the table. The Dawsons laughed, and as soon as she recovered, Dinni did, too. It was a great icebreaker; it is also the only positive memory Dinni says she has of social contacts with her professors during her three years at Harvard Law School. In socializing with the professors, Dinni thought she had a double disability: she was a woman and she was married.

Even in her last year, some of the male students continued to ask Dinni what she was doing at law school. One opined, "You're not contentious enough." He meant it as a compliment, that she was gentle, compliant, not a ball-breaker type, but Dinni knew that it was also dismissive: "We didn't have a vocabulary in those days to resist typecasting." Another guy accused her of taking a man's slot at law school, challenging the proper order in society, and holding men back as a class. Dinni was appalled:

"It was my first real consciousness of this kind of discrimination. You would have thought that he might pause and remember that, after all, I'd gotten to the third year, so I must not be a total dope. And yet his comment made me feel guilty that I wasn't doing all the things I should as a wife— that I wasn't darning Jim's socks, so to speak. I still bought into the idea that the men would make their mark in the law but that, for the women—well, law school was still a sort of frill."

It was vitally important to our future careers to have a good job during the summer between our second and third years of law school, and to receive an offer of full-time employment when the summer ended. Many of us headed to New York, or to big corporate firms in other major American cities. We knew that having a few months' training and experience at a Wall Street–type firm would give us a taste of what "big law" was all about, and that, if we got an offer, we would be all set after graduation.

After our first year, Ann Dudley had wangled a job with O'Melveny & Myers in Los Angeles. Warren Christopher (later U.S. Secretary of State) was her boss. That summer was her first inkling that she wasn't going to like the practice of law. She found it repetitive, with a lot of make-work. It was also nerve-racking: "You were dealing with large amounts of other people's money, and the issues were just drop-dead boring to me." By the end of the summer, it was also reasonably apparent to her that she had been hired because everybody there knew her family: "I was like a pet. They weren't taking me seriously, and it appeared to me that this was not only not going to be fun, but dull and ultimately humiliating." Ann Dudley decided not to go back the next year.

The following summer, she tried clerking for a federal district-court judge. He was a political appointee and a close family friend. He was from her parents' Republican circles and had often been at their home for dinner. Ann Dudley loved the work but not the judge: "The man was a social-climber who loved parties. He had the criminal calendar that summer and often just told me to handle the basics." The most controversial decision she drafted was whether a local men's club, the Jonathan Club, had to allow women members. "That was a sensitive thing for him to ask me to do, wasn't it?

Under the law then [1963], it became perfectly obvious that they could exclude women. So that's what I wrote. But I didn't like having to do it."

I was in the same fix. The summer after my first year, my mother had helped me land a job at the Fuller, Seney firm in Toledo, Ohio. I spent a fascinating summer working on a federal antitrust case against the Libbey, Owens, Ford Glass Company, trying to prove that glass bottles were interchangeable with plastic and paper containers. I might have gone back, except that they told me it was their policy not to make full-time offers to women.

By January of my second year in law school, I was looking for that all-important second-year summer job. Many of the Wall Street firms that conducted interviews on campus declined to grant me—or any other woman in my class—an interview. It may have been our grades—none of us was on law review—but we thought it was our gender. After all, they were interviewing men whose grades weren't as good as ours. I surmised from this predicament that I, as a woman, would just have to do better than a man to get to the same place. I wrote letters to firms in Toledo, Cleveland, and Denver, but struck out: either they didn't interview women law students at all, or they were willing to talk, but warned me that, even if I got a summer position, their policy was not to give permanent-job offers to women.

The spring wore on with no luck. Finally, in desperation, I called Amalya Kearse, a good friend from Wellesley who'd finished a couple of years ahead of me, then graduated from Michigan Law School and landed a job with the Hughes, Hubbard firm at One Wall Street in New York City. (Amalya is now a highly respected judge of the United States Court of Appeals for the Second Circuit.) Amalya said she'd see what she could do. Within a day, she phoned to say that if I would come to New York at my own expense, they would grant me an interview. As soon as my mother wired the money for the train ticket, I headed for New York. Amalya introduced me around the firm, sat in on the interviews with me, told everybody that I was "brilliant," and, I suspect, more than anyone else, made sure that I got an offer. It was a great firm, and I was elated.

My first assignment was to help draft the final documents for the initial stock offering for the first American cable-television company, CATV. On the final morning before the documents were to be filed with the SEC, I carried stacks of contracts into the main conference room, where lawyers from the firm and representatives of the client had assembled. I had just finished distributing copies to each man at the table and started to sit down when CATV's president, Matty Fox, turned to me:

"Honey, could you get me a cup of coffee?"

"This," I thought to myself, "is the biggest entrance exam you're ever going to take."

Gritting my teeth, I responded with my softest voice and sweetest smile, "Yes, sir, Mr. Fox, how do you take it?"

I don't remember his answer. I just remember that I hustled out of the room and headed for the elevator. In those days, Hughes, Hubbard had no coffee machines. In the summer, iced coffee was delivered on silver trays to the partners twice a day, midmorning and midafternoon. The rest of us had to go down twenty-six floors, cross Wall Street to the Chock Full o' Nuts, stand in line, and buy a paper cup full of java to bring back to the office. That morning, there was a long line. It took me half an hour to fill Matty Fox's order. When I finally delivered it, he looked up from his papers and asked:

"How much do I owe you, honey?"

"Twenty-five dollars," I replied.

"What!"

"Mr. Fox, I'm a summer lawyer here. My rate is fifty dollars an hour. Half an hour is twenty-five dollars. Plus, of course, fifty cents for the coffee. But don't worry about it. We can just put it on your bill. Let's get back to work."

Nobody laughed. More important, nobody got mad. The men around the table just looked at me hard, appraisingly. I must have passed: I was given great assignments for the rest of the summer and received an offer of a permanent job after I graduated from law school.

Classmate Terry Lenzner, an all-Ivy football star who'd been captain of the Harvard College team (and who went on to found the premier global investigative firm, Investigative Group, Inc. [IGI]), spent the summer of 1963 working at Paul, Weiss, Rifkin, Wharton & Garrison in Manhattan. The offices there were all connected by vacuum tubes. For the entire summer he received his work assignments that way: he'd sit at his desk and wait until a canister came popping out of the tube with a note

Terry Lenzner

telling him what to do: "Go research the contract on the issue of jurisdiction and give me a three-page memo by tomorrow at noon." He would go to the library, do the research, prepare a memo, and send it back through the vacuum tube to whoever had made the assignment: "Unless a lawyer in the firm had a question about the memo, you never saw him. And, of course, they were all *hims*."

For a man used to a lot of action, Terry found Paul, Weiss too structured. In August, he and a couple of the other summer clerks there decided to go

Washington, D.C., to join the March on Washington for Civil Rights. When he told his parents he was going, they objected: "No, you're not going. It's going to be dangerous, there're going to be riots. You're risking your career, not to mention your life." Given Terry's fearless personality, that warning made it absolutely mandatory for Terry to go. He drove to D.C., met up with leaders from the Student Nonviolent Coordinating Committee (SNCC), and joined the march. Terry was moved by what he saw and heard: he was standing near the steps of the Lincoln Memorial when Martin Luther King gave his "I Have a Dream" speech and remembers that, for the first time, he knew with total clarity why he had gone to law school. He decided to forget Wall Street and went to talk with Burke Marshall and John Doar about a full-time job with the Civil Rights Division at the Justice Department. He got an offer right away.

The next spring, Terry called Doar up: he'd just won a Fulbright Fellowship to Denmark, "with all those beautiful blondes." He asked to postpone starting work for a year. Doar responded, "You can wait a year, but you'll be making a total mistake, because this is going to be a hell of a summer. It's already starting to heat up." Terry turned the Fulbright down. On June 21, 1964, a week after he graduated, Terry found himself in Philadelphia, Mississippi, working on the unexplained disappearance of three civil rights workers, Goodman, Schwerner, and Chaney. It was Freedom Summer. Instead of writing memoranda about jurisdiction, he was gathering evidence for a grand jury in Biloxi, Mississippi. His work culminated in the indictment of twenty-one people for murder, including the local sheriff and deputy sheriff. Seventeen of them were convicted. Most nights when he was in the South that summer, Terry slept *under* his bed in the local motel. The experience of leading investigations into the flagrant civil rights abuses he uncovered in the South changed Terry forever. He had always been a maverick, but now he was angry as well and vowed to dedicate his talents and his tenacity to leveling the playing field for all Americans.

On Wednesday, August 28, 1963, Judy Wilson (Rogers) also joined the March on Washington for Jobs and Freedom. The next month, she spoke with classmate Dan Kucera, a reporter for the *Harvard Law Record,* about her experience: "I kept reading about plans for the march. As time passed, I seemed closer and closer to it, and it to me. I felt that if one really believed in it, [s]he ought to participate in it. . . . It was a sporadic, calm, slow walk. Singing enveloped me."[37]

Now, forty years later, Judy vividly recalls the march and the emotions that overwhelmed her that August day. "It was something I knew I wanted to be there for. I didn't say anything to anybody else about it, which surprises me. It was a hot summer day. I was walking down the middle of the street with thousands of people and suddenly there beside me was Professor Arthur Sutherland from the Law School, small and slight, marching in the middle of the street. We chatted. We heard the 'I Have a Dream' speech together. I was moved to tears. I was so glad to be there. It was one of those pivotal moments: if I hadn't gone, I would have been sorry for the rest of my life. There was a reaffirmation of a very positive attitude that, while there were serious problems, there was violence, some people were even losing their lives, it was a wonderful moment to be alive because we could be part of the effort for positive growth and change."

Like the rest of the country, the Harvard Law School community was electrified by the March on Washington. Professor Mark de Wolfe Howe, who had authored the 1949 report recommending the admission of women to Harvard Law School, took the bus from Boston to Washington to join the march. As he told the *Harvard Law Record* at the time: "It was a stroll. I walked slowly with the others from the Monument to the Memorial. There was no pushing; no incidents. It was peaceful and friendly. . . . The march educated the public and aroused the nation's concern for civil rights. It was a very moving expression of national opinion."[38]

Classmate Joe Austin was there, carrying a huge sign: NO U.S. DOUGH TO HELP JIM CROW GROW. Classmate Aurelle Smoot, who was working at the Treasury Department that summer, told the *Harvard Law Record*: "I saw history being made before my eyes. . . . We saw the buses come in. A strange feeling went through my office—we wondered if there would be violence. . . . We just walked and watched. The march came off well. . . . It brought much national publicity and made a favorable impact for the Negro case."[39]

Tony Bloom entered Harvard Law School from South Africa in September 1963 as a candidate for the master's of law degree. There, for the first time, he read the writings and speeches of Nelson Mandela in the Harvard Law library. They had been banned in his homeland, and it would have been a criminal offense for him to obtain them there. As he told me later, "Suddenly, the penny dropped. Reading law and talking with my professors and classmates about civil rights shaped my views and made me determined to do what I could to abolish apartheid in South Africa."

Tony Bloom

Tony earned his master of law degree in 1964 with our class and returned to South Africa, where he practiced law for a few years before joining one of the country's largest corporations, Premier Milling. He immediately began to implement nondiscretionary, racial neutral policies. Despite the hate mail and the death threats he and his family received as a result, Tony never backed down. In 1979, when he became Chairman and CEO, Premier Milling was the only company in South Africa that had totally integrated facilities, hired detainees, promoted blacks to senior management positions, and gave financial support to the families of those who were tried for treason because they opposed apartheid. To this day, Tony attributes his inspiration to bring essential change to his homeland to the year he spent at Harvard Law School as part of the class of 1964.

In June 1964, it was over. Fifteen of the twenty women who had begun in September 1961 had made it through. Like the men in our class, we had passed all the academic challenges put before us. But we had also passed a test that only the women were given: we had disproved the assumption that marriage would lay waste to a woman's law school education and a career thereafter. Many of us had married during law school or would do so within a few months of commencement, and all of us expected to work as lawyers. In fact, we were eager to begin. We had survived the pressures, the humiliations of a few of our male classmates, and the efforts of legendary teachers to outwit us as they were opening our minds to the magnificence—and the limitations—of the law. With brains, intuition, tenacity, humor, and a fair amount of courage, we had run that fearsome gauntlet successfully and mastered not only a body of law but a way of making our way through the male preserve. We were ready. And yet, in many ways, we hated to leave. Our classmates and teachers had become not only our comrades in arms but our confidants, our friends. The fifteen women of the class of 1964 had also forged an alliance out of common experiences and battles fought and won that would last a lifetime. Despite—or perhaps because of—its very rigors and challenges, we realized that Harvard Law School had been one of the best times of our lives. We might not have learned it all in kindergarten, but by the time we graduated from Harvard Law, we had learned almost everything we would need to know about life, work, and love.

Our class dedicated the 1964 Harvard Law School yearbook to President John F. Kennedy:

> Our class emerges from the Law School scarred by an experience not shared by our predecessors. For who among us shall soon forget the unbelief with which we sought to protect ourselves that stark Friday last November, the unwonted silence in Langdell, the tears flowing on that tragic afternoon marked by the violent death of a young President. . . . Is it not incumbent upon us to devote a portion of our talent and skill to keeping alive that

spirit? An accounting ten or twenty or thirty years from now will reveal whether our class rose to the challenge and carved a fit memorial to the President out of that most malleable of materials—our careers. . . . Perhaps we shall, like the generation which followed Lincoln, turn away from the paths illumined by the late President, turn inward in pursuit of private fortune or backward in conformity to comfortable, if hardly serviceable, ideas. We may do so, but no longer in innocence.[40]

Commencement day, Thursday, June 11, 1964, was balmy and bright. Crimson banners displaying the coats of arms of each of Harvard's nine schools waved in the breeze as forty thousand graduates, family, and friends celebrated. The Harvard marching band played the university's rousing fight song: "Ten Thousand Men of Harvard Won Victory Today." The fifteen of us thought that we had won a victory, too.

My parents brought my Welsh terrier, Cappie, along. He was the only dog at the Harvard commencement that day. My dad was true to his word: a brand-new navy blue sports car with white leather seats and a red steering wheel was waiting for me outside Harvard Yard after commencement. It was the only one like that they ever made. I drove it back to 64 Frost Street for the last time, loaded my suitcases and books into the trunk, plopped Cappie on the front seat beside me, and headed west, to Ohio and home.

PART THREE

The Real World:
June 1964 Forward

CHAPTER 16

"Women Unwanted"

The year I entered Harvard Law School, 1956, 3 percent of the nation's law students were women. The proportion was even lower at Harvard, closer to 2 percent. When I graduated from Columbia Law School in 1959, not a law firm in the entire city of New York would employ me. I struck out on three grounds: I was Jewish, a woman, and a mother.

> —Ruth Bader Ginsburg, Associate Justice of the United States Supreme Court, at Harvard Law's celebration of forty years of women law graduates, 1993

"Women Unwanted." That was the December 1963, page-one headline in our law school newspaper, the *Record*, just at the time when all of us were scanning the want ads, looking for jobs as lawyers. It was six months before graduation and I, like most of the fifteen women in the law school class of 1964, had not yet lined up a permanent job. On a scale of plus ten ("definitely does get job") to minus ten ("definitely does not get job"), 120 major U.S. law firms ranked women lawyers at minus 4.9. Only two groups were rated less desirable than women: "lower one-third of class," minus 6.7, and "badly groomed," minus 5.5. "Lower one-half" of the class, at minus 4.5, and "Negro," at minus 3.5, outranked "female." According to the survey, belonging to the "weaker sex" was a "highly relevant, though not all-controlling, factor *against* giving an applicant a job." The firms' stated rationales (anonymous, of course) were quite extraordinary for a profession that prides itself on being analytical: "women can't keep up the pace"; "bad relationship with the courts"; "responsibility is in the home"; "afraid of emotional outbursts"; and the ultimate cop-out: "I have enough problems in life."

Harvard Law Professor Frank E. A. Sander, then a member of President

Lyndon Johnson's Commission on the Status of Women, commented, "Discrimination against women, unlike other forms of bias, is based partly on myth, but partly on relevant considerations. The firms know best how to run their own offices, and they are justified, if it is true that women tend to leave firms quickly, though no empirical study seems to have been made on this."[1]

The women in my class paid little, if any, attention to the poll or to Professor Sander's comments—we just kept going. We knew we probably weren't going to find a job in the want ads of our law school newspaper anyway, or, for that matter, at the Law School's Placement Office, which offered us little encouragement and virtually no help. Nancy Kuhn, who worked in the Placement Office to help pay her tuition bills, had a front-row seat to watch how the office operated when we needed, but couldn't get, help there. She recalls: "I never heard anyone say that having criteria such as 'We don't interview women' was unacceptable behavior for people who used the services of the Harvard Law School Placement Office. Some firms were even more restrictive: they would only talk to members of the most selective social club, Lincoln's Inn, which was all male and generally drawn from the Ivy League and the so-called upper classes. It wasn't fair."

Eleanor Appel, the Placement Office director, thought she was doing her job when she explained to us which firms not to waste our time with because they wouldn't consider hiring a woman. According-ing to Nancy, "She had no concept of trying to change how things worked. But if she could just convey how they worked, then she believed she had done what she was supposed to." Nancy also remembers when I came into the Placement Office one day after failing to get an interview with the Manhattan law firm, Sullivan & Cromwell, although male students with lower academic averages had been given interviews slots: "You were standing at the counter, and you were agitated, you were very upset."

Eleanor Appel

When I asked the Placement Office about judicial clerkships, they told me, "You're not on the *Law Review.* Forget it." I was too unimaginative to figure out for myself that my grades were good enough to qualify me to clerk for a trial or appellate judge, and that hundreds of them around the country needed law clerks.

Despite the barriers and biases, somehow all of us were confident that we would land jobs, good jobs, and that, as our mothers had always promised us, "everything will be all right." After all, we had gotten into Harvard Law School and taken everything it had dished out for three years. Most of us had not only survived but found law school one of the most stimulating times of our lives. We each had somehow finagled summer jobs in government or private law firms. We had come to know an exceptional and diverse group of people. We had had fun in the classroom and outside. We had a strong network of friends from law school, male and female. And many of our professors had befriended us, quietly helping us behind the scenes. It may have been cockeyed optimism, but we believed that we could not fail with all of that backup.

Individually and collectively, we had also found time not only to learn the law but to go to the Boston Pops, take in a few Red Sox games, ski in New Hampshire, and date a rather substantial percentage of our male classmates (as well as men in the other graduate schools in the area). A majority of us were married or engaged to be married. We thought we had balance in our lives, and that it would help us on the road ahead. We never questioned that we should and would have fulfilling personal lives and productive professional lives—despite the hazing of a few of our classmates and teachers, despite the hostile job market, no matter how many times we were rejected personally and professionally.

Our Harvard Law School training and degree helped immeasurably: our future employers knew we had survived running that rigorous gauntlet. But we would have made it if we'd gone to Podunk U.—it would just have been harder and taken longer. The changing political and social climate in America actually helped us: it was a time for restless spirits, people who wanted to make a difference, and who would not permit themselves to be hampered by traditional views or roles or obstacles. Almost without exception, all of us—and the men we married and those we worked for—were unconventional and restless just as we were. We took our chances, going against the tide—as it turned out, that tide was going out anyway. There was no affirmative action or mandated diversity in the workplace we were entering. The only quotas that existed were meant to exclude us. We had no choice: we had to use everything we had. Fortunately it was enough.

Just as the women in our class went where few, if any, women had gone before, the men who graduated with us in the class of 1964 headed in new directions, rejecting the Wall Street big-firm expectation in unprecedented numbers, choosing instead to go to Africa to write constitutions for new nations or to serve in the Peace Corps, to Thailand and Indonesia to start the first American law firms there, to Mississippi and Alabama to fight for civil rights, to California and Washington to join the government and develop programs to give the poor and disenfranchised access to the legal system.

Pat Scott Schroeder

Pat and Jim Schroeder had worked in Colorado the summer after their second year in law school and decided to move there. They thought Denver and its more relaxed Western lifestyle was just what the doctor ordered. That year had been traumatic, not only because of the unrelenting academic pressure but also because Jim's father had died suddenly of a heart attack the night before one of Jim's final exams. As Pat remembers it, "It was a total shock. We were reeling. And we were in stark terror of what to do about his exam. As the only son, Jim had to go to Chicago immediately." Pat called Jim's professor, explained the situation, and asked if Jim could postpone taking the final for a few days. The professor expressed his condolences, said that he understood Jim had to go home, but told Pat that Jim would lose credit for the whole year if he didn't take the exam as scheduled.

Pat was dumbfounded: "Wait a minute! We'll pay to send a proctor with us."

"No, Harvard doesn't do that."

"Well, can we pay somebody out there to get the exam and monitor it?"

"No, we don't do that, either."

"Well, why don't you do that?"

"Well, what if people started using this as an excuse?"

"How could they? How do you phony that up? Bring a forged death certificate?"

"Mrs. Schroeder, it's just like life. You may have a situation one day when your father dies and you're in the middle of a trial or a deal, and you have to find a way to handle it. The law school's rules about exams are not fixable. There are fixables and nonfixables in life, and we're all operating under the same nonfixables with respect to final exams."

Pat couldn't believe the debate she was having: "Am I out in space somewhere? This is unbelievable."

For her, it had been the final straw at Harvard Law School. Somehow she and Jim got through it:

"We flew out, we flew back so that Jim could take the exam. We flew out again, we flew back again. And by the end of that week, I thought, 'I'm out of this place and the East Coast as soon as I can get out.' "

After graduation, they decided to move to Denver and then find jobs later. They'd find a place to live, then find a way to exist. But there were a lot of things they never thought of.

"As we were preparing to take the Colorado bar exam, we decided we would go and find out what kind of jobs were available. Denver was not a huge city at that time. The law firms certainly weren't large by today's standards. They had absolutely no idea what to do with us. I talked to a number of firms in Denver. Almost all of them asked me if I could type. Many said they did not and would not hire a woman. A lot of the big firms told us they were afraid to hire only one of us without hiring both of us, because they were worried about conflicts of interest. I ended up deciding that there wasn't any firm that was really going to let me be active trying cases or anything else, and that if they hired me at all, I was going to be doing research, wills, or family law—and I didn't want to do that. So I decided to go to work for the federal government.

"We went over to the federal building and I filled out all of their little forms. I wanted to work for the IRS because I had basically made taxation my specialty in law school. The IRS interviewer told me that they would be happy to hire me, but that if my husband practiced law in Denver, I could not work for them in Colorado; I could, however, work in the IRS office in Albuquerque. They said it was required because of potential conflicts of interest in the Denver regional office with whatever law firm Jim decided to join. Whether that was the real reason or just the reason they gave, I'm not sure, but whatever it was, I knew that they weren't going to change their policy for me and I knew I wasn't going to live in Albuquerque. So I went over to the regional office of the National Labor Relations Board in Denver, which covered cases in Wyoming, Utah, and Colorado.

"I had never even taken a labor law course. I hadn't even thought of labor law. But they said, 'Sure, we'll hire you.' I thought, 'Okay, that looks interesting. Try some cases. Move around through the region. Learn more about the Rocky Mountains.' So I did it. That actually helped Jim: he could say to firms, 'Okay, now she is doing labor law for the NLRB.' Most of the firms weren't doing labor law cases, so they were no longer worried about the potential conflicts of interest. Eventually it worked out, but it was a lot more awkward and difficult than I thought it would be."

Pat didn't find any discrimination against her as a woman at the NLRB. But there was discrimination because of her law degree. At that time, Harvard's first law degree was a bachelor of laws, LLB, not the Juris Doctor, or JD, that Harvard awards today. Pat found herself working with men who had gone to a night school and gotten a JD. Under federal law, theirs was a doctorate and hers was a bachelor's degree; they got two pay grades higher than she did.

Dinni Lorenz (Gordon)

As a married woman and law student, Dinni's travails in getting a job were, if anything, even more difficult and, at the same time, even more confusing than those the rest of us lived through. When her husband, Jim, had an interview, she would go along as "wife." At Jones, Day in Cleveland, they entertained her lavishly, hoping to recruit him, but when she asked for help in finding a legal job if Jim ended up in Cleveland, they were totally thrown: they finally said that they would be happy to help her find a house, a good plumber, and the right doctor, but they couldn't promise anything in the job marketplace.

As things worked out, Jim decided to go to Los Angeles, and with his firm's help, Dinni got a job at a small litigation firm there, spending the first year reading and summarizing documents in connection with a private antitrust case involving the monopolization of the citrus fruit market.

It was a bad time: She hated her job and didn't want to spend the rest of her career helping fat cats get fatter. Her marriage was in trouble. And she had flunked the California bar twice.

Pulling herself together, Dinni got a divorce, quit her job, and moved to Washington, D.C. Once there, she looked for jobs in government and had a number of interviews on Capitol Hill. One congressman declined to hire her as a lawyer because he would have to pay her more than the secretaries. When Dinni answered, "I should hope so," he elaborated, "Don't you understand that some of these secretaries have been here a long time? They are older women and would be very upset if you, a bright Harvard Law woman, came in and immediately took precedence over them."

When Dinni interviewed with Senator John Tunney, he not only warned her about potential trouble with the secretaries if he hired her, he also inquired if she would be prepared to work until two in the morning. After she assured him that it wouldn't be a problem, he shifted gears: "Don't you think it might be kind of hard on the guys to have an attractive woman around after midnight?"

Dinni ultimately went to work for the newly established Office of Economic Opportunity, overseeing demonstration projects in legal services. One of the first grant applications she reviewed requested funding to establish California Rural Legal Assistance, a legal-aid program for California's migrant workers. It was signed by James D. Lorenz, her ex-husband. Somehow Dinni managed to get through the analysis without conflicts or rancor and eventually approved the funding for what became among the most controversial of the legal services programs of that era, CRLA.

Ann Dudley Cronkhite (Goldblatt)

After two problematic summer job experiences in California—as a summer clerk at a law firm that didn't take her seriously, and as a judicial clerk for a federal judge who did the opposite and delegated much of his work to her—Ann Dudley decided to head to Wall Street after law school. It was a serious and exciting place and had the advantage of being three thousand miles away from her prominent family: she wanted a place where she would rise or fall on her own merits. Her mother had sat by Randall LeBoeuf, founding partner of LeBoeuf, Lamb and Leiby, at a fancy New York dinner party and bragged about her brilliant daughter. LeBoeuf, a liberated man at a time before we had any concept of what that expression meant, said he was interested in interviewing her.

Earlier he had encouraged his secretary, Sheila Marshall, to go to law school at night. While taking dictation, typing his letters, and answering his phone, Sheila had also made herself indispensable on the biggest matter in the office, an original Supreme Court case on how much water could be diverted from Lake Michigan to serve the city of Chicago and the state of Illinois. According to Sheila, "Randall was very much interested in having a lawyer as a secretary. He encouraged me and, in fact, offered to pay for law school. I went to New York University Law School at night. In the daytime, as senior secretary, I was doing a lot of what today we regard as associates' work. Of course, by the time I got out of school, I didn't want to be Randall's secretary. So I talked to him about coming to the firm as a lawyer."

LeBoeuf announced to his Executive Committee that the firm had to hire Sheila Marshall. "What! Hire a woman? And not only a woman, but a little shanty-Irish woman who went to night law school, while everybody else has gone to Harvard, Yale, or Cornell?" LeBoeuf insisted, "She's the only person who knows everything about the Lake Michigan diversion case. If we don't hire her, she'll go somewhere else and take the case with her." There was no further argument. Sheila had her job and her chance. (Today, she is a senior partner, one of the leaders of LeBoeuf's insurance practice.)

Sheila Marshall's courage and outstanding legal work opened the door for Ann Dudley at LeBoeuf: she received a job offer the day after she was interviewed. She took the New York bar exam and joined the firm's corporate department, the second woman they had ever hired. She was dazzling—brilliant, beautiful, and not exactly the quiet, gray wren some of the partners had expected. As Sheila Marshall recalls, "She showed up in short white boots, and short skirts, dressed in the latest style. She came from a lovely family and was absolutely adorable. She was just a big hit at the firm, she really was."

Ann Dudley had come a long way from Pasadena, debutante balls, and weekends in the Turf Club at Santa Anita. Although, truth be told, when the races were running in New York, Ann Dudley sometimes snuck out for an afternoon at the Aqueduct "law library," then stayed up the rest of the night finishing her work for the next day. When then New York City Mayor John Lindsay heard that Ann Dudley was a champion backgammon player, he sent a car and driver to bring her to Gracie Mansion for a late afternoon backgammon tournament. She was smart enough—and charming enough—that no one objected. The LeBoeuf partners helped her in other ways, too, introducing her to clients, acknowledging to them the work she did, and even advising her on her wardrobe.

Ann Dudley remembers, "In those days, it was a benefit to have the female lawyer look very much like the client's wife or daughter or friend. I can remember my supervising partner, Cameron MacRae, actually telling me what suit he wanted me to wear to specific meetings. Which didn't seem at all strange to me then. It was only later that I thought that if somebody did that today, they'd get slammed or sued. Which, actually, is too bad. First, it was a compliment that somebody actually noticed your suit. Second, women lawyers were rare then, and clients could object. He was doing everything he could to build their confidence in me. If dressing conservatively made the client more comfortable, that was good for the firm and good for me."

Rosemary Cox Masters

On November 2, 1963, the middle of our third year, Rosemary wrote her parents about her search for a permanent job:

> The job hunt in New York had the exhilaration of a big game hunt. It was stalking the Wall Street lawyer—a lure of charm, a flash of wit, and wham! Before they knew it they walked blithely into the trap saying, "Now if I can just convince my partners that a woman of your ability can do a trememdous [sic] job here . . ." The rest depends on whether the daze wears off before the prey can convince his partners to send off that offering letter. I enjoyed it fully. I remember my plaintive attempts last year and realize what a lot I have learned. A woman looking for a law job must cut a fine path between assertiveness and feminine appeal—too much of either is fatal. . . . Despite my

wretched grades I've had more 'Come to New York so that we can take a closer look' offers than have any of the other girls in our class (a slim boast, alas).[2]

The first year after Rosemary graduated from law school was probably the most miserable of her life. She and her husband, Jon, had each passed the New York bar examination, then moved to Washington, where Jon had lined up a job traveling with Lyndon Johnson's presidential campaign. Rosemary found herself a camp follower: Jon was gone most of the time, and Rosemary was left to fend for herself in the tiny house they'd rented in Georgetown. She'd put her own plans on hold until Jon decided what his next move would be.

After the November elections, they traveled in Europe for a couple of months, then returned home to New York, where Jon had accepted a job as an associate with the Wall Street law firm of Shearman & Sterling. Rosemary started looking for a job. With the help of classmate Sheila Rush, who had already found a position there, Rosemary got an interview, but not a job, with the NAACP Legal Defense Fund. The man in charge told her, "I don't know what I would do with a white woman. We can't send you South—it would be too dangerous." Eventually, she received offers from both the city's Legal Aid Society and the New York District Attorney's Office. As she was weighing which one to accept, her father-in-law, a financially successful New York lawyer who often intruded into the decisions she and Jon were making, expressed his vehement opposition to both possibilities: "Why do you want to do that? Why don't you work at a corporate law firm?" His attitude was much like those Rosemary had encountered in the Harvard Law School Placement Office: in those days there had been little understanding of or support for Harvard Law School graduates going into the social justice world. Not wanting to exacerbate an already difficult family relationship, Rosemary declined both offers. Eventually, she landed a job at Webster, Sheffield, a small, excellent Manhattan law firm where she took a starting associate's position.

Although the people she worked with were great, Rosemary hated law practice. After nine months, she left to join the Vera Institute, funded in part by the federal government, to work on problems of juvenile justice. It was about as far from Park Avenue as Rosemary could get. One of her first assignments was to establish a voluntary detox program for derelicts and alcoholics in the Bowery area of lower Manhattan, rather than having them hauled off to jail, sobered up, and turned out. The headquarters was a former YMCA building with a huge gymnasium, which, on cold nights, took in forty to fifty men to sleep on the floor or to pick up tickets they could exchange for a $5 room in a nearby flophouse.

"It was a violent, crazy place because most of the alcoholics were mentally ill; they had schizophrenia, bipolar illness, organic brain damage, or just severe alcoholic deterioration. They would fight and get into screaming matches with each other and with the caseworkers, including me. I was five feet two and a half inches tall and several months pregnant. I would go there with my stomach a foot out in front of me, praying that no one would attack me. And yet it seemed to me that, at last, I was doing very important work."

Judy Wilson (Rogers)

Judy Wilson (Rogers) was one of the few women in our class who had her job lined up before the end of law school, and the only one to win a judicial clerkship. Immediately after graduation, she went to Washington, D.C., as law clerk to the three judges of the Juvenile Court of the District of Columbia. After working for the President's Commission on Juvenile Delinquency and Youth Crime during the summer after her second year, Judy knew that it was exactly what she wanted to do. She had chosen law because of her intense interest in helping children; a lot of them, often impoverished, abused, or abandoned, passed through the juvenile court in the nation's capital. It was the start of her career in public service.

Judy went on to become an Assistant U.S. Attorney in D.C. (only the third woman to be in the criminal division), a trial and legislative attorney with the Criminal Division of the U.S. Department of Justice, General Counsel to a congressional commission, and the first woman to be named Corporation Counsel of the District of Columbia (comparable to the attorney general of a state), before finding her life's work as a judge. But her year of clerking in the juvenile court made an indelible impression on her and helped chart her course for the less public side of her life, as Mary McGrory reported in the Sunday *Washington Post* on November 27, 1994:

> My favorite vignette of the marvels of personal attention comes from an encounter between a visiting judge and a homeless child at St. Ann's Infant Home. Judith Rogers, a District judge who has since progressed to the federal bench, met with the boy when he was eight and in big trouble. He was a big kid who looked as if he knew more than he did. School was hell to him. He was surrounded by smaller children who knew how to read, recite poems and do other things that exposed him for a dunce. He did the usual: He hit them. He was sent home, suspended. I asked Judge Rogers to speak to him.
>
> Beforehand, I took the boy aside and told him that the judge sat on a high

bench and sent people to jail for doing bad things—all familiar subjects to him. . . . They withdrew and sat on a bench in a long conversation. They came back looking very pleased. She had got it out of him that he wanted to be a fireman. She was inspired to say, "You can't just go and be a fireman. You have to take a test, and you have to study hard in school to pass it." It was as if a giant light had been switched on in his head. He had never associated school with anything good or important. He stopped hitting, and started bragging about "the judge who talked to me."[3]

Nancy Kuhn (Kirkpatrick)

Nancy Kuhn received offers of a job with the newly established Peace Corps and with the law firm of Covington and Burlington in Washington, D.C. Instead, she decided to marry classmate Doug Kirkpatrick and move to Buffalo, New York. The law firm that Doug had decided to join suggested several firms to Nancy that might be looking for new lawyers. In sharp contrast to Philadelphia, where she had worked as a summer associate during law school, the Buffalo law firms were not shocked at the prospect of hiring a female lawyer. The University of Buffalo had first admitted women in the nineteenth century, and some of the larger firms there actually had women partners! Nancy quickly found a good job with a fine small firm. Among her early accomplishments was her success in forming the first homeowners' association in the state of New York.

The openness of Buffalo's law firms came as a pleasant surprise to Nancy, who, when she interviewed for a summer clerkship after her second year in law school, had found that almost all the Philadelphia law firms that she contacted did not hesitate to inform her that they didn't hire female law students or lawyers. Fortunately, one firm told her that the Philadelphia firm of Pepper, Hamilton & Scheetz had hired a woman lawyer during the Second World War and might therefore consider hiring another. Nancy interviewed there successfully and worked there the summer after her second year in law school.

Alice Pasachoff Wegman

Alice graduated with the rest of us in 1964, but stayed in Cambridge for another year. During the spring of 1963, Dick Wegman, a first-year law student, had struck up a conversation with Alice in the Langdell library and asked her out. It was love at first sight. Alice and Dick were married in June 1964, just after Alice graduated from law school. They spent a summer working for law firms in San Francisco and returned to Cambridge for Dick's final year of law school. During that year she served as a research assistant to the most respected constitutional law scholar of that era, Paul Freund. In the summer of 1965, Alice and Dick studied for the New York bar examination together and started looking for permanent employment. It was not the first time Alice had come face-to-face with discrimination against women lawyers in the job market. She remembers going to lunch with a partner in a prominent Wall Street firm to discuss opportunities:

"I was focused entirely on getting a job. I remember taking off my eyeglasses, which I often do in a restaurant. Then the partner took off his eyeglasses. After lunch, he suggested that we go out for dinner to discuss the law firm. At that point the bell went off: he wasn't interested in me as a job candidate; he was just taking the opportunity to socialize with a woman. I was surprised and frustrated that I wasn't being taken seriously."

Another firm, with about twenty-five lawyers, complimented Alice on her résumé, but told her, "Unfortunately, we hired a woman lawyer several months ago and I'm sure you can understand how we would feel about having two at the same time." Eventually, Alice and Dick decided to look for work in Washington, D.C. They agreed that they wanted to explore a wide range of options, and that they might even apply to the same government agencies for jobs. They quickly discovered, however, that employers were so unsettled by the notion of a husband and a wife competing for jobs that they would reject both rather than make a choice. Having struck out with this approach, Alice and Dick decided to divide up the list of government agencies and law firms. At the top of Alice's list was Shaw, Pittman, Potts & Trowbridge, a law firm that now has several hundred lawyers but then had only five partners and one or two associates.

All five name partners assembled to interview Alice. They were seated in a semicircle facing her, asking her questions. As Alice remembers it, "I thought the interview was going quite well. At some point I was asked about my husband. I told them that we were both interested in working in Washington, that my husband had received several offers from federal agencies, but that he was also interested in exploring jobs with private law firms. At that point the five men began to glance at one another. One of them said to me, 'I hope you won't take this the wrong way, but would you mind very much if we interviewed your husband?'

"At that time, they knew nothing about my husband's academic record or how it might compare to mine. The only thing they could have known was that we were both graduates of Harvard Law School and that he was male and I was female. I told them that it would be all right if they spoke to him. I wanted both of us to succeed, and it wouldn't ever have occurred to me to deprive Dick of the opportunity to talk with them. I was not hurt because it didn't reflect on me as a person or as a lawyer. I felt confident of my own credentials and my record. I was frustrated—merely the fact that I was a woman was posing an extra challenge. I thought that succeeding would be particularly satisfying. It also would be particularly difficult."

Alice dug in her heels and kept interviewing. Like most of us from our class, Alice was determined and stubborn. She was unwilling to give up. She never seemed to get angry. And she kept going until she found a great job.

Alice did not receive an offer from Shaw, Pittman but Dick did. They told him that if he accepted the offer, the firm would help find Alice a job. Dick turned their offer down and took a job with the U.S. Justice Department. Alice accepted a position with a small firm doing primarily estates and trust law, "which was generally accepted at the time to be the area most appropriate for women lawyers." She stayed several years, then left for another job of greater interest to her, in the General Counsel's Office of the new, congressionally chartered Communications Satellite Corporation, COMSAT.

Arlene Lezberg (Bernstein)

Right after law school, Arlene Lezberg went to work for the Boston Legal Aid Society for $4,600 a year. She tried cases, and, as she was still single, she lived at home. In 1966, she met Jerrold Bernstein, also a first-generation American, who had become a doctor, finishing second in his class at the University of Kansas Medical School. They were engaged eight weeks later and married in August 1966. When Jerry entered the Public Health Service, he was transferred to the National Cancer Institute's branch at John Hopkins University in Baltimore.

Arlene walked in cold to one of Baltimore's best firms, Venable, Bajter & Howard, handed them her résumé, and asked for an interview. She can't remember how she finally managed to get that interview, but three of the firm's most senior partners met with her. As they were talking, one of them said, "How did you come here? We've not only never hired a woman, we've never even interviewed one."

The question sounded just like those over dinner at the dean's. Whatever Arlene answered, it passed muster. Frank Murnaghan, one of the partners interviewing her, had gone to Harvard Law School, and his wife had gone to Radcliffe, just like Arlene. He finally spoke up: "Wait a minute. I see some things on her résumé that resonate."

Arlene had found a job, and the firm had found a talented lawyer to help them in litigation and in banking law. She was not only the first woman the Venable firm had ever hired, she was the first woman ever hired by any major Baltimore law firm. Once she had the job, she was thrown in with the mix and never experienced any discrimination: "It was an exciting time. I was there during the civil rights riots. Various people were involved in representing some of the people who were arrested. Paul Sarbanes [later a U.S. Senator] had just finished his Rhodes Scholarship and was an associate, as was Ben Civilletti [later Attorney General of the United States]. It was a wonderful learning experience."

After work, she would go home, make dinner, clean the house, and do the laundry. She never thought twice about it: "That was what you did; you sort of did everything."

Marge Freincle Gibson (Haskell)

Like Alice Pasachoff Wegman, Marge Freincle Gibson (Haskell) stayed an extra year at Harvard Law until her husband, Dan, in the class of '65, graduated. The Wegmans and the Gibsons lived in the same building providing married students housing. After Dan graduated, the Gibsons moved to Washington, and Marge easily found a job, first with the U.S. Department of Defense (DOD), then with the Department of Transportation (DOT). By then, the Johnson administration was looking for women lawyers, and Marge had the right training and the right credentials.

When many of the military brass didn't take her seriously at DOD, Marge decided to have some fun at their expense. "What I would do, which was wicked, would be to take notes in a secretary's spiral-bound pad. Usually before the meeting was over, somebody would have a tough question. I'd look up from my notepad and answer it. They would be astonished, then decide I was a genius. I had an edge and I used it. I walked in knowing how they viewed me—as a secretary who didn't have any brains. If they were going to be so stupid as to view me that way, I thought I would take advantage of the situation. It was their problem, not mine. They never got a fix on me as to who I really was. That was fine with me because they didn't know how to deal with me. I had a lot of fun doing it."

Sonia Faust

Sonia Faust went home to Honolulu after graduation. She hadn't had any ugly experiences in law school and didn't expect that much fuss would be made about women lawyers when she got home, especially since the Civil Rights Act had just passed. What she found shocked her. The private practitioners who interviewed her were uncomfortable with the notion of women lawyers: two firms told her straight out that they would never hire a woman: "It wasn't at all elaborate. They just said they didn't want to hire women and they weren't going to do it."

Their blunt assessment of her employment prospects reminded Sonia of her mother's reaction to her daughter's legal aspirations: "Eventually, I announced to my mother that I wanted to be a lawyer even though I didn't know lawyers and I didn't know what really was involved. Being a person from the Depression era who had survived because she lived on a farm, she looked at me and said, 'You're going to starve.' It was clearly because I was a female and she doubted that I would be able to get work as a lawyer."

Sonia abandoned the idea of private practice and refocused her job search on the public sector. In contrast with the rigid views she had encountered at law firms, Sonia found the government offices welcoming. "I applied to the Attorney General and the Corporation Counsel of Honolulu, but the Corporation Counsel offered me a job first. I was so broke, I really needed to work. By the time I landed back home, I had two hundred and sixty-one dollars left to my name. I took the first job that was offered. I was the only woman there. Then I went out and rented a room for sixty-five dollars a month, and it was all up from there."

Liz Daldy Dyson

In Liz Daldy Dyson's last year at the University of Kansas Law School, she did what many third-year law students did: applied for a clerkship with two federal judges, one in Topeka and one in Kansas City. Although she had superb credentials and was sure her interviews went well, she was not hired: "I was shocked when I didn't get one of those jobs. I can't prove it, but I think they didn't hire me because I was a woman." However, as the saying goes, God closed one door but opened another for Liz: she became chief probation officer of the Juvenile Court of Douglas County, where the University of Kansas is located. Because there was insufficient money to pay her full-time, the job became part-time: "I had a twenty-hour-a-week job instead of a forty-hour-a-week job, which was good for me personally and good for my marriage." In her spare time, she made a comprehensive study of family courts for the Kansas League of Women Voters. It was fortuitous: when her husband accepted a teaching position at Boston University Law School, Liz gave up her job as chief probation officer and moved with him to Boston. She received offers from two law firms, Ropes & Gray and Nutter, McClennen & Fish. "The choice became very easy: Ropes & Gray offered a male classmate of mine two thousand dollars more than they offered me. My former law school classmate Barbara Margulies Rossotti was working at Nutter. She told me she really liked working there and that they didn't pay women any less than men. So I thought, 'Forget Ropes. I'm going with Nutter!'" Liz had a terrific year, doing interesting work and loving every minute. At the end of the first year, the senior partner she had worked for, John Hally, called her in: "You have done a spectacular job, and we're extremely pleased with your work. I just want you to know you'll be getting the same bonus that your male counterparts will be getting." Liz was especially pleased because she had done bonus-worthy work within the confines of a normal workday and had not worked nights and weekends as many of those "male counterparts" had.

A month later, she found out she was pregnant. She was actually relieved: as good as she was at it, Liz had began to find private practice somewhat stultifying. In addition, a professor at the University of Kansas Law School had read her family court study and was urging her to turn it into a book. It offered a perfect solution. In 1966, Liz resigned from Nutter, gave birth to Julie, and spent the next two years at home taking care of her daughter while writing a comprehensive study of the nation's family courts. As she told me, "Looking back, it was actually good that I didn't get the federal clerkships in Kansas. I was able to develop a specialty in juvenile and family law. I didn't have to go back to the law firm, I didn't have to hire a nanny, and I could write when the baby was asleep." Her work was eventually published in two entire issues of the *Journal of Family Law* and is still considered a seminal work in the field.

It was the beginning of Liz's long and distinguished part-time legal career. No matter what the cost to her career, Liz was determined to have plenty of time for her children when they were young: "I wouldn't take full-time jobs because of my own experience of my mother leaving me too early to go back to work. I was about eighteen months old when I was put into full-time day care; even before that, I had a series of different caretakers. My mother wanted to earn money for psychotherapy in order to strengthen her marriage. For her it was probably a good decision. For me it was disastrous."

The author
with her parents,
Joseph and Eve
Richards, at home
in the Methodist
parsonage, Defiance,
Ohio, 1950.

The Harvard Law School faculty, 1960–61.

Judith A. Wilson (*far left*) in a Harvard Law School seminar, 1963.

Classmates Sheila Rush (*center*),
Mike O'Neil (*left*), and Peter Oberdorf
(*right*), November 1962.

Ann Dudley Cronkhite dressed
for a costume party given by classmate
Bartle Bull in honor of Rasputin's
getting on at court, fall 1963.

Harvard Law '64 classmates Pat
and Jim Schroeder on their wedding day,
summer 1962.

Former classmate Katherine Huff O'Neil,
mom and Harvard Law wife, with baby
Will, January 1963.

Harvard Law '64 classmates Rosemary
and Jon Masters on their wedding day, summer 1962.

Twenty-four-year-old defense lawyer Judith Richards, "the blond Giancana mystery, totes her own bag" in Chicago's Federal Courthouse while representing Momo Salvatore "Sam" Giancana, June 3, 1965.

The author dances with her new father-in-law, Bob Hope, as the best man, playwright John Guare, looks on (Defiance, Ohio, December 1967).

The June 1968 wedding party of Ann Dudley Cronkhite (Harvard Law '64) and Stanford Goldblatt (Harvard Law '63). *(Left to right)*: Matron of honor Judith Richards Hope, the groom, the bride, and best man Charles Nesson (Harvard Law '63).

Newly elected Congresswoman Pat Schroeder at a "Welcome Breakfast" for new members of Congress, January 1973. (*Left to right*): Representative Gillis Long, Representative Pat Schroeder, Speaker Carl Albert, and Representative Jack Brooks.

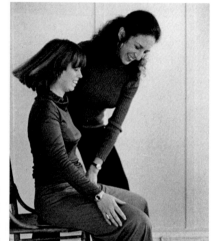

First-year classmate Eleanor Rosenthal teaching the Alexander Technique, San Francisco, California, 1977.

Pilot and House Armed Services Committee member Pat Schroeder talks with an Air Force pilot at a U.S. military base.

The members of the Harvard Corporation, 1990 *(first row, left to right)*: D. Ronald Daniel, Harvard President Derek Bok, Charles Schlicter; *(second row, left to right)*: Judith Richards Hope, Henry Rosovsky, Robert G. Stone Jr., Coleman Mockler.

The author with former Law School Vice Dean and Director of Admissions Louis Toepfer in Harvard Yard, April 1998.

The Board of Directors of Union Pacific Corporation at the 2000 Republican National Convention in Philadelphia, just before Director Richard B. Cheney was nominated as Vice President of the United States. *First row, left to right*: Elbridge T. Gerry Jr., Richard J. Mahoney, Richard K. Davidson (Chairman), Richard B. Cheney, E. Virgil Conway, Judith Richards Hope, and Ivor T. "Ike" Evans. *Second row, left to right*: Spencer F. Eccles, Archie W. Dunham, Philip F. Anshutz, Richard D. Simmons, and Thomas J. Donohue.

The D.C. Circuit en banc panel of judges hearing the Microsoft appeal, February 2001; Judge Judith W. Rogers is in the second row, far right.

Harvard Law '64 classmates and friends for almost forty years at the author's sixtieth birthday party at the home of Judge Judith W. Rogers. *(Left to right)*: Jim Schroeder, Eric Fox, Pat Schroeder, Steve Breyer, Judy Hope, Judy Rogers, and Terry Lenzner.

The author with her daughter, Miranda, and son, Zachary, near the top of Hickerson Mountain, Rappahannock County, Virginia.

The twenty-fifth reunion of the Harvard Law School class of 1964, April 1989. Nancy Kuhn Kirkpatrick (*third row, eighth from left*), Rosemary Cox Masters (*second row, right of center*), Judith Richards Hope (*second row, right of center*), and Patricia Scott Schroeder (*third row, right of center*).

In 1969, Liz and her husband moved to Washington, D.C. She undertook a series of challenging part-time jobs both in the public sector and for private law firms. She was the first part-time attorney hired by Arnold & Porter. Later, she became a consultant to the District of Columbia government legal department, working with the U.S. Department of Justice to reorganize the court system in the District of Columbia. Part of her responsibility was to draft a new juvenile code for the new D.C. Superior Court. Later, she was hired to draft rules for family law matters, including juvenile delinquency, child neglect, and mental health commitment and mental retardation proceedings.

Once again, Liz did a great job, but the D.C. Superior Court bureaucracy ultimately went after her, ruling that a part-timer was not "appropriate" for a project as important as the one pending before the Rules Committee. Judge Tim Murphy was furious, but couldn't find a way to stop her from being fired:

Superior Court of the District of Columbia. December 27, 1971.

Dear Liz: I cannot help but think that the final days of your employment with the Rules Committee were tarnished by the shabby treatment that you received relevant to your continuing with us on a part-time basis. . . . I am convinced that you could have easily been accommodated. . . . It troubles me that you, the loyal, trusted, dedicated professional, who have given the Court so much in the last couple of years, should have to leave the Court's employ as part of a bureaucratic bungling. You deserved so much better. . . . I wish to express my deepest personal gratitude for what you have done for the Court. . . . I shall make a particular effort to keep my eyes open for opportunities for you.

Sheila Rush

By the spring of 1964, our last year in law school, the civil rights movement had begun in earnest. Although Sheila never really liked the study of law, she found the civil rights movement fascinating and compelling. She became deeply involved, and deeply committed, joining with a university-wide group of Harvard students in starting the first black student union in the country. As Sheila remembers, "This was a very, very important development for black America. The country was finally taking notice of a lot of things that had been ignored for many, many years. I was connected with that whole movement, and, as a result, my last year of law school was just a ball. I went on marches. I got involved with civil rights conferences, and the Northern Student Movement [NSM], which was the Northern counterpart to the Student Nonviolent Coordinating Committee [SNCC]."

Sheila remembers that during the job-hunting season in our third year in law school, there was a lot of talk among the women and some blacks about the racial and gender barriers of law firms: "I knew all about that. That stuff was just so well known." But Sheila didn't like law enough to work for a big firm, so she never interviewed with law firms. Instead, she thought she could use her skills to make a contribution to the civil rights movement. She applied for just one job: lawyer with the NAACP Legal Defense Fund. "Jack Greenberg came up to Harvard to recruit and I interviewed with him there. He told me, 'When you come to New York, come and stop by and see the office and see what you think.' But there wasn't anything else I wanted to do. That was it. And they hired me."

After law school, Sheila moved to New York City, passed the New York bar, and went to work for the Legal Defense Fund, fighting for school desegregation and against housing discrimination. She particularly enjoyed working to change the policies and practices of the federal Department of Housing and Urban Development (HUD): "Many of the people who were administering urban renewal programs in the South were using them to uproot blacks from what were really nice black neighborhoods. They would evict the blacks and use the housing for some other purpose that wasn't going to benefit the black community. We were able to stop a number of those actions by showing how they violated the HUD guidelines, and how black citizens were being moved not to better housing but to worse. It was awful."

Eventually, the National Fair Housing Law passed and Sheila's work for the Defense Fund changed: she began focusing on how to enforce fair-housing laws, which were largely ignored. She even brought a mandamus proceeding against the fair-housing commissioner of New York to require him to do his job. The suit caused a big political stink; ultimately, he was forced to resign.

Judith Richards (Hope)

After graduation, I had headed home to Ohio. I planned to take the bar exam and to practice law for a few years, then run for public office. I signed up for a mail-order bar-review course and sent out my résumé—to Jones, Day and to Squire, Sanders in Cleveland, and to Fuller, Seney and to Marshall,

Melhorn in Toledo—requesting interviews for a starting associate's position. During the summer I was studying for the bar, I won interviews with a half dozen Ohio law firms. The hiring partners were polite, complimentary of my academic and work record, and curious about my personal life: "Are you engaged? Planning to marry? How do you expect to handle marriage and law practice? Do you intend to have children? And how in the world, Miss Richards, will you handle a husband, children, and a law practice?"

A couple of them even took me to lunch. It turned out they were looking for a date, not an employee. By the middle of August, I had passed the Ohio bar exam, finishing, they told me, second in the state. I didn't have a single job offer. What I did have was a stack of courteous letters from virtually all of the biggest firms in Ohio congratulating me on my accomplishments, wishing me good look, and explaining, directly and with no apologies, that they just didn't hire women lawyers. A couple offered a senior secretarial position if I passed the required typing and shorthand tests.

In the dog days of that particularly steamy August, I decided I had no choice: I abandoned my thoughts of a career in law and politics in Ohio and redirected my job search from the Middle West to the nation's capital. At least I knew that the Civil Rights Act, which had become the law of the land that summer, prohibited discrimination on the basis of sex. I figured that if all else failed, the U.S. Justice Department should know that, too, and would find a place for me. But my goal was not a job with the government. I decided to try to land a job at the eleven-lawyer law firm of the man I'd heard was the greatest trial lawyer in America, Edward Bennett Williams. I withdrew the last savings from my depleted law school account and bought a three-day bargain-fare plane ticket to Washington, D.C.: I would leave for Washington on Wednesday morning and return to Ohio Friday night.

There is no question that, at twenty-three years old, I thought I had everything I would need to get a job in Washington: a great education, a place to stay with law school friends Charlie Nesson and his then wife, Sally, a well-worn but acceptable navy cotton suit, my mother's three-strand pearl necklace, and two pairs of white cotton gloves—one to wear, one to wash. I had no appointments with anybody, but that didn't worry me. I'd been through that before. On the plane to Washington, I decided that if I had an offer or two in hand, I would be a more interesting prospect for Ed Williams. I decided to start my job search at the Department of Justice.

"Always start at the top," my father had counseled me. First thing Thursday morning, I took the bus from the Nessons' town house on Capitol Hill to 900 Pennsylvania Avenue, "Main Justice." I looked up Robert Kennedy's room number on the marquee at the entrance and headed for the elevator.

This was before metal detectors and Secret Service agents guarded the entrances to our public buildings. I stepped into the elevator, pushed the button for the sixth floor, got off, and walked—unannounced—into the office of the Attorney General of the United States. I handed my résumé to Angela Novello, the woman who appeared to be in charge of the front office, and asked to see Attorney General Kennedy about a job.

Although I learned later that Novello could be caustic and a tough guardian of RFK's door, she made a snap decision to help me. She told me that both the Attorney General and his deputy, Nicholas Katzenbach (with whom, twenty-five years later, I served on the IBM board), were busy. But, noting from my résumé that I had Ohio roots, she suggested that I talk with the assistant deputy attorney general for litigation, William Geoghegan, who hailed from my birthplace, Cincinnati. "I'd love to," I said. Within a few minutes, a tall, dapper, gregarious Midwesterner with the map of Ireland on his face walked into the reception room, shook my hand, and came right to the point: "I'm Bill Geoghegan, Miss Richards. Congratulations on your fine record. Why didn't you apply for the Justice Department's honors program? With your grades, you're a natural for it."

"Is it too late?" I asked. I didn't know it, but I had just met one of the pillars of the Kennedys' Irish mafia that was still running Washington, and he had the blarney down pat.

"Not at all," he answered. "We may have a few spots left and we've been looking for lawyers like you."

I thought he meant top graduates of top law schools, but what he was thinking was "female." He didn't tell me that in February of that year, Ralph Dungan, a former Kennedy loyalist who'd switched camps and gone to work in the Johnson White House, had sent Attorney General Kennedy a letter describing the Justice Department's record on hiring women lawyers as "disappointing." The letter told RFK that he had to improve and required that he make a weekly report to the White House on his progress.

As described by Evan Thomas in his book *Robert Kennedy: His Life:*

> Kennedy, who was paternalistic towards women, and did not regard them as victims of discrimination, replied to Dungan with dripping sarcasm. He informed the White House aide that he would consider it a "real favor if you would furnish me a list of girl lawyers who are qualified for GS-15 [a high civil service rank] or above. I would also appreciate an outline of your plan of how I am to hire them when there are no vacancies and there is an economy drive. You people think of wonderful programs which we over here want you to know we fully support.[4]

It was the first, but by no means the last, time that my gender would actually prove to be an asset. By the end of the day, I had five offers to work at the Justice Department, two from the Civil Rights Division, and one each from the Civil, Criminal, and Antitrust Divisions. The offers included a private office, the use of a shared secretary, and pay at the prevailing wage for first-year lawyers in the honors program, $600 a month.

I was ready to talk with Edward Bennett Williams. It was Thursday night. I washed my white gloves, pressed my only suit, looked up "Offices of Edward Bennett Williams" in the phone book, and silently rehearsed the remarks I thought might get me through his door. I left on the bus early the next morning and arrived at the Hill Building, 839 17th Street, NW, around 7:30 A.M. I handed my résumé to the receptionist, Frances Slaight. It listed my college and law school grades, my 1962 summer legal job on Wall Street, the offer I received there, and my part-time jobs as a fashion model in Toledo and Boston, which had paid almost as much an hour as Wall Street paid in a week and had helped me earn my way through college and law school.

"I would like to see the hiring partner about a position as a lawyer," I said.

"Mr. Williams is not in yet," she responded, not asking me to have a seat.

"That's all right. I have plenty of time. I can wait."

I took a seat in the small reception room near the elevators. To make the right impression in case anyone noticed, I read a recent issue of the *Harvard Law Review*, one of the best-researched, least-read magazines in the history of publishing.

A little before 9 A.M., a statuesque brunette arrived. "Good morning, Miss Richards. I'm Cathy King, Mr. Williams's substitute secretary. He is here but he's very busy today. It probably won't be possible to see him."

"Well," I answered, "I can wait. Perhaps he'll have a few minutes to talk with me when he takes a break." I had nothing to lose: with the Justice Department offers to fall back on, the fact that I was out of money and almost out of time no longer worried me.

About an hour later, Cathy came out again: "Mr. Williams has taken a look at your résumé. He congratulates you on your fine record. Unfortunately, his time is fully committed for today. Besides," she whispered, "we just hired our woman lawyer, Barbara Babcock. She's a Yale Law School graduate, has been clerking for Judge Bazelon, and will be arriving in about a month."

"Actually, that's great news!" I said. "If he's already hired a woman, he understands that women have the ability to be good lawyers. I'll wait a while longer."

I didn't know that Ed was married to a lawyer, Agnes Anne Neill, a brilliant, beautiful Irish-American redhead he had met while teaching at Georgetown University's law school. She had been in the first class with women at Georgetown Law and was the first woman ever elected to the *Georgetown Law Review.* Agnes had accepted a position as a fledging trial lawyer with Ed's young law firm and had retired a few years later when she married him and took on the responsibility of his home, including his three small children.

Around noon, Cathy approached me for the last time: "Mr. Williams really can't see you at all today. He thanks you for your interest." I didn't know then that she'd been working on him, urging him to "take a look at her. She may be something special."

Disappointed and more than a little frustrated, I said the first thing that came into my head: "I am grateful for his compliments but I am amazed that he can't see me for just a moment or two. In his book *One Man's Freedom,* he purports to believe that everyone deserves the benefit of the doubt. That should apply to me just as much as to some criminal defendant. Certainly the man who wrote that book, *if* he wrote it himself, could talk with me for five minutes."

I didn't know that Ed Williams was just around the corner. He had asked Cathy to get rid of me so that he could leave for lunch. He overheard what I said to her and came charging into the reception room, a big bear of a man with electric blue eyes, curly brown hair, and the disarming baby face of the Welshmen I'd grown up around on my father's side of the family.

"I'm Edward Bennett Williams. I wonder if you have the guts to say to my face what you just said to Miss King?"

"Well, I'm Judith Coleman Richards from Defiance, Ohio. I've read your book and everything else I can find by or about you. You believe that lawyers have a duty to take on unpopular causes. What's more unpopular these days than hiring a woman lawyer? You made your way here from Hartford, Connecticut, where your father was a part-time department-store floorwalker. It's been every bit as hard for me, a preacher's daughter from Defiance, Ohio, to get through Harvard Law School and now to your door as it was for you to get here from Hartford. If you don't understand that, you're not the man I thought you were, and frankly, I wouldn't work for you on a bet."

All he said was "What are you doing for lunch?"

It was the start of my career as a trial lawyer.

What would today be described as the ultimate power lunch was full of raucous male laughter, inside gossip about national political figures, and football trivia. There I was, eating the first square meal I'd had in three days with three legendary Washington figures: Edward Bennett Williams, who'd just beaten the rap for his client Jimmy Hoffa; humorist and syndicated columnist Art Buchwald; and *Washington Post* editor Ben Bradlee. I wasn't "in" yet, but I knew even before the coffee arrived that *that* was exactly where I wanted to work.

After lunch, Ed invited me to go back to his office for further "conversation." He grilled me about law, my background, aspirations, and experience, as well as about my marital status, including "your intentions in that regard."

"As for marriage," I told him with my fingers crossed behind my back, "I have a wonderful parental family. I like men, and I have even dated a few of them. But I decided when I went to law school that I had to choose either law or a family, because I knew I couldn't handle both. I chose law and that's still my choice." It seemed to be the answer he was looking for.

By four o'clock, we had covered every legal subject I could think of, and more. I was running out of time: my plane home was scheduled for 6:30 P.M.

"Mr. Williams," I said, "it's time for me to go. Have you made a decision?"

He responded, "I'd like to think about our conversation. Can you stay in Washington over the weekend and meet me again on Monday afternoon?"

I knew I couldn't stay. In addition to losing my cheap excursion fare, there was a football game in Cleveland on Sunday that I didn't want to miss.

"I'm sorry. I wish I could, but I have to go back to Ohio. I have a ticket to see the Browns play the Los Angeles Rams this weekend, and I have a lot at stake in that game."

That was the truth, but the "whole truth, so help me God," was that I was out of cash, and that my date for the game was a man I wanted to get to know a lot better.

Ed Williams surmised that I had figured out over lunch that he was president of the Washington Redskins football team (I hadn't) and that my interest in football was a come-on, meant to clinch a job with him. His expression changed and his eyes narrowed just a bit as he thought about my supposed dedication to football. He bored in with a quiet, paced, and potentially lethal cross-examination, the kind he had used to destroy witnesses during his winning defenses of Senator Joe McCarthy, Frank Costello, and Frank Sinatra. If I was bluffing, he would find out fast, and any chance I had for a job with him would be lost.

What professional players did I think had talent? What was a draw play?

What was a "lonesome end"? How did a "prevent defense" work? I knew the answers as well or better than I knew the law. For kids growing up in Ohio in those days, football was oxygen: you couldn't live without it.

Finally, with a roar of laughter, he stopped the interrogation. "I'll be damned. I've got a Gypsy instinct about you. I'm gonna make you an offer just like I would a football player. I'm gonna hire you for six months. If you don't make my team after six months, you'll be cut. Whadda ya say?"

It was almost the offer I had been waiting for. Almost, but not quite. "Mr. Williams, I accept your offer on these conditions: I will do my best to make your team in the next six months. If I don't, I know I'll be cut. But if I do make it, I don't want to sit on the bench. I want to go to court. I want to learn to be a jury trial lawyer, and I want you personally to train me. I also want to be paid the same amount as someone in the honors program at the Justice Department, six hundred dollars a month. Those are my terms."

With a grin as big as the Redskins' stadium, he agreed. "Well, Miss Richards, I must say you have balls. I'll take your terms. We have a deal. Oh, and just one thing, Miss Richards: a woman has the edge. Your job is to fig-ure out how to use it."

Ten days later, I was back at the Hill Building. Luckily, I had decided to arrive at the office at the same time as before, 7:30 A.M. Frances Slaight was more cordial this time: "Go on back. Mr. Williams has been waiting for you." That's when I learned that work started there as early as seven in the morn-ing. He said, "Hello! Let's get going!" We walked down the fire stairway to the ninth floor. He pointed out my office, a simply furnished, square room with a window facing 17th Street, and introduced me to my suite mate, Peter Taft, who'd graduated from Yale Law School and clerked for Chief Justice Warren. He told me that most of the secretaries had refused to work for a woman lawyer, but that twenty-year-old Betsy Pond had agreed "to try it for a couple of weeks." He pointed out a file cabinet full of documents on a crim-inal case he'd been working on for three years, assigned me to draft a Petition for Certiorari to the United States Supreme Court within two weeks, and left. I knew immediately that I was in over my head: in those days, law school trained us to think like appellate judges, not advocates. I had never seen a trial or appellate record, had no idea what would constitute "reversible error" in those proceedings, and had no clue as to how to start drafting a Petition for Certiorari. I picked up the phone and called my law school friend Charlie Nesson, who was clerking for Justice Harlan: "I need some help. Could you let me borrow a few Petitions for Cert. so I can see what one looks like?"

I had begun to learn why it's called "practicing" law.

Liddy Hanford (Dole)

In the summer of 1965, Mary Elizabeth "Liddy" Hanford came to Washington, D.C., looking for a job. She came to see me at the offices of Williams & Connolly. Just like the rest of us, she was having a tough time even getting interviews, much less a job in a private law firm. How had I done it? I told her my story, including the risk I took in signing on with Edward Bennett Williams for a six-month probationary period. Luckily, I told her, I had made the cut. I introduced her to Ed, told him Liddy was a gem, and left them to what turned out to be a lengthy interview.

A few hours later, Ed stuck his head in my office: "Did you coach her on how to get a job here?"

"Well," I said, "I told her of our initial conversations last year and that I'd come here on probation and it had worked out."

"Well, she made that same proposal. She wants a job and I think she'd be good. But we only have room for so many women from Hahvahd around here. What do you say, shall I hire her or do you want to stick around?"

"Well, all things considered, I'd like to stay. But let's try to help her find something somewhere else."

"Good! But just remember, she's smart, persuasive, pretty, and very ambitious—just the kind of lawyer I like. So keep pushin'." With that he was gone. Ed Williams often referred to his lifestyle as "contest living," as his approach to me about Liddy's job application demonstrated. Both Liddy and I were highly trained, competitive, and willing to work hard. I wanted her as a colleague, yet I found myself not so subtly being pitted against her in the tough job market for women lawyers. I hated it.

I called Liddy, told her that "we" didn't have an opening just then, and told her I would do what I could to help her find a job in Washington. She tried for a White House fellowship, but lost out in the last round. Undaunted, she landed a job with the Department of Health, Education, and Welfare organizing a conference on education. When that ended, she often volunteered as a pro bono lawyer for the poor and disenfranchised, before landing a great job in 1968 with Betty Furness, Lyndon Johnson's director of the White House Office of Consumer Affairs. In 1973, President Nixon nominated Liddy to the Federal Trade Commission, one of the youngest ever named. Liddy was on her way.

On December 6, 1975, Liddy married a highly respected, handsome senator from Kansas, Bob Dole. "*Tout* Washington" showed up for the ceremony in which she became Elizabeth Hanford Dole. I was there—it was clear that Elizabeth was not only on her way, she had arrived. Six months later her husband was named the vice presidential candidate on the Republican ticket.

CHAPTER 17

Work—and Marriage

Judith Richards Hope

In our last year of law school my roommate Ann Dudley had added Tony Hope, a second-year law student, to her retinue of beaux. From time to time, she had talked to me about him, saying that he was smart and funny, and that he was a great cardplayer who loved the horse races. It sounded like a wonderful combination. One night in April 1964, I saw Tony talking with Ann Dudley in our living room. We didn't introduce ourselves or even say hello. He told me later that, the same night, he called his best friend, John Guare (now a distinguished American playwright), in New York:

"I've just seen the woman I'm going to marry."

John asked sleepily, "What's her name?"

Tony said, "I don't know."

"Where's she from?"

"I don't know."

"Have you talked with her?"

"No."

John summed up the situation, "You're not doing very well," and hung up.

Law school was about over. After final exams, we would scatter to the four winds. There was no time for new relationships, and besides, I was in love with Joshua, whom I'd been dating off and on since our first year.

But Tony was persistent, and crafty. Over the next three and a half years, he occasionally turned up, generally unexpectedly, at my parents' house in Ohio or at my office at what was then called Williams & Wadden in Washington, D.C. He always had some glamorous plan or other—Redskins football games or canoeing on the Potomac or running over to the White House for a party with Lynda Bird Johnson, whose parents were friendly with Tony's folks, Bob and Dolores Hope. It was always exciting when he was around. But most of the time I was busy learning my craft, trying cases around the country, and in the little free time I had, going out with Joshua.

Then, in early 1967, I got into what seemed to me then like a series of world-class problems at my law firm and decided it was time for me to evaluate my options. I had found out, by chance, that Michael Tigar (who went on to defend some of the more notorious figures in the annals of the criminal law), who'd joined the firm after I had, was making $100 more a month than I was. When I asked Ed Williams about the disparity, he told me that Mike was married with two children and needed the money more than I did, as a single woman. "That's not the point," I retorted, forgetting my usual Pepsodent smile and little-girl voice. "I graduated from law school earlier, I have more experience, and I'm carrying more responsibility. I'm entitled to a raise." I won the battle, but lost the war—at least temporarily. Ed moved me off his team that afternoon saying, "You need to work with others for a while."

I was quickly assigned to assist with the final preparations in a high-profile case involving racketeering, extortion, and bribery, which was on the fast track for trial in the federal courthouse in Manhattan. I packed my clothes and my briefcases and moved for the duration to the firm's four-bedroom apartment at East 55th Street and Lexington Avenue in the heart of the city. The trial team would be working there around the clock. Just before the trial was to start, I found myself face-to-face with a different kind of trial, one that I had never anticipated.

Our team was, as usual, eating a late dinner together at what Toots Shor called his saloon, a well-known Midtown restaurant that specialized in the prime beef and lobster favored by the athletes, sportswriters, and celebrities who frequented the place. That particular night, I was sitting in the middle of a black leather banquette with my boss, a highly regarded partner in my firm, on my right, and another lawyer, as well as our client, across the table. Toots joined us, sliding into the banquette on my left, and ordered a third round of martinis for everybody except me—Toots knew that I didn't drink. Just as I started to look at the menu, I felt a hand on my right knee, which started creeping up my right inner thigh. I froze. I was in shock and also scared—this was a test for which I had no training, and no easy defense. Just as I started to remove my boss's hand, I felt Toots's hand on my left knee, which began to move up my left inner thigh. I did the only thing I could think of: I reached under my skirt, joined their two hands together, slid out from under their now clasped hands, stood up on the banquette, stepped across Toots, and jumped to the floor on the outside of the banquette. Without even stopping to pick up my coat from the coat check, I ran out into the street to catch a cab with my boss in hot pursuit, yelling at me, "Don't you ever do this to me again." I didn't respond. I jumped in a cab, raced back to the firm apartment, threw my clothes in my bag and my papers in my briefcases, and raced down the street to the Drake Hotel. It was the last night I ever stayed in the firm apartment. I never mentioned the incident, nor did my boss. We continued to work together as if nothing had happened. Except for "Keep your hands off me!" there was nothing I could have said anyway, and I decided that, if I had said that in front of our client, one way or another I would have lost my job.

Several months after that case ended, I was just back in Ed Williams's good graces when Ed and I had another disagreement. I decided to stand up for Ed's partner, Tom Wadden, who'd been shunted aside to make room on the firm's masthead for Paul Connolly in the newly christened Williams & Connolly.

At the time it happened, I was sitting "second chair" in the trial of "Johnny C," an up-and-coming twenty-five-year-old bookie charged with interstate gambling. He was a special protégé of some of the Runyonesque characters we represented in those days, including Milwaukee Phil, Ice Pick Willie, and the three Franks: Frank Sinatra, Uncle Frank Costello, and Frank Erickson, the greatest oddsmaker of all times. Most evenings during the trial, we had dinner at the same restaurant in lower Manhattan. It had great food and was reputed to be a Cosa Nostra hangout—there certainly seemed to be a lot of wise guys hanging around on one particular night.

I was seated on Ed Williams's right, directly across from Uncle Frank, who was Johnny C's mentor. Costello leaned across the table to me:

"Tell me why Eddie dropped my pal Tommy Wadden. Tommy does a lot of good work for my boys."

My first response was the one I should have stuck to: "I really can't discuss that; you'd have to ask Ed."

Costello kept pressing. Ed finally turned to me in exasperation: "Tell him why I did it. Go ahead and tell him."

Foolishly, I decided to speak my mind: "I'm really upset about it, Uncle Frank. Tom helped train most of us and gave us chances to be first chair, to stand before the judge and the jury and make the mistakes we have to make in order to become trial lawyers. But it was Paul Connolly's price to join our firm."

Ed was rightly furious. Within hours, I was again back on Ed's "shun" list: no more lunches at Duke Ziebert's hash house in Washington, no more tickets in the president's box for the Redskins games, and no more work with Ed—at least for a while. Being in legal Siberia at Williams & Connolly in those days was about as bad as it got: I was still working on great cases, but I was no longer sitting at the side of the master.

After dinner, Johnny C's car was waiting to take me back to the hotel.

One of his boys held the rear door for me and, after I sat down, handed me a stack of seven large white boxes, tied together in *Breakfast at Tiffany's* style with blue satin ribbons.

"What's this?" I asked.

"Johnny has something special for you."

When the firm won a particularly difficult case, the grateful clients frequently gave the winning lawyers presents—cashmere sport jackets, star sapphire pinkie rings, or, if it was a really big win, color television sets. They had never offered me anything, and I was just as glad—sport coats and pinkie rings weren't my style, and color TVs, expensive and hard to come by back then, were too lavish for a young associate.

"That's very nice," I choked, "but I don't accept presents."

"Please take the presents."

"No, really, that's all right. But you can give them to Mr. Williams."

"You don't get it," the man answered with just a touch of menace in his voice. "Johnny wants you to take the presents."

"Oh! Well, in that case," I gasped, "I'd be delighted."

When I got back to my hotel room, I opened the boxes. Inside each one, wrapped in tissue paper, was the most beautiful silk lingerie I had ever seen: nightgowns, peignoirs, slips edged in lace, and transparent panties and bras. "So," I thought to myself, "this is what a lady lawyer gets when the case is going well." I didn't know what to do about my presents, so I shoved them under the bed and went to sleep.

Early the next morning, room service delivered coffee, toast, and the tabloids, which carried a blaring page-one story, HEIST ON SEVENTH AVENUE: "Yesterday in a daring daylight stickup, two masked gunmen hijacked a truck loaded with expensive French lingerie and drove off through the crowded streets of lower Manhattan."

"I've got hot underwear!" I thought. "Now what do I do?"

I was at least temporarily on the outs with the senior partner of my law firm, I had been accosted by another partner, and I had a hunch that it wouldn't help me to disclose that a client was now giving me intimate apparel. I decided to ditch the boxes in the janitor's closet down the hall, put the underwear in the bottom of my suitcase, and figure everything out later. But to the extent I had time before court to begin to think clearly about my situation, I figured I was in big trouble. For the first time since graduating from law school, I felt insecure and scared about my future: "Maybe I wasn't cut out to be a lawyer after all. Am I strong enough to handle all this? And what about clients? Will they ever take me completely seriously?

What kind of lawyer gets underwear as a gift from a client anyway? An ex-lawyer," I decided. It had been hard enough to get my first full-time job. If I lost it, I thought, it would be curtains for my career.

After court that day, I started seriously thinking about going in another, more traditional direction—I'd given law my best shot, but maybe it wasn't for me after all. I was also starting to experience what I described to myself as my "salmon swimming upstream in the spring" feeling. Joshua and I had always been out of sync: when he wanted to get married, I didn't, and vice versa. But maybe I was wrong to be indecisive, I thought. At the moment, he said he was ready, and while I wasn't, marriage was getting more appealing by the minute. I called Ann Dudley and told her I was thinking of getting married. All she said was "Don't do anything in haste. Marriage is forever. Take your time. And have a little faith: things will get better at work."

Then she called Tony Hope in California and told him I was getting married to someone else.

A few weeks later, Tony blew into Washington unannounced, took me to breakfast, dropped to one knee, pulled a large emerald engagement ring out of his pocket, and asked me to marry him. He said that, on his $18,000-a-year salary, he could take care of both of us. We hadn't lived in the same city or even on the same coast since I left law school—but I thought he was a great guy and that his parents were wonderful. His father, Bob, was one of the bigger-than-life heroes from my childhood, and his mother, Dolores, was a lot more than a beautiful Hollywood babe—although she was that, too. She was a gutsy girl who'd grown up in the Bronx and made her own way since she was sixteen. Just like my mother.

After Tony proposed, he started to cry. When I asked him about the tears in his eyes, all he said was "I hate to see a great guy like myself go down the drain." I laughed. Although a warning was hidden in his bon mot, I ignored it. Forgetting Ann Dudley's profoundly good advice, I leapt into the abyss and, on the spot, accepted Tony's offer of marriage.

I asked Ann Dudley to be my maid of honor. I knew that she, too, had decided it was time to get married—she had just turned twenty-eight and was ready to uncomplicate her life. She expected to marry a doctor-politician from Kentucky, but I had a better idea for her, one that I planned to put into action the night before my wedding.

I asked Ed Williams to move my admission to the United States Supreme Court on the morning I was leaving Washington to go home to Defiance. I was relieved—and proud—when he agreed: I thought it proved he wasn't angry with me anymore. I should have remembered my evidence professor's lesson: "You aren't paid to assume anything." At 7:30 A.M. on the appointed day, my phone rang. It was Ed: "I'm too busy to go down to the court today. Maybe you can find somebody else."

I didn't have time to be upset. Or angry. I started scrambling. At the last minute, I found a senior associate at Williams & Connolly who was willing to move my admission. To this day the Supreme Court certificate on my office wall is a subject of curiosity. "Who in the world is Thomas Dyson?" Chief Justice Earl Warren administered my oath as a member of the Supreme Court bar. After I was sworn in, I walked down the court's white marble steps for what I thought would be the last time, got in my navy blue sports car, and headed home to Ohio to be married.

There was a terrible snowstorm in Ohio the weekend of my wedding, and the airports in the vicinity had closed down. Ann Dudley, my maid of honor, took the train from New York with John Guare, then a promising young playwright, who was heading out to Defiance to be Tony's best man. They arrived just in time for the rehearsal dinner at the Toledo Club, a century-old men's club with lots of maroon carpet, located sixty miles east of Defiance. Ann Dudley quickly changed into a slinky, robin's-egg-blue silk sheath that just matched her eyes and swept into the dinner on John Guare's arm.

The first thing she saw was a huge cluster of Bob Hope's cronies standing around smoking cigars, even though it was before dinner. Bob himself was doing a show in Peoria that night and wasn't arriving until the next morning. As Ann Dudley remembers it, "There were several hundred people there. The Hopes had chartered a 727, or something like that, and brought an entire planeload of people from California to this tiny Ohio town. Everybody was dressed to the nines: Mrs. Bing Crosby, the governor of Ohio and his wife, Senator Stuart Symington and his wife, Eve, and Toots Shor and his wife, Baby. It looked as if Hollywood had been transplanted to the banks of the Maumee River."

Unbeknownst to Ann Dudley, I had quietly invited her old flame from law school Stan Goldblatt and placed his seat next to hers at the head table. She looked ravishing—and it was clear that Stan was still smitten.

There were a lot of toasts at the dinner, almost all of them to Bob Hope. Ann Dudley finally had enough. "I got up and said, 'It's time to remember who this party is for.' I was really pissed off. Bob Hope wasn't even there, but everybody was toasting him, saying how wonderful he was. The worst part was that there was almost nothing about Tony and Judy and nothing at all about Judy."

The wedding was set for noon the next day in Defiance. It had grown from the planned one hundred people to nearly six hundred. My longtime friends Hans and Kathie Jones had turned over several floors in their Toledo hotel, the Commodore Perry, for the out-of-town guests. My parents had borrowed a fleet of Toledo city buses to transport everyone the sixty miles down the Anthony Wayne Trail to Defiance and then back to Toledo for the reception. Although my father, a prominent Protestant clergyman, was originally going to officiate, Dolores Hope, a devout Catholic, was eager to have the wedding in the Catholic Church. Out of love and great respect for her, we agreed. We settled on an interdenominational-cum-Hollywood-style wedding ceremony: it would be performed in Saint Mary's Catholic Church in Defiance by twelve priests and my father.

Nobody in Defiance had ever seen anything like it, and given the history of conflicts and suspicions between the Catholics and the Protestants in many small towns in the Midwest in that era, everyone was more than a little nervous about what would happen when all the potentially combustible elements got together. Defiance went wild with gossip: It was scandalous! Sacrilegious! And delicious! They couldn't wait to see what happened next.

Harvard Law Professor Charlie Nesson remembers the beginning of the ceremony: "Bob Hope comes down the aisle walking with his wife. He's just one of the wedding party, but he's shaking hands with everybody as he goes. He's the total star of the show."

The first thing Ann Dudley saw as she walked down the aisle in front of me was a photographer on the altar under the Communion table: "I was convinced that God was going to strike us all dead. Then the ceremony began. I remember that you had signed the pledge that you would raise the children Catholics and then gone back like the good lawyer you were and crossed out and initialed everything you didn't agree with—which was everything. I thought that was just terrific."

After Monsignor Vogel pronounced us man and wife, my father ascended the pulpit with robes flying, to give the blessing. Charlie Nesson remembers Papa's grand finale:

"Your father is this wild guy, just wild. It builds up to the point where the groom is kissing the bride. Your father goes into this big metaphor about rocket ships, then he starts this countdown: 'Ten, nine, eight, seven, six . . . ,' and he comes right down to zero. 'Blast off!' And outside his friends Butch Schultz, the local plumbing contractor, and his wife, Marvel, fired off the cannons from Fort Defiance twenty-one times in the church parking lot.

"Some of the people in the sanctuary dove under the pews for cover.

Eventually the firing stopped, and the trumpeters started playing the recessional. We walked outside the church and there was a huge children's choir singing 'High Hopes' in the middle of the blizzard."

Tony and I took a late plane to California. He carried me over the threshold of our new oceanfront home in Malibu and brought my suitcases into the bedroom. I opened the closet to hang up my clothes and found a waist-high pile of dirty laundry.

"What's this?" I asked.

"Oh, just the laundry from the last few weeks. I knew you were coming, so I let the cleaning lady go."

I may have come a long way from Defiance, but I immediately realized that I was also a long way from Harvard Law School and Washington, D.C.—and from the dreams I'd had since I was twelve. Within a month, I went back to work. I wasn't admitted to practice law in California, but, with the help of classmate Jim Lorenz, by then Dinni's ex-husband, I found a job starting and then running a self-help housing program for California's rural poor, California Rural Development Corporation. Instead of hanging out with the movie stars in Hollywood, I started commuting to Modesto to help Caesar Chavez and Ernesto Loredo provide decent housing for migrant workers. I used the money I earned to hire somebody else to do the laundry.

Ann Dudley Cronkhite Marries Stan Goldblatt

On Saturday night December 2, 1967, after my wedding celebration ended, Stan invited Ann Dudley to drive to Chicago with him before she headed back to New York. She quickly agreed: they had been having a wonderful time and both realized how much they had missed each other since law school ended.

They were married six months later, on June 17, 1968. Their only real problem was finding someone to perform the wedding. As Ann Dudley recalls, "All the Anglicans and the Episcopalians said they'd love to do it, but they had to mention Jesus. And all the Jews said, 'We don't do that,' including Rabbi Magnan, who wanted us to get married in the Max Factor Chapel in Hollywood. He said he would make it 'as sincere as possible.'" Stan and Ann Dudley finally persuaded a young rabbi to preside over the vows. Like them, he was willing to cross the traditional religious barriers that most clergy of that era held sacrosanct.

As Stan and Ann Dudley's son Jeremy says now, "For Mom's parents, it must have been outrageous for her to marry this Jewish guy from Chicago.

My Pasadena grandparents were very Waspy, and I understand my grandmother Cronkhite never quite got her mouth around *Goldblatt*. I'm sure my
father's parents didn't really like the fact that my dad was married to a WASP,
but I think that they were both strong-willed enough that all four of their parents knew if they drew a line in the sand and said, 'Them or us,' they'd both
go with 'them.'"

Both Ann Dudley and I had broken a barrier: she was the first person in
her family to marry outside the Christian faith; I was the first in mine to
marry a Catholic.

CHAPTER 18

Trying to Do It All

Alice Pasachoff Wegman

Because both roles were important to her, Alice structured her career to accommodate both a professional life and a family life. Alice worked at COMSAT until 1971, when her daughter Laura was born. She thought about returning to work part-time two years later and actually sought part-time employment, but that choice proved particularly difficult: the Federal Part-Time Employment Act had not yet been enacted. (It passed in 1978.) Ultimately she opted to stay home until David, born in 1974, was a year old. Although she was eager to return to work, she thought carefully about the nature of the legal work she would undertake: "I was looking for something that would be both at a very high intellectual and professional level, but at the same time, was not time sensitive."

Alice recognized that it would have been difficult to meet her requirements in a law firm: "I never regarded the role of homemaker as one that was imposed on me, but as a role that I have actively sought out and enjoyed thoroughly and would not have wanted to give up. Inevitably you wonder, 'Could I really have done more?' but in my case, the answer is no. I was not prepared to give up the pleasures of family life in order to take on enormous career responsibilities. These are very difficult choices for women, but I don't think that it really is possible to do it all. There are certain levels of responsibility that I made a decision not to look for. If I had to do it again, I would make the same choices, I would do exactly what I did."

After working for several years for the Consumer Product Safety Commission, Alice joined the U.S. Environmental Protection Agency in 1979, first in the general counsel's office, then as one of three assistant judicial officers for the EPA's chief judicial officer. Since 1992 she has been a counsel to the EPA's Environmental Appeals Board, working on significant cases involving issues of first impression in interpreting federal environmental laws.

When Alice's children were very young, she worked three eight-hour days

186

a week. As they got older, she switched to four shorter workdays, allowing her to be home in time to take Laura and David to music and art classes, and to attend swim meets and soccer games. Alice considers herself "very lucky that I was able to create work schedules that were driven by the needs of my children." She knows all too well how uncommon day care was in the 1970s. She relied on a succession of college-student baby-sitters, providing her with a challenge and a constant source of tension when their schedules changed or they didn't appear at all.

Her husband, Dick, was working long hours during those years as chief counsel and staff director of the Senate Government Affairs Committee. Without ever discussing it, Alice and Dick both assumed that child care was primarily her responsibility: "This is a wonderful man that I'm married to, and a fabulous father, but I don't think he's ever once cooked a dinner or stayed home with a sick child. It would never have entered his mind, nor, for that matter, mine."

Ann Dudley Cronkhite Goldblatt

After four years on Wall Street, it was clear that "powerful corporate lawyer" was not Ann Dudley's only cup of tea. With three married sisters and thirteen nieces and nephews whom she loved being with, she wanted to start a family of her own. As mentioned earlier, in June 1968, Ann Dudley resigned from her law firm, married Stan Goldblatt, and moved to Chicago. She didn't even try to get a job there: "I didn't want to work. I wanted to have babies. I had always thought I would stay home with my children." Alexandra was born in May 1970; Nathaniel in November 1971; and Jeremy in June 1974.

Although Ann Dudley was happy, she felt just a little guilty. Her life of wife and mother seemed living proof of the accuracy of Dean Griswold's prediction that women law students would abandon their profession for the home. "I felt guilty, not because I had taken the place of a man at Harvard Law School, but because I had been given this great gift of rigorous and analytical thinking, a gift I shouldn't be wasting."

After five busy and fulfilling years at home with young children and laundry and cooking and waiting for Stan to come home, Ann Dudley was also—yes—bored. "For all the talk about being a mother and staying at home, there was something to this 'quality time' concept. Not a lot, but something. In fact, I had begun taking my kids for granted. I didn't pay as much attention to them if they were always there and I was always there."

She started volunteering twice a week at Children's Memorial Hospital, where she studied the medical records of infants with congenital anomalies and began to confer with the doctors about better ways to communicate with the infants' parents on diagnoses and treatment. Before long, she had created an entire program of liaison between the hospital's intensive-care and surgical units and the parents' waiting room. Stan, meanwhile, had become a trustee of the University of Chicago. He and Ann Dudley often had dinner with the university's professors: "Being a woman was a great advantage: you didn't have to sit next to some trustee's boring wife, you were some trustee's boring wife."

Because of her volunteer work at Children's Memorial Hospital, her conversations turned to medical-legal issues, particularly in the new field of bioethics. Ann Dudley was fascinated and quickly decided to return to school part-time to study theology, philosophy, and political science. After three years as a student-at-large at the University of Chicago, she knew she wanted to work in a field where law and medicine intersected. She also knew that her legal skills were rusty. She enrolled in law school to be recertified, this time in bioethics, not corporations. She had three small children, her husband was changing jobs, and her parents were failing in California. Nevertheless, one year later, in 1978, she received her master of laws degree. At commencement, she realized that she was the only LLM graduating from her class: only then did she learn that her classmates were taking two years to do what she had just done in one.

Ten years after retiring from law to start a family, and with her new credentials in hand, Ann Dudley returned to work. She took a part-time job at DePaul University, teaching bioethics. Her reputation as a gifted teacher in a hot new field spread quickly. In 1979, the University of Chicago asked her to teach there, but, to avoid any appearance of nepotism because of Stan's trusteeship, made their offer contingent on her successfully giving a public lecture to the college faculty, who would then have a secret ballot on whether to confirm her position. "There were about a hundred people there, some friends, some colleagues from classes, and some professors whom I knew or who knew Stan. In the middle of it, I remember thinking that I had on a maroon silk blouse that exactly matched my nail polish. I felt like saying, 'I don't suppose it's escaped your attention that my nail polish matches my blouse?' but I didn't. It was actually a very good lecture and it got me the job. The funniest thing was that I think it is the only public lecture ever given at the University of Chicago where the speaker kissed eighty percent of the audience at the end."

As her reputation grew, Ann Dudley expanded her teaching, adding courses in the humanities and biological sciences in the undergraduate college, and eventually teaching graduate medical students at the MacLean Center for Clinical Medical Ethics. She had worked herself into more than a full teaching load, but she never applied for tenure: she liked her life the way it was. She didn't want to appear to presume on her husband's fiduciary responsibilities to the university, and she always wanted the option to cut back, or even quit.

Ann Dudley knows how blessed she was that Stan earned enough money so that she could hire a full-time au pair to help her with the children and the house when she went back to school and then to work. Her academic schedule also meant that she could be at home a lot of the time, preparing for classes and grading tests and papers. Her children adjusted well to their mom's new schedule. She didn't go to many of her sons' baseball games, but she somehow found time to drive her daughter, Alexandra, to and from horseback-riding lessons and performances every week.

Her son Jeremy began to realize in the sixth grade that his mother's life was different from that of the mothers of most of his friends: "The first thing my friends noticed in my house was all the books. Upstairs. Downstairs. Reading was a value I got from both my parents early on, although I wasn't a big reader. In our house, people who did well in school were to be looked up to. We talked a lot about the University of Chicago over dinner. I remember when Hannah Gray became president—it was a big deal that they chose a woman, and my parents were really pleased. I also remember Mom was talking a lot about euthanasia, and that it was a hot topic. But I couldn't figure out what that meant. I thought it was 'youth in Asia.' Like 'Eat your food! There are starving youth in Asia.'"

Grace Weiner (Wolf)

After a year in India with her then husband, classmate Joel Henning, Grace and he returned home to Chicago, where she found a position with the Legal Aid Bureau. She worked until her first child was born in the summer of 1966 and, among other things, filed more divorce petitions that any other lawyer in the city of Chicago.

Women lawyers were still a rarity in the Chicago courts in the midsixties, and Grace was frequently mistaken for a lawyer's clerk when she appeared in court. When the judges found out she was in fact a lawyer, they sometimes embarrassed her by making her stand up and then introducing her to the entire courtroom. Although they were probably trying to help her, she felt as though she were a trained dog instead of a fellow professional. When her daughter Justine was a year old, Grace returned to work part-time as a researcher with the National Legal Aid and Defender Association, which was then located in Chicago. After the birth of her daughters Sarah-Anne and then Dara, Grace stayed at home for several years, during which she chaired the local cooperative nursery school and then became active in the parents' association at the University of Chicago Laboratory Schools, eventually serving as treasurer of that group. She reentered the workforce when her youngest daughter was in kindergarten, finding, with the help of classmate John McCausland, a half-time, flex-time job managing a shopping center complex in Chicago's Hyde Park neighborhood, where she continues to live.

In 1980, Grace and Joel founded LawLetters, a company that published newsletters and books and sponsored conferences for lawyers. The first few years, Grace was working sixty-hour weeks. She was editor of the *Henning CLE Reporter* and also had responsibility for editing other publications, bookkeeping, budgeting, project development, and conference planning. Because the offices were at first in her house, Grace managed to do all this and still keep tabs on her children without a nanny or full-time housekeeper. She frequently returned to her desk after dinner. By the time the business moved to downtown offices, the girls were old enough to manage after school without outside help.

Even while working full-time, Grace found time for demanding volunteer activities. She became a member of the board of directors of her synagogue and then served for two years as president of the congregation, a twenty-hour-a-week commitment.

After Grace and Joel divorced in 1987 and LawLetters was sold, Grace worked as a freelance editor and consultant. While at LawLetters, she had created a bimonthly newsletter for the Business Law Section of the American Bar Association, and she continued to edit that newsletter and the quarterly journal *The Business Lawyer* for several years.

June Freeman Berkowitz

After Mort's two-year tour of duty in the Public Health Service in San Francisco ended, the family moved to Springfield, Massachusetts, where their third child was born when June was twenty-six years old. June continued to stay home with the children and Mort practiced orthopedic surgery, devoting 40 percent of his time to volunteer work with the Shriners, rehabilitating crippled children. Living in suburbia, June began, for the first time, to get restless. "The women were older than I was. They were very concerned with the right furniture and the right clothes and the right club. There were lots of parties, often with the same guests and the same caterers. They were very nice people, there wasn't anything terrible, but it sure wasn't for me."

On a lark, June and Mort bought a small summer house by the ocean in Gloucester, Massachusetts. "We didn't have any money. We borrowed the whole down payment and we pretty much ate bread and water for a long time." June also started taking classes in Springfield and earned her master's degree in guidance and psychological services. She loved counseling, but kept thinking about law school and that she had quit. She regularly read the Harvard Law School alumni news and decided that she had probably missed the boat.

In 1971, June wrote to Harvard Law School that she was ready to come back. The Law School Admissions Office replied, in its own lawyerly way, that an eleven-year hiatus was "somewhat longer than a reasonable time," that she would have to reapply, and that she should apply to several other law schools as well.

June bought LSAT cram-course books, did better on the LSAT than eleven years before, reapplied to Harvard, and was readmitted. Mort backed her all the way. To make it work, he suggested that their family move to Gloucester full-time: he shifted his medical practice to work nearby.

In September 1972, at the age of thirty-two, June Freeman Berkowitz started at Harvard Law all over again. The children's schools were on the way to Cambridge, and most mornings, she would drop her children off, then turn up the rock 'n' roll on the car radio, and sing along all the way to classes. Dressing for class was more relaxed than a decade before; instead of high heels, dresses, and pearls, June wore slacks, sweaters, and flat shoes. "I had a wonderful time. It was sort of a vacation to do it."

June and Mort already lived informally, and they stuck to it while June was in law school. What would be a daunting schedule for anybody else was exhilarating for June. Mort already did his own laundry, and their meals were simple: "How long does it take to shove a chicken in the oven? Essentially, I went to school and eliminated everything else that wasn't necessary. I didn't read magazines, I didn't hang out with people, I didn't shop. We felt we should be with the kids, so that's what we did." Mort describes June during this period as "extraordinary. I couldn't believe what she was doing. She went to law school, and when she came home, she was good to me, to our three children, even to our two cats and a dog. She never bragged about going to law school."

June says that, in returning to law school in 1972, she didn't want to be a symbol of anything, she just wanted to study law. In the 1960s nobody had made much of an issue of her being in law school, but eleven years later consciousness had been raised. "There was a Women's Law Association. Everybody seemed to have an opinion about what I was doing. Some people would be offended, some would think it was wonderful. I got a lot of attention the second time, a lot more than I had planned for. Or wanted. What upset me most was people who said I was neglecting my children, who said, 'You have a nice house, what a shame you're not home to enjoy it.'"

During the summer between her second and third years, June worked for a prestigious Boston law firm. Big-firm law was a lot different from Harvard Law School: "I would leave home at seven in the morning and get back at seven-thirty at night. Basically, I just had time to pull myself together in time to get up and do it again the next morning." She was drafting long memoranda by hand; after the secretaries had typed her work, she would edit it, and they would then retype each memo. It would, she decided, be easier to simply type her work herself. But when she commandeered a typewriter, she got some odd looks. "I think," she says now, "I was not supposed to do that."

By the end of the summer, June knew that big-firm practice was not for her. If she practiced law in Boston, she believed, she would miss much of her children's growing up. The work didn't interest her, either: "I was writing memos and memos and memos. I was writing down how many minutes of time that I spent on every project! I hated keeping time. And I missed my old life. To be really honest, it didn't thrill me—it did not." June asked the firm not to consider her for full-time employment.

In 1975, June graduated from Harvard Law School with honors. She had not interviewed for any jobs. She passed the Massachusetts bar and went home to hang out her shingle in Gloucester. Much to her surprise, people began to call her to talk about business, to ask about a divorce, even to start a church. There was so much to learn. "I realized almost immediately that I was going to be totally miserable. I'd be working long hours, because I'm not the kind of person who's going to wing it. I was so unhappy. I felt trapped into doing what I didn't want to do. Trial work sounded like fun, but I knew if I did it, I would be stressed my whole life. I thought, 'I don't want to do this.' I realized that I was only doing it because I was ashamed to say I wasn't going to practice at all. Everyone had made such a big deal about my going to law school, and about how I was representative of the whole corps of women coming behind who wanted to be lawyers. You feel you're letting them down if you quit. But what I really, really, really wanted to do was just be a mom, because I loved doing that. I loved carpooling, the gossip of the kids in the car, going to their games. So I finally said, 'No, I'm not going to do it.' People seemed disappointed. It was like telling them I had an illness. It made me feel very, very bad, but I was very, very happy that I was back at home."

Marge Freincle Gibson (Haskell)

Marge worked at the Matson Navigation Company in San Francisco, one of the first women in their law department, right up until she gave birth to her first daughter, who promptly refused to sleep through the night. As a result, after a few months, Marge had to move her practice to her home for a while before establishing an office in downtown Oakland, where she specialized in real estate and small-business practice. She gave birth to a second daughter and continued working part-time with citizens' groups and Oakland lawyers she'd met in the corporate world. The Oakland city administrators knew the quality of her mind and soon appointed her to the City Planning Commission, the first woman to hold a seat there. At first, she had no child care at home, so she just took her daughters with her.

One evening, a few days after Marge's second daughter, Debbie, was born, the Planning Commission called an emergency meeting. They needed a quorum and Marge decided she had to be there. Marge took Debbie in her baby carrier, placed her on the floor behind the long blanket covering the commission table, and rocked her with her foot throughout the two-hour meeting. Fortunately, Debbie wasn't like her sister: she slept through the entire proceeding. At the end of the meeting, a local news hen approached Marge:

"Didn't you just have a baby?"

"Yes."

"Well, what are you doing here?"

"Well, the baby's right down there."

The reporter was astonished and wrote a story about Marge and her newborn. The headline was DEBBIE GIBSON SLEEPS THROUGH PLANNING COMMISSION MEETING.

Patricia Scott Schroeder

Pat Schroeder was elected to Congress from Denver, Colorado, in November 1972, the first woman ever chosen from that district. Her son, Scott, was six years old; her daughter, Jamie, two. When her husband, Jim, had run for state representative in 1970, Pat had come to the campaign offices every day, made the coffee, and brought the doughnuts. Jim lost by forty-two votes. Now their situations were reversed, and the family dynamic was totally different. Jim was thrilled that Pat had been elected and backed her all the way. "Her career was suddenly the primary one. People said to me, 'Wasn't it great of you to give up your practice and move to Washington.' Well, what was I supposed to do? Stay in Denver with my little two-year-old daughter in diapers? And my six-year-old in first grade? No, of course not."

The family moved to Washington, D.C., where the children entered public school in the middle of the year. Jim was a great lawyer, but now it was his turn to have a difficult time finding a job that he could accept: many law firms wanted him to use his connections in the Congress to lobby for firm clients. Jim wasn't about to do that. Eventually, he became a partner in a highly regarded firm specializing in international law. He was on the road a lot, but also at home for long stretches of time. He purposely cut back on his career to make sure that at least one parent was around for their children. As Pat recalls:

"Because of the ethical restrictions Jim imposed on himself due to my position in Congress, he couldn't make a lot of money. But he had partners all over the world, traveled around, and had a lot of fun. He never played the role of the trailing spouse where he walked around carrying my purse. I didn't play the partner's wife, and he didn't play the congresswoman's husband. He also helped put together a group of men, the Dennis Thatcher Society. All these guys like Marty Ginsburg [spouse of Justice Ruth Bader Ginsburg] and John O'Connor [spouse of Justice Sandra Day O'Connor], who thought their wives' jobs were more fun, would get together and bitch and moan over dinner. Jim also totally enjoyed having the kids around on his own, without me there. They became very close, and I don't think he would have traded that for anything."

Pat tried in every way possible to make the children a part of her work, and to include Jim as often as his time permitted. As her daughter, Jamie, remembers:

"She was the only mom who consistently tried to pick me up from sixth-grade dance class on Friday afternoons. I remember one mom saying how overwhelmingly intimidating it was to see my mom's face pressed against the glass every Friday. She was thinking, 'How does that woman have time to do this?' She dragged me everywhere, and my brother, Scott, everywhere. There are pictures of me playing with pipe cleaners in the Arms Services Committee meetings. Scott and I roller-skated all around the Rayburn House Office Building. I was taken places where kids never went—refugee camps in Thailand, for example. I knew that if I was ever sick or anything went wrong, I came before the job. I think that one thing saved it more than anything. I wouldn't have traded that for the world."

One of Jamie's earliest memories is the day she first realized that there was cultural bigotry, and that it could turn violent. Pat was scheduled to give a speech at a synagogue in Denver and had taken six-year-old Jamie along. "The Ku Klux Klan was picketing outside the synagogue. They all had their white, pointy hoods on and were carrying signs saying, 'Schroeder is bad. Schroeder is a friend of the Jews.' To see these men in their scary suits, marching in a circle screaming names about your mother, was terrifying. The cops came over and said, 'Now, Mrs. Schroeder, we're going to take you in the back exit because we cannot guarantee your safety. We don't know what they're hiding in those robes.' My mother said, 'No way. I'm walking right through the middle of that picket line.' Then she tried to have me go with the policeman. 'Mother, Eleanor Roosevelt would roll over in her grave. I'm coming with you.' She let me come. And so on we went. She met a friend in the middle of the circle. They hugged and then both of them started sobbing. It was just so powerful."

Pat also made sure to involve her kids in her version of housekeeping. When Jamie was growing up, a lot of her friends lived in fancy houses and had plenty of spending money. The Schroeder family never had the time or the money to gussy up their houses. Besides, their already tight budget was made tighter by having to maintain two homes, one in Denver, one in Washington. As Jamie remembers: "Mom and I used to get down on the floor and color in the bald spots in our red shag rug that was like fifteen years old. There were plastic and silk flowers from Pier 1 stuck in the yard because nobody had the time to garden. I could hardly ever find sheets that matched. But even my friends who have terribly wealthy parents haven't traveled like my brother, Scott, and I have. It's all in the priorities, and my mom and dad had that figured out just about right."

Sheila Rush

Sheila began teaching at Hofstra Law School in 1972 when her son, Joseph, was six months old. They asked her to teach administrative law, consumer credit law, and law and psychiatry, subjects she had no experience in outside of her administrative law battles with HUD when she'd worked for the NAACP Legal Defense Fund.

"It was grueling. I was learning the material as I was teaching it. My husband and I were having difficulties. And Joseph was a baby. I had a live-in housekeeper and paid her out of my earnings. It was the only way my life worked. I knew that I could not manage without someone there all the time, except on weekends, when I was free in the sense that I was not teaching, although I was still preparing for class, taking care of the baby, and often cooking. I don't know how I did it. I practically killed myself."

Judith Richards Hope

In 1975, when I joined the staff of the Ford White House, my son, Zachary, was six and a half, my daughter, Miranda, four. There was nothing gradual about my return to full-time work: I went from a laid-back life in Malibu, where I taught one class of constitutional law at Pepperdine University and spent a lot of time with my children, driving carpools, cooking, and teaching them to swim and play tennis, to what can only be described as fourteen-hour days of total immersion in policy and political issues. I had less time for family, but enough (especially if I cut back on sleep) to never miss a school play, a children's soccer match, or an overnight camp-out. I also drove carpools and did most of the cooking, but it seemed completely normal: that was what women did. When I had to work on Saturdays, which was most of the time, I brought Zach and Miranda in with me whenever I could: they each had a tiny table in my office with a drawer with crayons, paper, paste, and blunt-nosed scissors. They were absolutely great about it: they would go to their "desks," color and paste and cut out characters, and then we'd have lunch together in the White House mess, where other staff members with children generally showed up around noon.

I learned a lot about juggling in those two years, which helped me for the rest of my complicated life of family and career. I hired a wonderful house-keeper who loved children and could drive. I paid her as well as I could, even if it took most of my take-home pay. Which it did. We deliberately chose to live close to work and close to the children's schools: neither was more than fifteen minutes from home. I cut out shopping (except for groceries) and most socializing, except for occasional Sunday-night Chinese dinners with Zach and Miranda's friends and their parents. And I found a sensational assistant, Ruth Drinkard (Knouse), who promised me that—no matter what I was doing, even if I was in the Oval Office—she would interrupt me whenever either of my children or their teachers called.

That finally happened half an hour before the 11 A.M. bill-signing ceremony for one of President Ford's biggest achievements, railroad deregulation.

I was in charge of managing the ceremony, to which four hundred or so members of Congress and railroad bigwigs from around the country had been invited. I was coordinating among the VIPs, the White House Press Office, and the Oval Office. I was just heading over to the East Wing of the White House for the ceremony when Ruthie put an urgent phone call through. The school nurse was on the line:

"Miranda has a fever and is throwing up. We can't reach your housekeeper. You will have to come and get her right away."

"Listen, I am really, really busy right at this particular moment. Could you call her dad?"

"I'm sorry. The school policy is to call the mother. You will have to come. Now."

I called her dad's office. He was in a meeting and his secretary said he couldn't be interrupted. I was frantic—worried about my daughter and torn by my obligations to President Ford. In desperation, I asked Ruthie if she could race to the school, pick Miranda up, and bring her back to the White House while I stayed close to the phones to handle the last-minute details of the ceremony and respond if the boss called. Ruthie made the round-trip in a record twenty-five minutes. It was 10:55 A.M. Miranda was pale, sick to her stomach, and frightened. I hugged her, then carried her to the ladies' room, held her head, washed her face. I got her some ginger ale and saltines from the White House mess and made a bed on my sofa out of coats and winter scarves. It was 11:10 A.M. Miranda had stopped throwing up and had started to look a little better. She said she was "okay now." Ruthie offered to skip the ceremony and stay with Miranda as long as I needed. I raced the two city blocks to the other end of the White House complex in my high heels. When I arrived, sweating and with my jacket and scarf askew, the chief usher removed the red velvet rope from the bottom of the stairs up to the State Dining Room, quietly informed the Marine Corps Band, "Mrs. Hope is here. You may begin," and motioned to me to lead the throng of VIP guests upstairs for the ceremony. President Ford was waiting at the top of the stairway. Smiling benignly, he whispered quietly, but with steel in his voice, "You're seventeen minutes late. Don't let it happen again."

Of course, it did happen again, both in the White House and in private practice, but I learned to fudge: I was never officially at a school event or a parent-teacher conference; I was always "at an appointment out of the office." I was never at home with my children when they were sick; I was always "working at home to complete the materials you need ahead of schedule." And I was never having my hair done or shopping; I was always "doing research in the field."

When I reentered private practice, my assistant Betsy Pond, from my earliest days at Williams & Connolly, joined me once again. She knew the ropes, and the rules about my kids: "You used to go to their school a lot. On Halloween you dressed up as a bear for one of their classes. And I remember when Zachary left his worms in the station wagon you drove to work, and you went racing out of a meeting to get the worms to him. You were totally serious about the law, but the kids were always the most important thing— you were like a mama lion about your kids. There were certain responsibilities that you had as a powerhouse, and it was tough, but when it came down to the bottom line, it was always the kids."

For forty years, I've been blessed by talented, smart assistants, without whom I couldn't have survived either professionally or personally: Betsy Pond, who started with me at Williams & Connolly, and worked with me over the years both in nonprofits and in private practice; Ruthie Knouse, who was my right arm at the White House; and Dona Brown, Doreen Wood, Charlotte Stewart, and Rosie Daniels, who together backed me up for more than twenty years at Paul, Hastings. They became, in a real sense, not only partners in my work and lifelong friends, but also close to my children. At the same time they kept the work flowing and the clients well cared for, they also honored my priority to put my children first. Even though both "children" are now over thirty, the rules are still the same. Over the years, my assistants covered for me when I was having a picnic lunch at the school instead of a business lunch at the club. With great sincerity and crossed fingers, they regularly said I was at a meeting out of the office when I was at Zachary's baseball games or Miranda's elementary school plays. I often finished the work for the next day by rising at four in the morning, which gave me nearly three hours of uninterrupted time before breakfast and carpool.

Shortly before Zachary and Miranda left for college, I ran into my pal Muffie Brandon Cabot at a small grocery store in Georgetown. She was Nancy Reagan's social secretary at the time, and she was juggling four children, a busy husband, and the social schedule of the White House. We were both exhausted and looked it. Somewhere between the cheese and the cereal, we decided that if we were determined to try to do it all, we had to expect that we would be tired for twenty years.

Until a few months ago, when I pressed my adult children to tell me candidly how they feel about having a mother who was also a busy professional woman, I believed that I had managed pretty well to do it all. Month after month, they hedged: they were "really busy right now," or they needed "more time to think about it," or they'd "really rather not say." But I thought it was important to know—for myself as well as for them. So I kept asking. Finally,

I received such candid responses from each of them that I wished I hadn't asked.

Zachary, now thirty-three and an investment analyst and hedge-fund manager in California, wrote me his "top-of-the-mind thoughts." He told me how his friends viewed me and how that jibes with his own recollections about having a mother who worked as a lawyer:

"When my best friend from high school, Frank Harmon, lost his dad when we were in ninth grade, he ended up spending a lot of time at our house. In terms of Frank's relationship with 'my dad,' Frank was totally comfortable. But when the topic of 'my mom' comes up today, Frank doesn't refer to 'your mom' but to 'Judy.' Judy took things very seriously, herself included, which seems almost absurd to Frank in retrospect. He has a pretty clear perspective that Judy is the one who wore the pants in the Hope household, and it was Judy who provided the role model and the direction. I had all the right discipline and experience to be able to get into the colleges of my choice. And Miranda had the same. He thought Mom was the real driver behind accomplishment and preparedness.

"Mothers of my friends knew other mothers who worked, but it was clear from the way they would ask about my 'mother' that they placed you in a different category. They respected you so much that any comparison between themselves and you was beyond one that could create jealousy. They were very curious and focused on you, as if you were a far-off fantasy, maybe even an antenna of some kind that caught hold of and became symbolic of a variety of unrelated thoughts or wishes or dissatisfactions. But certainly there was tremendous admiration. And always, whether expressed or implicit, there was the additional thought of 'And she's so nice'—as if they would expect otherwise.

"I remember a neighborhood party in the summer of 1991, when Mrs. Sander Vanocur, whose journalist husband broke the initial Watergate story, shared her perspective with me that what my father lent to my mother was 'lightness.' Implicit in what she said was that my mother was very serious—more serious than I would recognize her to be. For her, my mom had the kind of career and the kind of respect from men like her husband that those men normally only accord other men—respect that they may not have accorded their own wives.

"My main reaction to the conversation with Mrs. Vanocur was of pride that my parents were both so well liked and, it seemed, loved, by a woman I had never met, a woman who seemed sophisticated, smart, and elegant. Mrs. Vanocur's main reaction, which came on my bearing the news that my parents had separated, was of regret and sadness.

"The bottom line is that, to the extent that having a 'mom who worked' had an influence on the family dynamics, the influence was not as much from the location of the mom at certain times of the day but rather the chemistry of the mom, the nature of the mom, the personality of the mom that drove that mom to work. And drove us to excel. It was so much more extreme than having a mom who works. It was more that my mom was 'Judy Hope.'"

My daughter, Miranda, now thirty-one and a teacher, singer, songwriter, and poet, married to Andrew Smith, a boat builder and musician, finally leveled with me by handing me a long letter one day while we were sitting at a lunch counter eating vegetarian burritos:

"I am uncomfortable talking about you and your choices. What do I know about your life really? Not much. But, because you asked, twice, I will try.

"For a long time, I believed that I needed a mother, not a trial lawyer. But maybe a mother is a very rare thing to get. You came to every play, drove carpool, drove us to soccer games, bought me beautiful dresses, went to parents' night, checked my homework, served on the boards of my schools, paid attention. I never *consciously* felt abandoned or neglected. You edited my research papers, organized the neighborhood Easter egg hunt, and sewed Halloween costumes. You planned and paid for trips to Colorado, Maine, Wyoming, Nantucket, Europe, and Japan. You cared for your mother when she was dying, and you care for your father every day of the year. You do not put yourself first. Many women work. But your particular job and the training that led to your success in this job gave birth to—or gave reinforcement to—a woman too invincible, too pushy, too isolated, too sedentary, too tired. A woman I have never seen truly laugh or truly cry. A woman without needs. A tank.

"For better and for worse, you pushed me hard. You love the answer that a Harvard dean gave to a student when asked, 'Should I take the hard class and get a B or take the easy class and get an A?' And you always smile, secretively, when you whisper the answer: 'Take the hard class and get an A.' This is one of your core beliefs. I hate it. The answer should be, 'Grades are stupid. Life is short. What do you want to learn?'

"I remember standing by the sink in the bathroom of my elementary school. You were in court that day and you had asked me to send you good ESP. So I stood in the bathroom during lunch, closed my eyes, and whispered, 'Let my mom win her case today!' I was seven.

"You kept money for the housekeeper in an old mustard jar in the spice cabinet. Our metro tokens always smelled of old mustard. Every so often I would secretly put my allowance in the mustard jar so you wouldn't have to work so hard. I was eight.

"You convinced us that you hated the long hours, that you wished you could be at home with us. I understand the impulse, but what I absorbed was not a message of your love for me, but instead the notion that a high-powered job was an endless string of enforced days that tore a woman away from her family: 'Mom's evil job.' When my friends were admitted to law school, all I could think of was the horrible dungeon of a life that lay before them.

"My friends' mothers often talked about how impressive you were, how they wished they could have done something other than laundry with their lives. They'd cook me perfect grilled-cheese sandwiches and play James Taylor on the car stereo—with you, we only listened to classical music. I'd listen to their regret, in mild shock that a mother could honestly express any emotion at all.

"When I think of you, I see a woman in a turtleneck T-shirt and underpants cleaning out the clogged drain in the pond in the backyard, stopping to talk on a cell phone to the president of Harvard. A woman calling herself a 'street fighter from Defiance' playing two hours of Chopin études on a Sunday morning. A woman who went to law school with a blazing sense of justice, now representing the Mob, now prosecuting the Mob, now working for giant corporations. A woman who taught me how to knit, plant bulbs in the fall, cook, clean, work hard, design a home with beauty and simplicity. A woman who will win an argument against her daughter at any cost.

"Good God! Every morning at seven A.M. you came into our rooms, pulled up the blinds, and sang, 'It's a beautiful day, but it's cold. Rise and shine! Another day in which to excel!' You finally admitted, proudly, that you picked that last part up from a friend at West Point. At seven twenty-two A.M. WTOP would play a march and you would march around the kitchen in your high heels and your suit with a spatula in your hand. You packed our lunch bags, and there was usually a drawing in crayon covering each bag—drawings of me and the dog and swings and trees—and always 'I love you' written across the bottom. Then you drove our carpool, and we played an elaborate, thrilling game of 'submarine' all the way to school—captains and bombardiers and enemies approaching. I went to school and you went, with your spatula, your crayons, and your imaginary periscope, to—oh—take on the Federal Aviation Administration. Twelve hours later, you would drive into the driveway and honk the horn—'shave and a haircut'—then come inside and sing a loud, ridiculous greeting to the dog. You must have been exhausted, but I think you felt you did not have the right to be tired.

"You chose to work and to be a mother, and so there was this carnival of silliness every night when you came home. Zachary and I had to come down to greet you. You would have a big smile on your face that seemed incongruous because of how tired you looked. There was mandatory hugging and mandatory sitting on your lap. Enforced quality time. Eventually, of course, we refused.

"When you said that you were going to lighten your workload and build a house in the country so you could practice the piano and plant a garden, I thought, 'Great,' and I gave you a trowel with a note that said, 'For your new life.' That was five years ago. I imagined that you would finally melt, soften, relax, live, listen, talk, breathe. I imagined you—smiling. But, alas! . . . You. Cannot. Rest. The trowel is now a paperweight on your desk. Something in those ancient neural pathways that guide you, perhaps toward some notion of survival, takes over. You did so much. You worked so hard. You did so well. Intellectually, I am very grateful and proud. But in my heart, there is a large sad hole. I fill it with acting, yoga, hiking, songwriting, tai chi, teaching, laughing, loving, and still it rarely gets full. When I spend time with you, your philosophy, your drive, your big plans—they drain my heart, and I have to start again."

I have thought a lot about Zachary's and Miranda's views of me. They make me indescribably sad. I thought I had successfully navigated the two demanding worlds of motherhood and law practice, that I had hidden my struggles, my fatigue, and my concerns from them. I thought they knew without any question how much they were loved and cherished. I was wrong about all of those things.

I saw myself as Joan of Arc, vindicating my father and protecting my children. They saw me as a tank and perhaps saw themselves as just another couple of important files in my file cabinet. I worked at not letting troubles get inside and pull me down. My children came to believe I had no feelings. I have thought hard about whether I would do it differently if I could do it all over. Given the choices I thought I had, and acknowledging, too, the drive that had been part of me since my nursery school races to the top square of the jungle gym, I believe I made the decisions I thought were right for me and best for them. If I had my life to live over again, I hope I would take things a little easier, that I would attempt a little less, aim just a little lower, take more time just to sit with my children by a stream with our toes dangling in the water. I hope I would delete the word *push* from my vocabulary. But I am not sure I would be able to. The repeated losses of homes and security over the years took a toll and drove me to try both to support and care for my family and to honor my commitments to myself, my parents, and my alma mater. Besides, I love being a lawyer, representing clients and figuring out how to win for them. It's the endless years of long hours that I regret. Perhaps the two are inseparable. Young children need their mother close by. Clients need their lawyers to be open twenty-four hours a day when there is a crisis. It's a tough—perhaps impossible—balancing act.

Although I failed at trying to do it all, I think I am a better person for having tried. For better and for worse, my two children had to find a lot of their way on their own. They are stronger for that. My clients and the young lawyers I have mentored are also, I hope, better for our work together, and I am certainly better for having worked with them.

Perhaps, as my father still tells me so often, "Angels can do no more."

PART FOUR

Bumps in the Road

... I'll tell you
Life for me ain't been no crystal stair.
It's had tacks in it
And splinters,
And boards torn up,
And places with no carpet on the floor—
Bare.
But all the time
I'se been a-climbin' on,
And reachin' landin's.
And turnin' corners,
And sometimes goin' in the dark
Where there ain't been no light.
... [D]on't you turn back
Don't you set down on the steps
'Cause you finds it's kinder hard.
Don't you fall now—
For I'se still goin', honey,
I'se still climbin',
And life for me ain't been no crystal stair.
                              —Langston Hughes[1]

Despite and perhaps even because of our ambition and the complicated lives we have lived, the women lawyers who graduated from law school in the early sixties were not—and are not—always as strong and as invincible as we may have appeared to the outside world.

We have all had setbacks. Even Justice Ruth Bader Ginsburg had bumps on the road to the United States Supreme Court. In 1971, then Harvard Law dean Albert Sacks invited her to teach at Harvard Law School for the fall semester as a visiting professor. The invitation was essentially a semester-long audition to become a full-time faculty member. At the time, Ruth was simultaneously teaching law at Rutgers University in New Jersey; living in New York with her husband, Martin, their daughter, Jane, and son, James; and working on the ACLU's Women's Rights Project. She and Marty talked it over and decided that, between them, they could manage it. Ruth accepted the invitation.

One morning in the late fall, after she had pulled an all-nighter on an ACLU brief, Professor Phil Areeda showed up as she was walking to Pound Hall to teach and said that he would be observing her in class that day, a day on which, as Justice Ginsburg told me later, the definition of success for her was to remain standing at the end of the class." After class, Areeda apparently reported to Dean Griswold that her performance was not up to snuff. The dean asked her, "Could you return in the spring semester for one more semester's tryout?" Ruth already had an offer to teach at Columbia Law School, but she told the dean she'd talk with her husband about it. Marty had already agreed that if she received an offer from Harvard, he would move to Boston with her and retool himself. After a full family discussion, Ruth decided that her life was complicated enough without further excursions to Cambridge. She turned down Harvard's offer for a second semester-long audition and accepted Columbia Law School's offer of a full professorship.

Our generation was never one to "let it all hang out." Even those women in my class who have become the most public remain essentially private people. Only our parents, children, husbands, and closest friends see through us and know the price we have paid—as well as the enormous sense of accomplishment we have had—in trying to do it all.

Candidly, most of us were a mess at one or another time in our lives. Among us, we have suffered through attempted suicide, serious depression, nasty divorce, life-threatening illness, and the loss of close family members. We have asked for child support and been denied because we had a good job. We have been double-crossed, sexually harassed, defeated, passed over, and fired. We have experienced searing religious, gender, and racial discrimination. All these things and more have hurt us, but, in the end, have also made us stronger. Although the hurts were often personal, we eventually learned not to take them personally, following the old adage that all the water in the ocean cannot sink your boat unless it gets inside. When all else failed, our sense of the absurd, our instinct for survival, and our trust in and reliance on each other have saved us time and again.

Early on in her career, one of us became completely overwhelmed by the dual responsibilities of a demanding job and a busy overcommitted family. She found herself increasingly unable to manage the inevitable conflicts between her professional commitments and the very real needs of her preschool-aged children and her husband, a brilliant lawyer whose work and ambition kept him at the office most nights and weekends. She was desperately unhappy and, having recently read Sylvia Plath's biography, concluded that suicide was her only escape. But even at this lowest point in her life, she somehow retained a certain sense of black humor.

"I decided to turn on the gas and put my head in the oven. Not wanting to roast myself to death, I put out the pilot light. But it turned out that our oven had some kind of fail-safe mechanism: without the pilot lit, the oven wouldn't turn on. 'Damn!' I said to myself. 'At least the Brits have the good manners to design their ovens so that an unhappy housewife can kill herself.'

"Next I decided to try the stovetop method. I managed to turn on the unlit gas on all the top burners. I put a sheet over my head and started to inhale. Just as I was going under, my husband unexpectedly came home early from the office. He discovered me in the kitchen, which was rapidly filling with gas. He was frightened and screamed my name. I pulled the sheet off my head and told him: 'This is ridiculous. There has to be a more efficient way to die.'

"Although I probably would not have gone through with the suicide, it was the only way I could think of at the time to reclaim myself for myself, to do something for myself alone. The attempt also revealed to both me and my husband that I was not the strong professional woman I seemed. We needed help and we got it. After my brief hospitalization and months of counseling for both of us, we rediscovered our true selves, and realized that family and friends were, for us, the first priority. We changed the way we lived and worked. Things ultimately got much better for both of us and we are still happily married to each other several decades later."

Pat Schroeder

In 1987, eight-term congresswoman Pat Schroeder decided to explore a run for president of the United States. Because a lot was going on in the Armed Services Committee and in her district, and she hadn't found the time to tell Jim, who was in Bangkok working on a big case for the World Bank. One of his partners there brought in USA Today and said, "Oh, I see your wife is running for president."

And Jim said, "What the hell is this?" He took the next plane home. When he arrived, he asked Pat, "What's going on?"

Pat chuckled. "I got bored while you were out of town."

Jim knew that he would have to be involved in the campaign, and Pat knew how much she needed him: in every one of her campaigns, he had worked side by side with her and helped her win. According to Pat, "Among the many strengths that Jim brought was that he could deal easily with the male half of the world. There is absolutely no question that if journalists like Jack Germond had to pick between us as to who he'd rather talk to, he'd rather talk to Jim. It was a Washington thing, not a Denver thing: 'What's she doing now? Have you talked to her about this bill that's before the Armed Services Committee?' Jim was an ex–navy guy. They could talk military with him, without having to put me on the spot—or on the record."

Jim told his partners at the law firm that he would be taking a leave of absence for the duration of the campaign, however long it lasted.

Pat's daughter, Jamie, found out her mom was thinking of running for president when she answered the phone at home to find Bella Abzug on the other end of the line:

"Where's your mother?"

"She's not home."

"Well, tell her I think she should run for president. What do you think about that?"

It was the first Jamie had heard of it, and she stuttered a reply: "Ah, ah . . . well, I, ah, don't, ah, know."

"Well," Bella replied, "I think she should do it, and you'd better think about how you can help her."

A couple of days later, Pat and Jamie were on the plane to Denver, where Pat would announce her exploratory campaign. "Mom turns to me and says, 'Sorry I didn't have time to talk this over with you, it's been such a rushed week. The minute the plane lands, we're having a press conference. Somebody leaked that I might be running.'"

Pat's announcement was electric: a few other women had tried a presidential run, most notably Congresswoman Shirley Chisolm of New York, but for the most senior woman in the U.S. House of Representatives and a member of the Armed Services Committee to take a crack at the nation's top political job was serious and significant. A lot of folks, including newsman Jack Germond, thought she might just make it.

From the outset, Pat promised that if she didn't raise $2 million by September, she would not go forward: "No dough, no go." David Brinkley commented dryly on ABC that if Pat actually kept that promise, it would change the course of American politics. But Pat was not about to run a crusade, particularly a crusade just for women. If she ran, it would only be as a real, full-fledged candidate with realistic expectations of being competitive, of trying to win.

Pat and Jim had always tried to protect their children from the ugly side of politics—the unfounded charges, the hate mail, and the threatening phone calls. But a presidential run was different. Jamie overheard more than one discussion that because Pat had had so many death threats, the Secret Service wanted to put a security detail on her immediately. Jamie was scared for her mom and worried for herself: "If she wins or even becomes vice president, there goes my adolescence. I was sixteen and just coming of age. I was looking forward to going to college, which is supposed to be the best time of your life. I did not want that scrutiny. But at the same time I was very supportive of her. It was an opportunity not to be missed."

By September, Pat's exploratory committee had raised more than $1 million, but not the $2 million she and Jim had decided was necessary for her to have a chance. Jim had been at her side every step of the way and was constantly working the phones on her behalf. On the Friday morning when Pat was to decide "go or no go," Jim received three calls. Lou Harris told him, "Your wife is now at fifteen percent and she's number three in the polls. I think she can be a strong number three if she stays in this thing." The ex-chairman of the Democratic Party in New Hampshire called: "We're ready to go up here. We're on board. I'll have the organization for Pat's primary if she runs." And the president of the independent oil producers called from Dallas: "We know it's time. We know Pat, and we think she's all right for independent oil. We're ready to go. Let us know what you want us to do."

The night before, Jim had drafted a memo for Pat on yellow paper, acknowledging that he knew she was not going forward because the money wasn't there. Now he revised it. She seemed to have a real chance to win: "You're up there ahead of most of these guys. Everybody's been saying it's Snow White and the Seven Dwarfs, and Snow White is looking good. We've got grass roots, and some more money coming from down South. You're number one in the polls on believability and trustworthiness. You're the one who's going to have to do this, not me, but I think probably you should go ahead and do it."

It was Jim's last memo to Pat about the presidency. She had already decided that if she couldn't raise the money, the country wasn't yet ready for a woman president: "It just wasn't going to happen. And, in the interim, I would have had to give up the seat in Congress."

For Pat, the hardest part was the feeling that she'd let her supporters down.

That afternoon, as she headed for the microphones in Denver, the crowds were cheering "*Run, Pat, run.*" Pat thanked all those who'd worked so hard, then announced her decision: she was not going to run. Some people shouted, "*No! No!*" while others kept on chanting, "*Run, Pat, run.*" Pat repeated her decision, and the crowd began to groan. Pat broke down. She started to cry. As she said later, "It was my tears, not my words, that got the headlines. One good result of my tears was that crying came out of the closet."[2] Jamie remembers, "She was in front of the television cameras. There were protesters holding up dead babies, there were cameras and reporters everywhere. It was just this wild, surreal media circus. And Mom couldn't get it together to finish her speech. I'm looking at my dad and he's got this look of pain . . . it was such public pain. It caught her so off guard, because she had been trying to be everybody's pillar of strength. There we all were, standing right behind her. As her child, to see Mom cry was so hard. I've only seen my mom cry a handful of times in my entire life. It was awful."

Twelve years later, our friend and former law school colleague Elizabeth Dole, Harvard Law class of '65, almost threw her hat in the presidential ring. Pat thought Elizabeth had a great chance: "The polls showed that she got many more independent voters than [her opposition]. People were excited about making history. I had a carpenter working in my house . . . and after the Monica Lewinsky thing, he decided to vote for Elizabeth Dole. She was a fabulous candidate. She went out there . . . quit her job, killed herself, everything. If I were Elizabeth, I would have pushed it all the way. But she had a problem: Bob Dole is thinking about giving money to one of her opponents, McCain. What is the message there? That she wasn't going to raise the money. I was stunned. And even more stunned that the media didn't go after him. If a woman had acted like that when her husband was running, they would all have been raging."

Rosemary Cox Masters

After her first child, daughter Brooke, was born, Rosemary took a three-month leave of absence from the Vera Institute's Bowery Project, where she'd been helping derelicts recover their sobriety and their lives. When Rosemary was ready to return to work, she hired an old-fashioned British nanny to care for Brooke while she was at work: Rosemary's salary was just enough to cover the cost of the nanny and her own transportation back and forth to the office. The nanny quit a month later. Rosemary scrambled, found a mother's helper who was "okay," and kept on going. But she was exhausted most of the time: the minute she got home from work, the nanny left. Rosemary's husband, Jon, was rarely home: as a young associate at Shearman & Sterling, he was working terrible hours, often not getting home until three or four in the morning. According to Rosemary, "It was basically me, and I was getting more and more tired. And then Brooke started to mind it when I left. She would cry and I felt horrible whenever I left the house. Then Brooke essentially fired her nanny—she was one year old and she refused to eat. She would only eat for me."

A few months later, Rosemary quit her job. Rosemary and Jon's son, Blake, was born two years later. Rosemary loved her children and her husband, but felt more and more trapped by her life, particularly by the social expectations Jon's parents were thrusting on her. To make matters worse, both children were vulnerable to croup and although Jon tried to help out, many times Rosemary was the one who stayed up with them all night or rushed them to the hospital when steam from the shower failed to open their lungs. Rosemary remembers her anger when she bumped into one or another of her Harvard Law School classmates on the street after she had been up all night and having them say, "Oh, so are you working? Or are you at home with the kids?" Their derision felt a lot like law school. "For them, there was work, and then there was everything else. It didn't seem to matter that I had been helping my child breathe for most of the night . . . to them, it wasn't important or even legitimate."

At the same time, Jon's parents were pressuring him "to fit in, to be this upper-class Wall Street lawyer," even though he was dissatisfied with the endless hours and repetitive work of a large law firm. Simultaneously, they kept pushing Rosemary to help his career by making the "right" friends, joining the "right" social clubs, buying a house in the Hamptons and entertaining the "right people." Rosemary was ambivalent about their demands. As she admits today, she was drawn to "a Jackie Kennedy vision of life as the glamorous supporter of a successful man," but even if she had wanted to comply, doing those things on a law firm associate's salary was impossible. The cumulative effect of all these competing pressures—the exhaustion of caring for young children, confusion about her professional goals, and the expectations (her own as well as her in-laws') that she should be a traditional wife—pushed Rosemary into a serious clinical depression. Eventually, individual psychotherapy and medication helped. "I am one of the earliest success stories for antidepressant medication," she commented.

But the big breakthrough came when Rosemary and Jon sought counseling together from a family therapist who helped them create clearer boundaries between themselves and Jon's parents. As a result, Jon began to resist his parents' demands and to create a more independent life for himself and his family.

Meanwhile, Rosemary struggled and finally put herself together in a way that made sense to her. She came to understand that life in the New York social elite—the Junior League, planning benefit parties, and serving on charitable boards—would never challenge her. Despite her love for the precision and clarity of legal thinking, she also concluded that criminal justice administration no longer suited her. Her personal struggle with depression had made her aware of how crudely and superficially the law often evaluated people and how ineffectually it often responded to illegal conduct. With a sense of renewed purpose and restored self-confidence, Rosemary decided to return to graduate school to gain the skills needed to become a psychotherapist.

Rosemary's daughter, Brooke, now a reporter for the *Washington Post*, remembers how her mother ultimately managed her busy life of work and family: "Mom worked four and a half days a week. She was usually at home in the early mornings. She would get us going and we would eat breakfast together. Coming home in the afternoon, we had caretakers. When we got my report card in the mail, I would take the envelope and call Dad to ask if I could open it and read it to him. That was the rule—we couldn't just randomly tear open our parents' mail. That's how my parents balanced: my mother in the morning, and then my father during the day. My parents were the original quality-time people, before quality time was the thing. We had breakfast together, which was not a painful meal. Breakfast was just breakfast, and everybody was kind of there. But we always had to have dinner together, and it got later and later and later, like nine o'clock. By that hour, it was like a spotlight: 'It's your turn, we are focusing on you, now tell us about your life, what happened to you today.' It was 'Okay, here comes the interrogation.' It made me a bit of a drama queen.

"But, on the things that mattered, my parents showed up. Mom also played stay-at-home mom for half a day a week, generally when my brother Blake's chess club came over. We went to our cottage in the Berkshires every weekend, and that made a huge difference. We did everything together as a family. In spite of all the really hard work that both of my parents were putting in, they really enjoyed parenting. It was important to them, and we knew that. That was what made the difference."

Liz Daldy Dyson

In 1980, as a divorced mother of two needing a steady income and health insurance, Liz took a three-quarter-time job in the General Counsel's Office of the U.S. Office of Personnel Management (OPM). Although OPM depicted itself as a model employer seeking to promote part-time career opportunities in the federal government, Liz ran into one brick wall after another because of her part-time status: "I had supervisors who were jealous when I left promptly at three o'clock because I had to pick up my son from school at three-fifteen P.M. They were chained to their desks until five P.M., and until six or seven P.M. if they especially wanted to look good. They could not stand it; I didn't get promoted, even though I always met my deadlines and was always told I did outstanding work. Everybody said, 'You know, we're not going to promote you until you work full-time. You might as well face it.' This was especially galling because Congress had passed the Part-Time Career Opportunities Act in 1978, specifically exhorting the federal government to provide part-time career and promotion opportunities at all professional levels. Finally, in my last three years there, I capitulated and went to work full-time since, by then, I needed the extra money for my son's college tuition."

After converting to full-time, Liz won a long-deserved promotion to GS-15 rank. Within a month, however, the acting general counsel, who had been her supervisor when she had consistently been denied promotions, pressured the personnel office to withdraw the GS-15 promotion. Liz had had enough: she filed a sex-discrimination case under the Equal Pay Act and won the support of the Washington Committee for Civil Rights Under Law. After a painful four-month battle, she won: she got her GS-15 back, retroactive to its original date. After that, she found working under the same officials who had discriminated against her was not pleasant. In 1995, she eagerly accepted a buyout offer and took early retirement.

Liz's story is one of grit, determination, and courage. When people demanded that she work full-time, she refused—determined to take care of her young children. When she was fired by the District of Columbia because she was a part-timer, she bounced back, finding other rewarding part-time jobs that kept her mind alive and helped pay the bills. When she was unfairly demoted by the federal government, she fought back, winning back the promotion she had long been denied.

Even today, Liz is not sanguine about the chances of other women being able to carve out successful part-time legal careers: "Prejudice against part-timers is still unacceptably strong, and not only on the part of men. Many women who have had to work full-time to advance up the career ladder seem to be at least as unsupportive as men, if not more so."

Dinni (Lorenz) Gordon

After Dinni's stint with the Office of Economic Opportunity in Washington, D.C., she went on to a number of demanding public interest jobs. She served three years in Mayor John Lindsay's administration in New York City, during which time she married a Harvard graduate student, David Gordon, who later became a well-known Marxist economist. She also won a fellowship to the Institute of Politics at Harvard, where she wrote her first book, City Limits, about the limits to municipal reform possibilities in the Lindsay administration. The book was well received and opened new employment opportunities for Dinni. Several years later, she was recruited for the job of president of the National Council on Crime and Delinquency.

By the time the selection committee had narrowed the field to three candidates, Dinni was still in the running. But there was trouble brewing, as Dinni recalls: "Somebody on the executive committee said, 'Don't we really want a man?' Another group on the board objected to me on the basis of my writings—I had been critical of one of Attorney General Griffin Bell's reports, and there were friends of his on the board. Somebody else brought up the fact that my husband was a Marxist economist. It was like red-baiting. It turned into a very, very ugly scene."

After a rancorous discussion, Dinni was selected, but the battle had left terrible scars. She wanted to turn the job down, but having won, she felt she had an obligation to take it on: "I longed to give it up, but I couldn't in that situation. I had to stand my ground or I would be really cooked. I certainly wasn't going to admit that I had done anything seriously wrong, because I hadn't. And I certainly wasn't going to be red-baited."

Of the twenty-four board members, eight resigned when Dinni accepted. Two of those went to the federal government and tried to have the program defunded on the basis that Dinni was a wild radical and would destroy its purposes. The battle went on for almost two years until the dissidents' unremitting attacks finally succeeded: the organization was losing money and contributors, and Dinni was out of strength and out of resources. Even though the board initially refused to accept her resignation, she insisted that it was in the council's best interests. After she resigned, she took a position as a visiting professor at City College for a year: she thought it would be an interesting thing to do while she healed her wounds and figured out where to go next.

Six weeks into her teaching year, she realized that she liked having the time to write and enjoyed teaching the upwardly mobile working-class students in her classes. Disaster was also on the horizon. Her husband, David, was diagnosed with a potentially fatal heart condition. Dinni decided to stay at City College, City University of New York, agreeing to a salary 50 percent lower than that of her previous job.

Sonia Faust

Not long after starting with Honolulu Corporation Counsel's office, Sonia contracted a serious illness, requiring major surgery. The operation and the lengthy recuperation period precipitated a deep depression, one that may have been made worse by some of her experiences at Harvard Law School:

"Many of us at Harvard probably came away from the Law School thinking less of ourselves, less of our intellectual abilities, than we had thought when we started. There was, at that time, the sense that if you didn't do really well, then you weren't as wonderful as you used to think you were. You weren't always smart enough to get the analysis right, but you were always smart enough to figure out how you had messed up, to ask yourself, 'How could I have been so stupid?'"

With determination and a lot of good professional help, Sonia made a complete recovery from her illness, overcame her depression, and went on to a great career in public service in Hawaii.

Sheila Rush

Early in her career as a lawyer for the NAACP Legal Defense Fund, Sheila argued a housing discrimination case before Judge Carswell in the federal district court in Florida. "I started out scared. Then the judge was so rude to me. He was whistling when I was making my argument. He swung his chair around and turned his back to me. I stopped being scared and got mad. So I said, 'Let the record reflect that I am trying to make this argument, and the judge is whistling,' I stood up to him in a kind of dramatic way, and the story got around."

When President Nixon nominated Judge Carswell for the Supreme Court, Senator Cranston called Sheila and asked if she would prepare an affidavit about how she had been treated when she appeared before Judge Carswell. She agreed. Senator Cranston told her later that her affidavit, detailing the disrespect Carswell had showed to a black member of the bar, was a key document in defeating Carswell's nomination.

Nancy Kuhn Kirkpatrick

Unbeknownst to her clients, and to her colleagues at her law firm, Nancy Kuhn Kirkpatrick had broken her back twice when she was young and had suffered from degenerative disk disease for twenty years. The doctors warned her that surgery could result in paralysis, so she just kept working and hid her condition from everyone but her family. "If clients or colleagues think you are in terrible pain all the time or not at their disposal, they're not going to want to work with you. Just trying to keep my practice going and my family going was all I could do and survive."

One morning, she woke up and realized she had absolutely no feeling in her legs. Her husband, Doug, stuck her legs with pins—still no feeling. She stumbled in to work and called the doctor. He was away. She went home, didn't sleep, went to work again the next morning, and called again. After a series of medical runarounds, one of the many doctors she was trying to reach called back and told her to go to the emergency room. A younger resident there looked her over and sent her home with some painkillers. By the next morning, Nancy could not walk at all. Doug raced her back to the hospital, where an emergency CAT scan revealed a ruptured disk as large as an apricot that was severing her spinal cord. The doctor couldn't believe it. "I expected you to be screaming in agony and you're sitting here watching Saddam Hussein on the news?" Nancy answered, "You kept telling me that I had to learn to live with it." "Well, I know you said it was unbearable," the doctor replied, "but there you were in your gray suit, looking ready for business. Besides, you never even cried." Nancy's last words before they quickly wheeled her into the operating room for what turned out to be an eleven-and-a-half-hour emergency operation were "Next time you don't believe a female patient, tell her."

Nancy attempted to keep her law practice going from her home for the next few years while undergoing several more operations on her back. After the final operation, the surgeon told her, "You'll never be able to go back, and it will be five years before you can even do something part-time." That was when Nancy resigned from her law firm.

Barbara Margulies Rossotti

Barbara Margulies Rossotti has had an extraordinary career, successfully and with no apparent difficulty combining her roles as high-powered corporate lawyer, glamorous wife, community volunteer, and devoted mother. Classmate Charles Buffon remembers an early setback in her career and how courageously she handled it: "She worked at my firm, Covington & Burling, for a while. We had no women partners at that time—Barbara would have been the first. She left fairly quickly when she didn't become a partner. Now, there were a lot of people who didn't become a partner that year, including me. There was a bloodbath. Barbara quickly went on to Shaw, Pittman and became one of their brightest stars. She has become their most senior corporate lawyer—chair of their corporate department, a leader in the community, all that. One of Covington's senior partners was talking about Barbara recently and said what a big mistake it was not to elect her to the partnership."

Barbara just quietly packed her briefcase and moved on. The firm she liked best was Shaw, Pittman, Potts & Trowbridge. Her negotiations with them had only one small and quickly overcome glitch: noting that she was a mother with two young children, the name partners who were interviewing her inquired, "Just one last thing, Mrs. Rossotti. Do you plan to have any more children?" With her softest voice and biggest smile, Barbara replied, "Well, gentlemen, if I do, I don't plan to consult with you about it."

A few days later, she was unanimously voted into the partnership. She has been there ever since.

Alice Pasachoff Wegman

In 1975, after several years at home with young children, Alice decided to go back to work as a lawyer. She wanted to work only part-time, not an easy thing to negotiate in the midseventies. After a number of interviews and false starts, she received just the offer she wanted from the Consumer Product Safety Commission, with one exception: the pay was too low. She just said:

"No! I won't accept the position at that salary."

"Why do you think you should have a higher salary?" they asked.

"Because, with my credentials and experience, I am worth more."
"Okay."
They raised the salary and Alice took the job.

Judith Richards Hope

When I think back on my own bumps in the road, there seem to have been a lot of them, so many that sometimes the patches of smooth going seem short and far between. I think of the courageous battle my mother fought with cancer, and my commuting from Washington to Ohio weekend after weekend during her last year of life. Even as she was dying, my mother tried to comfort me by reciting one of her favorite poems:

"Pain is sometimes heaven's kick at the hinder parts of man to wake up the fool. But sometimes it is a deep and awful mystery which little minds must leave alone, for pain is nearly always birth."[3]

My mother was, and still is, the greatest woman I have ever known: beautiful, brilliant, extraordinarily talented, and a wonderful mother to me. I miss her every day of my life.

In remembering the troubles that have come my way, I think, too, of the loss our young family suffered in Malibu in April 1975, six weeks after we had finished remodeling our A-frame home overlooking the Pacific. We completed the work just in time to celebrate our son, Zachary's, sixth birthday on Valentine's Day 1975. Our daughter, Miranda, was four and a half. I was loving being at home with them and, in my free time, teaching a course in constitutional law at nearby Pepperdine University. It seemed like the perfect balance: just as Tony and I had agreed when we married, I was mostly staying home, making sure our children got a good start while still finding a way to keep my brain active and the rust off my credentials. Besides, we needed the money I was earning to make ends meet. It was ironic: I was married to the eldest son of a world-famous show-business icon, yet my part-time job was absolutely essential to help pay our bills.

On April 25, 1975, our home burned to the ground in the middle of the night. Although nobody was hurt—even the cat got out alive—the fire was devastating for us, both emotionally and financially. The next day, I took a hard look at our financial situation and discovered that we were nearly broke, with huge bills owed to the builder and the bank.

It was the second time in my life that something beyond my control had taken my home away and threatened my family's security. Standing in the middle of the charred shell of our dream house, I vowed to myself and to my children that I would never let that happen again. I decided to do whatever it took to restore the family's security and make a new home for us. "And one day," I said quietly to myself, "I will rebuild our home." It was too soon for me and for my young children, but it was time for me to go back to work full-time. I decided that if I was going to work, I would try to "shoot the moon," going all out, as we sometimes attempted when we played the card game of hearts. (I should have remembered that, at least in the game, if you fail at shooting the moon, the penalties are enormous and it is usually impossible to win.) I called my great friend from law school Olivia Barclay Jones, Harvard Law class of '65, and her husband, Jim, a young but already highly regarded congressman from Oklahoma. I told them that, after eight years off, I needed help in finding my way back into the workplace, and would especially like to work for President Ford, whom I admired tremendously—and who had his own mess to clean up, Watergate. I said it was urgent, but I didn't explain why, and they didn't ask.

Olivia and Jim arranged a meeting with the White House director of Presidential Personnel almost immediately. After several intense discussions about what I'd been doing with myself for the last eight years, and what I thought I was qualified to do in government, President Ford named me associate director of the White House Domestic Council. I would be the first woman ever to hold that position.

My parents agreed to care for Zachary and Miranda in Ohio until we could get back on our feet. I enrolled them in school there and drove on to Washington with everything we owned in the trunk of the car. Almost every weekend for six months, I went home to Ohio to be with my children, arriving late on Friday night, and leaving Sunday afternoon to return to Washington and work. By Christmas 1975, we were as ready as we were going to be. We hung a life-size plastic Santa on the front door, called Ohio, and told Zachary and Miranda we had made a new home for them. My parents borrowed a neighbor's van and brought them to Washington, D.C.

I trudged through the next dozen years. On November 13, 1981, for example, I wrote my parents a quick note: "I had a complete physical today. Health: excellent—blood pressure 110/70—just like 20 years ago—BUT: Rx is: get more sleep, lose 15 pounds, and laugh more." I didn't follow my doctor's advice for a long time. Much of the time, I was still working too hard and exhausted by my attempts to juggle the demands of work, the needs of my children, and my own need to be with them and a part of their lives. I wasn't looking to get to anywhere except home in time for dinner. Like the Red Queen in *Through the Looking Glass*, I was running as fast as I could to stay in the same place.

In the spring of 1988, I was summoned from a Paul, Hastings partners' meeting by what the messenger claimed was a call from the White House. I thought one of my friends was playing a joke on me, but I left to take the call anyway. When I said hello, the White House operator said, "Please hold for President Reagan." He asked me if I was willing to have the administration submit my nomination for the U.S. Court of Appeals for the District of Columbia Circuit, the second-highest court in the land. Even though I had a thriving law practice and was serving on the boards of several publicly traded corporations, I agreed immediately. It was a call to serve the country and the law. I could not refuse.

On March 28, 1988, the *Legal Times* headlined: REAGAN TURNS TO "INSIDER" REPLACEMENT FOR BORK

> Judith Richards Hope is the consummate Washington insider, the kind of establishment Republican that the President has often shunned in favor of young, movement conservatives. For some Reagan loyalists, her appointment to fill the shoes of the revered Robert Bork is a bitter coda to the Bork debacle.... But the confirmation of Hope, a 47-year-old veteran of the Ford Administration and a major rainmaker in the D.C. office of Los Angeles' Paul, Hastings, Janofsky & Walker, is expected to proceed smoothly.

My nomination was announced April 14, the same day the Union Pacific Corporation named me to its board. The *Omaha World-Herald* for Friday, April 15, 1988, carried the story:

> Judith Richards Hope, Union Pacific Corp.'s first woman director, said Friday she would have to resign from the board if the U.S. Senate confirms her nomination to the federal judge's position vacated by former Supreme Court nominee Robert Bork. "These things didn't come in any order that I could control," Mrs. Hope said of her nomination to the Union Pacific Board. She will serve as a Director while the Senate considers her nomination to the Court.... Mrs. Hope's election ... follows a long-standing association with Union Pacific chairman Drew Lewis. Lewis appointed her to the board of ConRail when he was Secretary of Transportation.... She also was chairman of the Railway Law Section of the Federal Bar Association.

Senator Alan Simpson of Wyoming, the ranking minority member of the Senate Judiciary Committee, volunteered to be my Senate sponsor and to shepherd me through the confirmation process. He took me to meet with the acting chairman of the Judiciary Committee, Senator Edward Kennedy of Massachusetts. Ted told me, "You're a respected member of the District of Columbia bar, a trial lawyer, a woman, and a graduate of my alma mater,

Harvard. I'm not only going to support you, I'm going to take credit for you."

Because it was an election year, the administration put a rush on my paperwork. Nineteen FBI agents fanned out across the country, completing their full field investigation of my life—from kindergarten on—in record time. There were absolutely no problems. The American Bar Association investigated me and found me qualified. The Judiciary Committee staff investigated me, too, and came up with nothing but a clean bill of health.

My confirmation hearings were set for June. Then for July. On August 11, 1988, Senator Simpson complained on the Senate floor, "We have a nominee named Judy Hope, who is a superb woman, a superb lawyer . . . a lawyer's lawyer. And where are her papers [ordering her confirmation hearing]? Lord knows. We will find them one day. At least [the Senate Judiciary Committee staff has] promised or say that they will produce a hearing for her in September. It does not leave much time. . . . I hope that we will begin to deal with this nomination. . . . No one is well served by the present state of affairs—not the Senate, not the nominee, and assuredly not the American public."

September came. And went. So did October. On October 31, 1988, the Senate minority leader, Bob Dole, husband of my close friend from law school Elizabeth, addressed the Senate: "Mr. President, as the One Hundreth Congress adjourns, there is one piece of unfinished business that I would like to mention—the judicial nominations that were not completed. In particular, I am referring to that of Judith Richards Hope, who was nominated to the D.C. Circuit on April fourteenth, 1988, a year to the day after Ruth Bader Ginsburg was nominated [to the same court] by former president Carter. Judge Ginsburg was confirmed three months later; the Hope nomination was never acted upon—and for no reason. The Judiciary Committee found Judy Hope's record to be flawless and exemplary. Her nomination was widely viewed as excellent and noncontroversial. However, it was caught in the politics of an election year, which is a tragedy for the D.C. Circuit, because they still have a vacancy, which could have been filled by a woman of great talent and intelligence. It is rare that the Senate has the opportunity to act upon a judicial nominee with such impeccable credentials. Besides having a distinguished legal career, Judy Hope has managed to raise two fine children. . . . In effect, she has had it all and would have been a fantastic judge."

The Senate adjourned. My nomination lapsed. By the time President George H. W. Bush decided to resubmit my name for the D.C. Circuit, I had been elected as the first woman in history to serve on the Harvard Corporation. Much as I wanted to stand again for the judgeship, I decided that my best contribution to public service would be working for Harvard, the place that had taken a chance on a girl from Defiance in 1961.

President Bush selected Clarence Thomas to fill Judge Bork's seat. When he moved on to the Supreme Court, President Clinton named my law school classmate and dear friend Judith W. Rogers to fill the vacancy. Judy already had the enthusiastic support of the Democratic senators. I and other classmates and supporters lobbied the Republicans on the Senate Judiciary Committee, telling them what they already knew: Judy was a superlative judge and a great woman. Everybody agreed. Judy was confirmed unanimously. Judy asked me to speak at her formal investiture ceremony on May 6, 1994, when she was publicly sworn in as judge of the United States Court of Appeals for the District of Columbia Circuit. Pat and Jim Schroeder were there, as were Rosemary and Jon Masters, who had flown down from New York. Classmates Liz Daldy Dyson from D.C. came as well. I told the crowd in the Ceremonial Court Room: "Judge Rogers and I met . . . at Harvard Law School [as members] of the class of '64, which has been referred to—mostly by ourselves—as the class on which the stars fell. And certainly Judge Rogers is one of the brightest of those stars. . . . Now she has been named by President Clinton to the second-highest court in our land. It's virtually impossible to get here—believe me, I know. But, for Judge Rogers, it's a natural. She has paid her dues. She has overcome. It is with the greatest pride that I, on behalf of her classmates, and particularly the women of the Harvard Law class of 1964, salute Judge Judith Wilson Rogers. Woman. African American. Scholar. Leader. Innovator. Public servant. Friend. She has made the District of Columbia better. Now she will make our nation better. Talk about ladies' day! Isn't this great?"

So, despite the bumps, in the long run everything came out just fine.

PART FIVE

At the Table

Pat Scott Schroeder

First elected in 1972 to represent Denver, Colorado, in the House of Representatives, Pat quickly developed a reputation for integrity, straight talk, and skill as a legislator. No sissy Pat! She took all the tough assignments: Armed Services; Judiciary; the Select Committee on Children, Youth, and Families; the Post Office and Civil Service Committee; chairing the Subcommittee on Civil Service; founding the bipartisan Congressional Caucus for Women's Issues; and cochairing Gary Hart's ill-fated presidential campaign. She never pulled her punches and never lost an election in twenty-four years.

Pat's local office was famous for having someone at every event and making sure that every social security problem was corrected right away. But Washington was where she changed the national agenda: she successfully sponsored one bill after another that protected women and families: the Violence Against Women Act, the Child Abuse Accountability Act, and the Family and Medical Leave Act among them. As the *Atlanta Journal-Constitution* pointed out a year after she retired from Congress: "She made her mark. Because of her work, there isn't a candidate in either party today who turns a cold shoulder to issues that affect working women, family health care, child care, family leave and preschool education. Schroeder made those so-called women's issues everybody's issues. And she wasn't afraid to face off with those in her party who disagreed."[1]

Pat not only sat at the table. She reshaped it.

Diana R. "Dinni" Gordon

Dinni Gordon became a full-time professor and scholar at the City University of New York in 1984. Since then, she has written three highly acclaimed books on criminal justice, lecturing throughout the United States and Europe. In 1994, the United Negro College Fund awarded her a substantial grant to assist the University of Transkei in the Eastern Cape of South Africa, one of the poorest areas in that nation, in building an economics department. She is finishing a book on the role criminal justice plays in consolidating a democracy, using South Africa as a case study.

Ann Dudley Cronkhite Goldblatt

Jeremy Goldblatt says that his mother, Professor Ann Dudley Goldblatt, is an icon at the University of Chicago, revered by students and faculty alike: "I remember Mom putting together comments on people's papers which were longer than the papers themselves." She did the same thing on her children's homework: "We would show her our papers and she and Dad would rip them apart."

Ann Dudley's family was in great shape, and both her boredom and her guilt were gone: "I knew I was actually making some kind of contribution in return for my fabulous legal education. I'm a good teacher, maybe a really good teacher. I also look around at my female classmates from law school and realize that they are all incredibly accomplished. If you take any fifteen or twenty men from our class, you're not going to find the level of achievement or recognition that we have obtained as women."

Now in his midtwenties, her son, Jeremy, understands that women can handle anything in the workplace, but he has some of the age-old concerns as well: "There can be a default assumption that an attractive woman is not very smart. There is also the worry that women who get into power will bring other women up simply because they're women, and that could be emasculating to male subordinates."

Jeremy values and respects what his mother has accomplished: "Look at where my mom came from, the kind of family she came from. Going to Harvard was a stretch. Going to Wall Street was a stretch. When we visited her family in California, we were always referred to as 'the smart cousins from Chicago.' The kind of person I'm going to marry will be smart, outgoing, and aggressive in the sense that they are not going to stay home because I say so. In fact, if I said so, they would probably be more likely to go to work. There is no attraction to a passive person for me. In that sense, I hope to marry someone like my mother."

Rosemary Cox Masters

Seven years after Rosemary quit work, and a year or so after she had received treatment for her depression, she had more than recovered her strength. She took a part-time job with the American Bar Association and decided to go back to school in social work and psychology. Her career switch was reported by the *New York Times*:

> One of 15 women graduates in her Harvard Law class, Mrs. Masters was awed by "the masculine aura of the law, its power and rationality." After a year or so of corporate work, Mrs. Masters joined the Vera Institute, where she planned the Manhattan Bowery Project for alcoholics. "Doing that," she said, "I found what was most important to me—working with people directly, using that part of my mind that's intuitive, sensitive and all those feminine things." Although the feminist part of her mind told her she would be criticized for "selling out," eventually Rosemary Masters enrolled in Hunter College for a Master's Degree in social work. She reports that some friends— lawyers and social workers alike—still do not understand that career change is "a rounding out of our identity," she said, "and a completion of myself."[2]

With her degree in hand, Rosemary hung out her shingle as a psychotherapist and slowly built a preeminent practice in Manhattan. She is considered one of the nation's leading experts on victims of trauma and writes and comments regularly both in scientific journals and in the popular media.

Judith W. Rogers

> I am particularly proud to be making this appointment today. Judith Rogers's career has been one of historic firsts, and she will be only the second African-American woman ever to serve on a U.S. Court of Appeals. I am confident that she will continue the outstanding work she has done on Washington's highest court.
> —President William Jefferson Clinton,
> November 17, 1993

It is hard to pinpoint exactly when Judy Rogers "arrived," but from early on in her career she was clearly destined for big things. After her clerkship, her three years as an Assistant United States Attorney, and a stint as a trial attorney with the San Francisco Neighborhood Legal Assistance Foundation, a time when she also taught poverty law at the law school of the University of California at Berkeley, Boalt Hall, she returned to Washington, joining the U.S. Department of Justice, where she served as both a trial attorney and as a member of the deputy attorney general's four-person team that drafted and successfully shepherded the landmark 1970 legislation through Congress that established a state-type court system in the District of Columbia. After a lengthy search for a "superstar black lawyer whose appointment will have a big splash and ripple effect on the tone of the City's government,"[3] she was named Corporation Counsel of the District of Columbia, the top lawyer in the nation's capital, heading a staff of one hundred lawyers. She was the third black and the first woman ever to hold the post. At thirty-nine years of age, she had broken through into the top rank of Washington lawyers.

In 1983, President Reagan, with the approval of the U.S. Senate, named her an Associate Judge of the D.C. Court of Appeals, the highest court in the District of Columbia's judicial system, comparable to the Supreme Court of the several states. She was elevated to chief judge in 1987, where she served until her appointment to the D.C. Circuit. In 1988, Judy received a master of laws degree from the University of Virginia Law School. In 1990, the Women's Bar Association named her the Woman Lawyer of the Year.

In 1993, President Clinton nominated her to the United States Court of Appeals for the D.C. Circuit, the second-highest court in the land. Following unanimous confirmation by the U.S. Senate, she took the oath of office on March 18, 1994.

Nancy Kuhn Kirkpatrick

Nancy Kuhn Kirkpatrick retired from law the first time in 1969 to start her family. Although she thought she would take only a couple of years off, she ended up staying home for ten years. Buffalo was a small enough town, though, that Nancy had already become well known in the legal community. Every year, she received offers to return to work. Finally, in 1980, when her son, David, was ten and her daughter, Laura, eight, she returned to work as an associate with Cohen, Swatos, Wright, Hanifin, Bradford & Brett. A few years later she became a partner and, later, added a part-time professorship at the University of Buffalo Law School to her schedule, teaching future interests and estate financial planning. She was exhausted, but by 1984, twenty years after graduation, Nancy was at the table.

Barbara Margulies Rossotti

Barbara Margulies Rossotti became a member of the prestigious Washington law firm Shaw, Pittman, Potts & Trowbridge in 1973, nine years after graduating from law school. Specializing in corporate law, with particular expertise in technology and international transactions, she has built a substantial practice in technology, advising many of the senior executives in the field "on high-risk matters such as executive retention issues, strategic alliances, and resolution of major disputes." Lawyers on the other side of the negotiating table from her say that she often assumes the role of corporate clients' inside as well as outside counsel: "It [is] clear . . . that when you speak to her, you're speaking to a real player."[4]

Barbara served as a trustee of the Mount Holyoke board for fifteen years, during five of which she was chairman. In 2000, the college's distinguished president, Joanne Creighton, paid tribute to Barbara's extraordinary leadership when she stepped down:

"Mount Holyoke is a significantly stronger institution thanks to Barbara Rossotti. Much of what we have achieved in the little over three years I have served as president has been possible because of the leadership of what has become an engaged and effective board of trustees. I credit Barbara with helping to create a board that could see what was needed and provide it."

Sheila Rush

In 1968, Sheila was recruited by a group of Harvard Law School classmates from the Manhattan law firm of Debevoise and Plimpton to become the associate director of a pro bono law office in East Harlem established by a group of Wall Street and Midtown firms to demonstrate that it was possible to integrate civil rights cases into the firms' mainstream practices. They needed a minority lawyer to administer the program and supervise the staff attorneys who were involved in the full range of civil rights and poverty law cases. It was a great concept, and with Sheila's leadership, it worked. The office thrived, and two years later, Sheila was named its director. Under her leadership, a second office was opened in central Harlem. Six years out of law school, Sheila had become one of the people to turn to when New York City wanted to accomplish something in civil rights. In 1972, she became a member of the faculty of Hofstra University Law School.

232 • Judith Richards Hope

Judith Richards Hope

Judith Coleman Richards Hope, Doctor of Laws. Distinguished
advocate and devoted alumna, steadfast civic servant and ener-
getic entrepreneur, she has opened doors and minds through her
perspicacious Fellowship.
—LL.D., Harvard University, June 2000

Looking back over forty busy and productive years, I find that a couple of
lucky breaks early in my career helped me up the ladder in the law and the
corporate world: joining the board of the Budd Company of Troy, Michigan,
in 1978; and becoming a partner of Paul, Hastings, Janofsky & Walker in
1981.

On January, 17, 1977, three days before President Ford would leave
office and I would join the ranks of the unemployed once again, my assistant,
Ruth Drinkard (Knouse) (now director of the Executive Secretariat at the
U.S. Department of Labor), buzzed me: "There's a man on the phone who
wants an appointment to see you. He says his name is Gil Richards. Is he a
relative or something?"

"I've never heard of him. Could you tell him I'm totally booked, and
thank him for his call?"

A couple of minutes later, Ruthie buzzed again: "This Gil Richards character is on the phone again. He really wants to see you—says he's in town
and wants to thank you for all you did for transportation policy here at the
White House the last couple of years. He claims he's the Chairman and CEO
of some company called Budd. Don't they make beer?"

"Actually, Budd is a big auto-parts and rail-car manufacturer in the Midwest." With the hubris that only a thirty-six-year-old White House staffer
can muster, I told her, "Since his name is Richards, tell him I can see him for
five minutes—no more—if he can come within the next couple of hours."

Gil Richards showed up half an hour later, six feet two inches of blond
Welsh charm in a camel-hair cape. I had never seen him before in my life.
He thanked me. I thanked him for thanking me. We quickly explored our
lineage, his in Iowa and mine in Ohio, and decided that we probably
weren't even distant cousins. Ruthie buzzed me after five minutes. "Could
you tell Dick Cheney that I'm tied up and will be about ten minutes late?" I
bluffed.

After talking about the auto industry's problems—air bags and emission
standards and Japanese imports—Gil came to the point: "Out in Detroit,

we've noticed the job you've done here. When you're out of government, I'd like to talk to you about some possibilities with Budd, including going on our board. If you have the time, of course."

I told Gil it would be a pleasure to talk with him after I left government and thanked him, much more profusely this time, for taking time out of his busy day to drop by the White House. He gave me his business card; I gave him a piece of White House stationery with my home phone number on it. He wished me luck and promised he'd call me.

A month later, I was making the rounds of D.C. firms, discovering that there wasn't a whole lot of demand in Washington, D.C., for Republican lawyers at the beginning of the Carter administration. Having heard nothing from Gil Richards, I seized the initiative. Early one morning, I called him to ask for an appointment. His secretary put me right through:

"Judy, how have you been? Listen. You caught me at a bad time. I've only got five minutes. What can I do for you?"

"I'd like to take you up on your offer to come to Detroit for a visit."

"What about?"

It didn't take the proverbial rocket scientist to figure out that this was tit for tat.

"Well, I thought we might talk about the abysmal record of the Detroit Lions," I replied.

It broke the ice. He laughed, but he didn't let me completely off the hook:

"Okay. But I'm really busy. The only time I've got is this afternoon. Say, two o'clock?"

It was payback time. And a test.

"I'll be there," I replied.

I called one of the women in my carpool and asked if she could take Zach and Miranda home with her after school, called the school to let them know the plan, called my husband and told him that the kids would go home with a friend and that I'd be home late, donned my navy pinstripe suit and my mother's lucky pearl necklace, grabbed a cab to the airport, and caught the last plane out to Detroit that morning.

We met promptly at two. Fortunately, I'd done my homework—I knew a great deal about the Budd Company and even about Gil Richards by the time I arrived. We talked about the company's great history and the challenges ahead, particularly those presented by various pending government regulations. After an hour, he took me across the hall and opened the door to the boardroom, complete with a thirty-five-foot-long teak table surrounded by high-backed chairs upholstered in royal blue suede.

"How'd you like to sit here six or seven times a year and help us build this company?" he asked. "You'd be our first woman director."

"I'd love to," I responded enthusiastically.

"In that case, I'll send you back on the company plane."

Which he did. At thirty-six years old, I was about to become a director of a New York Stock Exchange company. It took awhile—Thyssen of Germany acquired Budd soon thereafter and had a say in who would be on the new board. But Gil was as good as his word: in early 1978, I was sitting at that long teak table, deliberating with a star-studded group of American and German businessmen about the future of the auto industry. It changed my image, my focus, and my life.

Three years later, Leonard Janofsky, Oliver Green, Bob Lane, and Bob DeWitt—one of the firm's founders as well as most of the executive committee of Paul, Hastings, Janofsky & Walker—came to Washington to talk with me about leaving my then law firm, Wald-Harkrader, and joining them to help my law school classmate Tom Lamia build a Washington, D.C., office. They'd heard of my record of winning cases, knew that I was a member of the D.C. and California bars, and that I had solid connections in both places. They believed that my experience in the Ford White House would be a big advantage in the new Reagan-Bush administration. Besides, they wanted a manager and thought that my work on the executive committee of my then law firm and my service on the Budd Company board demonstrated some managerial potential.

We negotiated for the next ten months.

In December 1981, we struck a deal: they would back the new Washington office to the hilt, including loaning it some of their best lawyers from California; I would do my best to recruit talented lawyers and blue-chip clients for the office and the firm. It was a crazy thing for both of us to do: I had no record in building a law office essentially from the ground up, and they had no presence in Washington. Even though they had opened a tiny outpost the year before, they were an unknown firm to most people in D.C.—they weren't even in the legal directory.

Against all odds, the combination worked. Five years later, the Washington office was thriving. Together, we had recruited a star-studded group of young lawyers from around town and were doing exciting work for big-time clients. My partners elected me to the firm's four-person executive committee, the first woman and first person from a branch office ever chosen. For months, I didn't tell my husband that I was now helping to manage the entire firm. There was already too much imbalance in our marriage. I was a rising star, he was still struggling. It must have been a bitter pill when Tony found out by accident one night over dinner: for most of his life, this talented man had been "Bob Hope's son." Now he was becoming "Judy Hope's husband," without ever establishing a prominent identity of his own.

I have gone on to serve on many topflight corporate and philanthropic boards—Conrail, IBM, Zurich Reinsurance, Union Pacific, General Mills, the President and Fellows of Harvard College, and the American Red Cross among them—but these two breakthroughs, one in corporate America and one in the law, laid the foundation for all that came later. With them, I was not only perceived to be at the table, I was actually there. At a time when few women were able to get to the top in either law or business, the men who recruited me flew directly against the prevailing wisdom that women weren't tough enough or dedicated enough to lead. They broke a hole in the glass ceiling not only for me, but for the legions of talented, ambitious women who would follow. They believed, as did the founder of my alma mater, Wellesley College, more than a hundred years before:

"Women can do the work. We give them the chance."

I did my best not to let them down.

PART SIX

Exit from the Fast Lane?
(September 2001)

We are at the age when we think—or think that we should at least start to think—about retirement. The thoughts come unbidden—when the notice from the Social Security Administration arrives in the mail, comparing your benefits if you retire at sixty-two and a half, sixty-five, or seventy; when the cashier at the movies asks if you qualify for the senior-citizen discount and you're relieved that you don't; when, in spite of yourself, you find the ads for plastic surgery in the Sunday papers riveting; when you flinch at auctions because things over fifty years old are described as "vintage" or "antique"; when younger folks—women and men alike—give up their seat on the bus for you and you are—yes—grateful; when you realize you are writing fewer letters of congratulations and more of condolence. We are trying to slow down, yet almost none of us is exiting from the fast lane just yet. Instead, we are shifting—or trying to shift—our priorities, valuing our friends and families even more, and making sure that we have the time for the things we still want to accomplish.

Ann Dudley Cronkhite Goldblatt
(Chicago, Illinois, and St. Malo, California)

At the top of her game, Ann Dudley found she was thinking more and more about the next phase—where she was going, what she wanted to do with the last third of her life. She knew it would be hard to stop being intensely involved in the academic world, but even harder not to. "I was never top dog in my profession. I was very good at what I did and very well respected. But it wasn't the ladder that I chose to climb or even thought I could climb. More, I didn't want it. I told everybody I didn't want it. Sixty hit me in a way that thirty or forty or fifty never had. I began to feel physically that I wasn't as strong as I had been. As with most women, my skin started to sag just a little. I realized that I wasn't immortal anymore. God willing, I've got about a

239

quarter of my life left, maybe a little more, hopefully a little more. There's no longer time to say, 'Well, I can always do that later, or I'll wait to do that in ten years.' I started thinking about what other things that I would really regret not doing. Something I wanted was not having to go to work every day, not always having to reinvent the wheel, which is what teaching is. I enjoyed every minute of it. But I don't particularly want to continue to do it until I get sick or something terrible happens. So, in the spring of 2000, I stopped."

That fall, Ann Dudley taught just a single course in bioethics at the University of Chicago, focusing on the top twenty cases in medical law for clinical students who are doctors. The issues were cutting edge: cloning, physician-assisted suicide, DNA manipulation. There were no papers, only a quiz or two. She spent the rest of her free time that semester doing research for her book on the American starvation experiments during the Second World War, spending more time with Stan and her adult children, and working out at the gym. She told me at the time, "My life has been a kind of serendipitous series of 'Would you like to . . . ?'s. Now I'd like to be a little more deliberate. There are, of course, some bad things to do: one is to retire to your garden. People who have worked all their lives sometimes die when they don't have anything to do. Why should you get out of bed every day if there is nothing tempting and hard? Not hard, but intense. Something that takes your whole mind to do. That's what I hope to do next."

On December 21, 2000, while lifting weights at the gym with her trainer, she felt a clinch and a pop in the back of her head at the base of her brain. Somehow, she knew instantly what had happened: she had suffered a subarachnoid hemorrhage. Her ability to diagnose her own condition probably saved her life. She put the weights down and headed for the stairs. The difficulty she had raising her left foot on each tread confirmed her thoughts. When she finally reached the top, she told the woman in charge of the ladies' locker room, "Call an ambulance fast. I've blown an aneurysm." The ambulance picked her up and raced to Northwestern University Hospital. Ann Dudley checked in, then, almost immediately, checked out, got back in the ambulance, and headed to the University of Chicago Hospital Center, where she knew the doctors and the staff well. Dr. Bryce Weir, chief of neurosurgery and holder of the Maurice Goldblatt Professorship, endowed by Ann Dudley's father-in-law, quickly confirmed her instinctive diagnosis: aneurysm. He told her husband, Stan, that a third of patients died, a third were significantly impaired, and a third recovered. The doctors took their time, waiting for three days to operate. Then, after a seven-hour operation,

Ann Dudley emerged from the operating room with a permanent titanium clip on the aneurysm in her brain. After three weeks in intensive care, she had two weeks of rehabilitation, where she engaged in all sorts of tasks, such as baking cookies, to determine whether her brain could still process information and follow directions. The doctors told her that she had made a miraculous recovery—"one hundred percent"—except for a slight "impulse control" problem characterized by her tendency to speak what she thought. But Ann Dudley told them that the aneurysm had nothing to do with that: she'd been speaking her mind all her life.

By the summer of 2001, six months after emergency brain surgery, Ann Dudley was—yes—bored. She called the University of Chicago and asked if she could have her old job back. They were elated. In September 2001, Ann Dudley once again became the assistant director of the MacLean Center for Clinical Medical Ethics, and a lecturer in the Social Sciences, Biological Sciences, and Humanities Divisions of the Department of Medicine at the University of Chicago.

Arlene Lezberg Bernstein (Wellesley, Massachusetts)

Arlene Lezberg Bernstein is still active in her full-time solo practice specializing in family law in Newton, Massachusetts. Her beloved husband of thirty-two years, Jerrold, died unexpectedly in September 1998 after a brief illness. When she isn't in court or serving on the Family Law Committee of the Boston Bar Association, she's visiting her four grandchildren in the Philadelphia area. It's a full and rewarding life, and she has no plans to retire anytime soon.

Aurelle Smoot Locke (West Granby, Connecticut)

Aurelle Smoot married classmate Arthur Locke in 1965. After working a few years for a large law firm and then an insurance company, she spent eighteen years as a full-time mother and part-time volunteer. She volunteered with the Girl Scouts, other community groups, church groups, and as a local politician. Eventually, she went back to school and earned a master of laws in taxation at Boston University Law School, then joined the faculty in the department of accounting and taxation at the University of Hartford. She retired after thirteen years, which included several years as assistant dean in the business school. Although she found Harvard Law School "one of the most painful experiences of my life," she has managed both a rewarding family life and a challenging career with grace. Aurelle has now returned to her volunteer activities and is using her creative energies in quilting. She and Arthur have three daughters, two of whom are pursuing degrees at Yale.

Alice Pasachoff Wegman (Bethesda, Maryland)

Alice continues to maintain a part-time schedule. Her job as counsel to the EPA's Environmental Appeals Board gives her the opportunity to combine her legal skills with her writing talents. She and her husband, Dick, married since their law school days, play competitive duplicate bridge and travel several times a year with friends to compete in national bridge tournaments. They enjoy day-hiking, particularly in the western United States, and have wonderful memories of hiking the Kalalau Trail on the island of Kawaii and the Narrows Trail in Zion National Park. They particularly enjoy traveling when the destination is San Francisco, to visit their daughter, Laura, an artist and exhibit designer; their son, David, a computer software engineer; and Laura's fiancé, Donovan, a city planner with the City of San Francisco.

Alice is still an avid knitter and designs her own sweaters for herself and her family. As she looks ahead, she thinks, "I continue to enjoy law but I would like to find some new outlet for my creative interests either in writing or the arts."

Barbara Margulies Rossotti (Washington, D.C.)

Barbara Margulies Rossotti remains a senior corporate partner at Shaw, Pittman in Washington, D.C. Both her children are happily married. She and Charles have a farm on the Eastern Shore of Maryland, where they retreat from their incredibly busy schedules. When Charles completes his term as Commissioner of the Internal Revenue Service, they will—perhaps—have a little more time to enjoy life, to travel, and to relax with their family. They will celebrate their fortieth wedding anniversary in the summer of 2003. Knowing Barbara, she will keep going professionally, representing her clients with skill and dedication, serving as a director of the Choral Arts Society of Washington and of the Advisory Committee to the D.C. Bar Foundation, and keeping an eye on the Charles O. and Barbara M. Rossotti Scholarship Fund at Georgetown University, established "as a way of sharing our blessings and good fortune with future generations of students who will benefit, as we did, from the best education our country has to offer."

Diana R. Gordon (New York, New York)

Dinni's husband of twenty-eight years, David M. Gordon, died in 1996 awaiting a heart transplant. He was the most important person in her life, always fully supportive of everything that she wanted to do, and proud of all she accomplished. At the end of 2000, Dinni retired as a professor at CUNY but continues as a research scholar in the Ph.D. program in criminal justice, with an office near the library. She still teaches one course a year at the Ph.D. level, with eight graduate students. She has made more time for research and writing and takes a little more time to smell the roses—to be with her surrogate grandchildren, and to work in her garden at her weekend home on Long Island. She recounts, "I don't think of myself as slowing down in the sense of having less to do, but I'm going to be able to focus on what I want to do more with. I don't serve on committees anymore—actually, what I did was retire from being a good citizen. In immigration studies, they talk about the 'push and pull factors' in migration: the pull factors are economic opportunities in the other country, and the push factors are the poverty or repression in your own country. For me, there was a very strong pull factor to focus on criminal justice, research, and writing. But there was a strong push factor, too: City College is getting to be a very difficult place for somebody who wants to be not just a teacher but an active scholar. They would rather have people who keep their noses to the grindstones, teaching big classes. And they seem delighted when the senior people retire: we are more expensive. They hired three assistant professors for my salary."

Dinni is going on a few more cruises these days. She's still running a program in South Africa and finishing her book on the South Africans' criminal justice system. As for her law school experience? "For a long time Harvard Law School was just a painful lump that seemed irrelevant in my adult life, but I feel quite differently about it now. It's not that I look back at it with fondness, but I know it's been very useful. To have that pedigree still makes things easier. It's silly, but the fact that I did it, that I got through, provides a kind of open sesame. More important, it has given me a kind of rigor, of precision, in the way I approach my work. I always felt like a fish out of water there, but now I have a comforting sense of continuity in my present and my past life. I'm proud to be associated with Harvard Law School."

Eleanor Rosenthal (San Francisco, California)

Eleanor graduated from Columbia Law School cum laude in 1964, and after much pavement pounding and many comments like "I'd like to hire a woman, but my partners wouldn't think of it" and "We can't hire you because you wouldn't be safe trying to find a cab on Wall Street at night," she found a great job in New York with Winthrop, Stimson, Putnam, and Roberts (now Pillsbury Winthrop); she was the first woman they had ever hired on the partnership track. In 1970, Eleanor moved to San Francisco to take a job with Bay Area Rapid Transit (BART), where she was the only woman in the legal department. Two years later, while working for BART, Eleanor discovered the Alexander Technique, a century-old, educational, hands-on method of changing people's habits of posture, movement, and thought. Her desire to teach the technique grew and, like an itch, wouldn't allow her to ignore it. In 1975, after extensive training, she was certified to teach the technique, one of fewer than thirty certified Alexander teachers in the United States at that time.

Now twenty-seven years into her third career, with a thriving practice of the technique and related disciplines, Eleanor has little desire to retire. She sees a variety of students, including actors and musicians, but many are people with severe pain problems who find that her hands-on work and the educational aspects of the technique offer them solutions they have not been able to find elsewhere.

In explaining how she ended up retiring from law and teaching the Alexander Technique for more than a quarter of a century, she says, "I've always had a facility for left-brain, linear reasoning, and that, plus the intellectual values I was brought up with, led me into my ten-year career in law. I don't regret my legal career for a minute. Although there were problems being a woman lawyer in the sixties and early seventies, it really was a wonderful adventure. What I do now is somewhat less linear and more intuitive, but seems to be a better fit with my basic nature. Also, while drafting perfect documents was rewarding, I find that doing the many different kinds of things I can do for people now is far more exciting."

Grace Weiner Wolf (Chicago, Illinois)

In late 1987, Grace married Rabbi Arnold Jacob Wolf, who had served as Jewish chaplain at Yale University in the 1970s. She continued her editing and consulting, with Sunday-school teaching added, until Arnold retired in 2000. Since then, she has limited herself to ongoing volunteer work—editing her synagogue's monthly newsletter, helping organize an annual neighborhood garden sale, leading book discussions, cooking for the homeless—so that she has time to travel with Arnold when he is invited to speak around the country. Other traveling centers around visits to children and grandchildren. As this is written, Grace and Arnold are looking forward to taking their nine-year-old granddaughter on an intergenerational Elderhostel trip to Oxford with a Harry Potter theme.

Grace is grateful that her decision to work mostly part-time gave her an opportunity to spend so much time with her daughters when they were growing up. She is now reaping the reward with the ongoing closeness they share, no matter how far apart they live. Grace feels that her sense of fulfillment has come from an ever-changing combination of family togetherness, paid work, and multifaceted volunteer activities. Even though she spent relatively little time practicing law, most of her paid work was law-related: "I am grateful to Harvard Law School for helping me develop a sense of confidence that, confronted with any sort of problem, I feel I am up to the challenge."

Judith W. Rogers (Washington, D.C.)

Judy Rogers has a lifetime appointment to the United States Court of Appeals for the District of Columbia Circuit and has no present plans to reduce her workload by taking senior-judge status or to retire from the court. She has a distinguished record, and lawyers who appear before her give her the highest marks:

She comes to court "marvelously well prepared," treats those who appear before her with courtesy and civility, and produces well-written, sound opinions. She is known for being highly intelligent and evenhanded. She has received dozens of awards from the organized bar, the federal and District of Columbia governments, and the community, including the D.C. government's Distinguished Public Service Award, the Chairman's Award from the Judicial Council of the National Bar Association, induction into the Hall of Fame of the D.C. Commission on Women, and an Honorary Doctor of Laws from the D.C. School of Law. But most of all she loves her job, her friends, and the children all over Washington whom she quietly—often anonymously—helps.

In 1997, Judy and I took up scuba diving and went off to Indonesia on a three-week odyssey with classmate Dan Emmett and his family to explore the Ring of Fire and the reefs of the eastern Spice Islands. We've since gone diving in the Cayman Islands and Bonaire. In November 2000, Judy threw a fabulous sixtieth-birthday party for me in her historic Georgetown home. Many of our friends from the class of '64 were there.

Judy has managed to strike the perfect balance: important, stimulating work dealing with some of the most challenging issues in federal jurisprudence, taking care of underprivileged children, and kicking back with friends.

June Freeman Berkowitz (Gloucester, Massachusetts)

In the late 1980s, June returned to Harvard Law School for the third time, this time to take a weeklong mediation course. Having originally trained as a volunteer community mediator in the early 1980s, she worked to resolve parent/child, landlord/tenant, and other community disputes. She also trained and served as a divorce mediator, bringing together her legal training and her master's degree in guidance and psychological services. Sometimes she volunteered; sometimes she was paid. She also took a turn at teaching family law to paralegal students at a local community college.

June and Mort celebrated their fortieth wedding anniversary on January 1, 2002. They have three grandchildren. She has no regrets about going to Harvard Law School, all three times: "I loved it, I loved it. But the main problem that I have with life is that there are too many things that I love. My life has been like a buffet . . . there is all this wonderful stuff and yet you have to choose, you can't eat it all."

Katherine Huff O'Neil
(Vancouver, Washington, and Portland, Oregon)

In 1986, Katherine and her second husband, John Paul "Toby" Graff, Yale '57, opened their boutique law firm specializing in civil appeals. In recent years, Katherine has redirected her practice toward work as an arbitrator and mediator to allow her the flexibility to spend scheduled and unscheduled time with her widowed mother, who lived in Pensacola, Florida. "In the end it comes down to the daughter taking care of the ill parent, even if they are a continent apart. I interviewed Janet Reno once for an ABA publication. Janet told about how her mother died in her arms. I didn't understand the emotion that came with that statement until my mother died, at almost ninety-three years old, as I held her hand."

Katherine is also grateful for the forbearance of her husband, Toby: "He kept the practice together and allowed me to continue my practice when I was traveling to Florida."

Katherine remains active in the Oregon State Bar and the American Bar Association. She's been in the American Bar Association House of Delegates since 1992 and, since 1995, has chaired Oregon's delegation as "state delegate."

She has enjoyed all the passages in her life and notes: "A friend of mine, Betty Roberts, the first woman on the Oregon appellate courts, told me once that you live your life in stages. You can do it all but not at the same time. I cherish the years I took off to be with my sons. Those are times that can never be replicated, even with grandchildren, and I'm grateful I was there with my sons day in and day out. You can always be a lawyer, but there's a very limited period in which you can be a mother."

Elizabeth Daldy Dyson (Washington, D.C.)

In 1985, Liz Daldy Dyson started taking piano lessons again for the first time since she was a child. At the age of fifty-six, retired from the U.S. government, she spent the next year playing chamber music with friends, swimming at a neighborhood health club, sorting out thirty years of files, and visiting family. After a year, she began to send application letters to various child-welfare organizations, hoping to reenter the juvenile-law field. But before she had fully explored the possibilities, she saw an ad in the *Washington City Paper*: "Wanted: Ballet accompanist. Will train. Near Cleveland Park metro." She picked up the phone: "I play the piano and I live near the Cleveland Park metro." Liz auditioned and got the job. She trained at a local studio and is now a regular accompanist for the Washington School of Ballet. She loves the work: "I don't have a lot of money. I have downshifted. I don't have a car anymore. My clothes aren't great. But every day that I trudge up Porter Street with armloads of music and open the door of the Washington School of Ballet, I'm in another world. I'm in a world where beauty is appreciated and hard work is appreciated, and teachers care about their students. I'm able to contribute a little bit and have fun playing the piano. I love my job." She also performs chamber music at weddings, parties, and nursing homes and coaches and accompanies singers.

Liz's daughter, Julie, is a tenured professor of classics at the University of Texas and the mother of Liz's grandchildren, Natalie, Anthony, and Nathaniel. Her son, Ben, who taught English in Japan for three years, does desktop publishing and graphic arts; he is considering applying for law school.

Liz has traveled a long way in forty years, and it hasn't been easy, but today she is content: "I have a lot of good friends. My piano has turned out to be one of the best."

Marjory Freincle (Gibson) Haskell (Oakland, California)

Marge served for six years on the Oakland Planning Commission, then for nearly fourteen on the Oakland City Council, including a term as vice mayor, before returning to private law practice. After a wildfire destroyed both of her Oakland houses (one she and her husband, Art, rented out and one they lived in), Marge spent two years rebuilding: "My law practice now has a sharp tinge of reality in that I can truly commiserate with folks going through the hairy process of settling with insurance companies, or not, and dealing with contractors, and mechanics' liens."

More important to Marge were the people who had also been wiped out by the fire. It was the biggest urban fire in fifty years and destroyed over three thousand homes, almost all of them in Marge's council district. From the first, she realized that she would have to rebuild an entire community. She told me, "All of the stress and the hours of concentrated effort I had endured at Harvard were the training ground for what I had to do for that year and a half. Many of the improvements that I had insisted on in the emergency facility were adopted by FEMA [Federal Emergency Management Agency] subsequently." She supervised the morphing of the emergency center into a facility in which people could easily get the necessary permits to rebuild. She went to Sacramento and worked with the insurance commissioner to put pressure on the insurance companies to obtain fair settlements for the fire survivors and then helped draft state insurance-policy disclosure legislation that was adopted. She worked with counsel from the Pacific Gas and Electric Company to get the area certified as a "new development," which entitled them to special funding for undergrounding utilities.

Marge now serves as a mediator throughout the Bay Area from her downtown Oakland office. She still keeps her sewing machine in her home office. Art has retired, both from the military and the shipping business. With tennis, skiing, and swimming, and—still—chasing Marge, he's in the best shape of his life.

Nancy Kuhn Kirkpatrick (Buffalo, New York)

Because of her spinal injuries and temporary paralysis, Nancy decided in 1992 that she could no longer provide her clients with the top-notch representation that they deserved. So, in accordance with her doctor's recommendation, she retired from the practice of law. Nancy's retirement has been fulfilling and joyous: "I was first inspired to attend law school because I wanted to be able to help others, thus earning me the epithet at law school of being a 'do-gooder.' In retirement, I have satisfied those instincts much more than I could when I was working full-time. I have no intention of retiring from my retirement in the near future." Nancy and Doug's daughter, Laura, is a reporter for *ESPN* magazine; their son, David, is a reporter for the *New York Times*.

Forty years after starting Harvard Law School, Nancy retains her enthusiasm about the education she received there: "If I could go back to Harvard Law School tomorrow and do it all over again, I would do it in a minute. It was one of the most stimulating and exciting periods in my life."

Patricia Scott Schroeder
(Arlington, Virginia, and Celebration, Florida)

In 1997, after twenty-four distinguished years of service, Pat Schroeder retired from Congress as the most senior woman and one of the most respected members of the U.S. House of Representatives. "I was over fifty-five years old. It was the speed limit." Pat took a year to teach at Princeton and collect her thoughts, then became president of the Association of American Publishers. In 2000, Jim completed his term as deputy undersecretary of agriculture and, at least temporarily, retired from full-time work. He and Pat celebrated their fortieth wedding anniversary in August 2002, on a cruise off the Turkish coast. Rosemary and Jon Masters, who will also be celebrating their fortieth wedding anniversary, will be there, too, as will classmate Judy Rogers.

Pat loves her job, but, like the rest of us, occasionally thinks about what comes next. "At some point you just decide, 'Okay. I'm ready. I'm ready to try retirement and just see what it is that comes out.' But if you insist that you are going to have a plan, then you carry your type A self into that part of your life that you don't want to be type A, you may never discover the parts of yourself that you've had to repress because you've had to be so goal-oriented.

When and if I get there, part of it will be my willingness to trust my hunches, and not plan too much. If all else fails, we can be greeters at Wal-Mart. But the question is, What do you do that engages you but does not capture you? That's the hard part. The first thirty years, you're captured learning; the next thirty years, you're captured earning. Now we're in the last third . . . God willing, we have a third to go. A lot of women, particularly, have the bag-lady fear—that they're going to wake up and be a bag lady. So we want to have enough to get out of this life without being a burden to our kids. And the second, equally important part is finding something to do so that you can continue to make a contribution. You can't just drop out. If retirement is dropping out, then that's frightening. Unnecessary. Unproductive. Retirement, I hope, will be a time for me to reorient my priorities and will be my time, for myself and for Jim, but it will still be as constructive as the work I've done all these years. Like they say in the old westerns, you've got to know when to hold 'em, and know when to fold 'em. I hope I will."

Rosemary Cox Masters
(New York, New York, and Great Barrington, Massachusetts)

Rosemary continues her work as a psychotherapist and legal consultant. She works four long days a week, arriving at her office by eight and typically working until eight or nine o'clock at night. On Friday afternoons, she and Jon generally go to their cottage in the Berkshires, where they take in the sunset over the mountains, cook for friends, and meditate. Rosemary is currently training with psychologists who have a strong connection to the Buddhist tradition: she finds it helps her both in her work and personally.

Freud said that analysis never ends—it's just the roots to your own self-analysis. That's what Rosemary's trying to accomplish these days—helping people disentangle. As she says, "All of us, especially women, have all of these inner voices that say, 'You should, you ought, and why don't you? Why don't you cook better? Why is the house a mess? How come you haven't written that article? What about the children—have you bought the Christmas presents? Why haven't you?' So we all have those voices that we acquired and took within. I try to help my clients listen to those voices and then say, 'You have to cook your own Christmas turkey? You couldn't possibly have it done at the deli?' I try to help the women I work with become aware that they can choose the expectation they decide to put on themselves."

In the spring of 2001, Rosemary attended her fortieth college reunion at Mount Holyoke. Everyone seemed to be talking about retirement; the college even provided retirement brochures and seminars as guides for those planning to retire soon. Just as forty years before, Rosemary was out of step with her classmates: "I've spent the last twenty years building what to me is a concept of the mind that feels relevant and powerful and useful. Through my work with the Institute for Contemporary Psychotherapy, I am introducing those ideas to people going through the legal system, and I am excited about that. I have been through this long sequence—law, social work, psychoanalytic training, therapy, and back to law. It's finally all coming together. I feel like I'm just getting started. I have absolutely no interest in retiring. Ask me in twenty years."

It all came together for Rosemary two days after the September 11, 2001, terrorist attacks. Marsh & McLennan had lost 340 of their 1,700 employees working at the World Trade Center and asked Rosemary to organize on-site crisis counseling interventions for two groups of Marsh employees: those workers who had survived the actual attack and the 2,500 Marsh employees who worked at the company's uptown office and watched with horror the destruction of the north tower, where their friends and colleagues worked. Enlisting the support of Manhattan's Institute for Contemporary Psychotherapy, Rosemary recruited and trained more than seventy-five social workers and psychotherapists who, within a week, provided group and individual trauma therapy to more than two thousand people. As Rosemary told me later: "My career as a psychotherapist and specialist in trauma had begun twenty-one years before with traumatized families of homicide victims. In September 2001, I 'came of age' in a literal sense. That terrible event provided me the extraordinary challenge and privilege of sharing the wisdom and skills imparted to me over the years by clients and colleagues. It was as if I had been preparing my whole life for the work of helping the victims of September 11."

Sonia Faust (Kaneohe, Hawaii)

In 1981, Sonia joined the office of Hawaii's attorney general. Over the last twenty years, she has supervised three different divisions. She is sixty-five now and serving ably in one of the most critical posts in the office, assistant attorney general for land and transportation, with full responsibility for Hawaii's aviation, harbors, and highways. The newspapers report that she is the highest-paid member of the attorney general's team and that many of the supervisors in the office are women.

Recently Sonia learned that she could receive retirement benefits without retiring. She applied and has just received her first social security check. She loves her job and what she has been able to accomplish for her home state. She has no intention of retiring. She also retains her high regard for Harvard Law School: "It is one of the best institutions I know about."

When young people today ask her how she managed to make it through Harvard Law School with no money, she tells them to go to the richest law school they can find: "They have money and they'll help you. The better the school, the better the assistance."

When—and if—Sonia retires, she's thinking about taking up surfing. "Me ke aloha!"

Sheila Rush (Nevada City, California)

In 1980, Sheila resigned from her tenured position at Hofstra Law School and, with her eight-year-old son, Joseph, moved to the foothills of the Sierra Nevada in northern California to become part of Ananda Cooperative Village, a spiritual community based on the teachings of the East. *Ananda* means "bliss" in Sanskrit. The Hofstra dean asked her to take only a leave of absence, but she declined: "I knew I had to burn my bridges. I knew it would be hard, but I had to do it. I hadn't even known that I was looking for anything spiritual, but when I discovered it, I knew instantly that it was the right thing to do. And, for twenty-two years, it's been very, very good for me."

Starting in 1986, Sheila spent twelve years at the Ananda community in Palo Alto, California, where she served as general counsel to the Ananda Church of Self-Realization. In 1998, she moved to the Ananda community in Italy, returning after a year and a half abroad to the Sierra Nevada foothills.

Sheila is no longer general counsel for the Ananda Church of Self-Realization, but she serves part-time as legal liaison with the church's outside lawyers. The rest of her time she pursues her first love, writing and editing, by editing the church's quarterly magazine, and also serves as a senior minister of the church. From time to time she leaves to lecture at various places in the United States, but she prefers staying among the tall pines with the friends and spiritual leaders she has known for a quarter of a century. Married and divorced, she is content with her single life. Her son, Joseph, graduated from Georgetown Law Center in 1999 and is practicing law in New York City. She sees him regularly at family events and when he visits Ananda: "He enjoys connecting with friends from his Ananda School days."

Sheila believes she inherited from her father, the self-made businessman who always used his political influence to help other blacks advance, her strong social conscience and her abiding desire to improve things for blacks. She believes she has made a difference, and a lot of us agree.

Now, just a tad over sixty, she reflects with great warmth on the friends she made at Harvard: "The relationships we formed in law school were a lot deeper and more enduring than the friendships we formed in college. At least for me they were."

Judith Richards Hope
(Washington, D.C., and Rappahannock County, Virginia)

In November 1991, almost twenty-four years to the day after our wedding in Defiance, Tony and I divorced. Both our children were in college, and I thought—wrongly, as it turned out—that our divorce would not hurt them as much then as it would have when they were living at home. Despite the widening and ultimately irreconcilable differences between us, we had grown together for half of our lives. When we made the decision, I felt as if I had just been through some primitive Aztec ritual with my beating heart torn from my body and placed on a stone slab in the sun for all to see. For months after the decree was final, I questioned my commitment to the law, blaming my ambition, my work schedule, and my competitiveness for the breakup of my marriage.

In 1992, I took a sabbatical from my law firm, traveling the world alone for the first time to see and do things I had deferred for a quarter century. When I returned, calmer and happy, my adult children were doing fine, my father was still, as always, 100 percent behind me, and my friends, including Judy, Pat, Ann Dudley, Rosemary, and Olivia, were there to welcome me home. My law firm and my clients seemed glad to have me back. And there was a wonderful new man in my life, a teacher who wasn't—and isn't—overwhelmed by me or by what I have accomplished. He takes me dancing and brings me buckets of daffodils in the spring. He beats me at tennis—and I don't even mind. If he hadn't gone to Yale, he'd probably be just about perfect.

In 1999, I bought seventy-five acres of pasture, woods, and orchards in Rappahannock County, Virginia—a tiny part of the original land grant of King George to one of his supporters. When it came on the market in 1999, the land had only turned over a few times since 1750. The original stone farmhouse had burned down in 1959, leaving a ruin, a tall stone chimney and pieces of two hand-laid walls: it was never rebuilt or replaced. On a clear day, you can see the Bull Run Hills of Civil War battles to the east, and the Blue Ridge, with the jagged peak of Old Rag on the horizon, to the south and west—a hundred miles or more, all the way to the Shenandoah. Halfway up the mountain, on a flat ridge that faces south and west, I am building a simple farmhouse with a big country kitchen and a music room instead of a living room. There will be a shed where, if they like, my daughter can teach yoga, and my son-in-law can work on his wooden boats when they are in the area. There will be a cottage with a wood-burning stove and a big porch for my ninety-seven-year-old father. I am putting in a satellite dish for high-speed Internet service so that my son, when he comes to visit, can temporarily run his hedge fund out of the library facing the sunset. As my classmate and friend Pat Schroeder knows, I will probably always have a bit of the "bag lady" fear, but I hope I will have the courage to slow my pace just a little and trust that, if I do, things will still be all right. I might even live to be 105, like my namesake Judith in the Old Testament.

Having broken through glass ceilings in the law and in the corporate world and—I hope—managed at the same time to rear capable and talented children, I find myself yearning to return to my beginnings—to the life I remember in rural Ohio at the time of my growing up—making gardens, hunting and fishing, knitting sweaters and scarves for the bitterly cold winters, helping with the harvest, and singing and dancing and laughing with a tall, handsome blue-eyed man. I have gone full circle.

Unexpectedly, when I started building, I found mounds of cacti and a huge colony of box turtles on the ridge. Turtle Ridge Farm sounds like a good name—after all, I am moving a little more deliberately these days. And, after forty years in the fast lane, I have learned that it is generally safer not to stick your neck out all the time and to take things a little slower.

Of course, being me, I also can't help but think that—in the end—the tortoise *did* beat the hare.

Coda

The last forty years have witnessed extraordinary changes for women in the law. The handful of women who entered Harvard Law School in 1961 were about 3 percent of the class; today, women are 48 percent of the student body there, and over 50 percent of all law students nationwide. The profession we entered in 1964 was 97 percent male; today, it is nearly half female. Instead of the all-male faculty of the early 1960s, 20 percent of the tenured professors, and 23 percent of the Harvard Law faculty, are women.

The fifteen of us who graduated with the Harvard Law class of '64, and the four who graduated later from Harvard and other law schools, have been privileged to participate in and even lead many of the dramatic changes in the landscape of the law over the last four decades, whether from the courtroom, the classroom, the boardroom, the city council chamber, the sanctuary, the government, or the floor of the Congress. We have done the best we could, not only in our own jobs, but also in working to open doors and opportunities for younger women as they pursue their careers and their dreams. After all, we've been over the road—we know a little something about handling its twists and turns.

In 1961, we really didn't understand that we were storming the barricades, or that we were joining—and to some extent even starting—what turned out to be a revolution. Back then, law was a fraternity in every sense, a brotherhood bound together by tradition, education, experience, and centuries of history. Except for the woman holding the scales of justice, "law" came complete with all of a fraternity's paraphernalia, too: the exclusive men's clubs where the deals were struck and the old boys' network parceled out the opportunities; the all-male lounges in many courthouses and legislatures where cases were settled and legislation negotiated; and the men's executive washrooms in law firms and corporations, not to mention in the robing room of the United States Supreme Court. We didn't let it bother us too much. We couldn't—it would have sunk us for sure.

257

Now all that has changed. Women lawyers may not always be welcome, but we are admitted everywhere.

When Sandra Day O'Connor, the first woman named to the United States Supreme Court, started her family, she longed for a part-time position as a lawyer, but none were available to her. For a while, she worked full-time, doing her best to become indispensable in order to have more bargaining chips in future negotiations about possible part-time status, but to no avail. Eventually, she stayed home with her children for five years. As she told me recently, she was "terrified" that she would not be able to reenter the profession.

In Justice O'Connor's view, things are much better today, but they are still not easy for women who want to have both a legal career and a family. The opportunities for women at the opening stage of the legal profession are wide. Then as they progress, the demands of law practice increase at the same time these women want to have a family and spend more time with their children. As Justice O'Connor says today, "Those problems never change and they never will."

In her twenty years on the Supreme Court, Justice O'Connor has had about an equal number of male and female clerks. Many of them go on to become law teachers, a profession that she believes is particularly beneficial for women because of the flexible time it gives them for their families.

Justice O'Connor is optimistic about the future for women in the legal profession, both in government, where there has been a "reaching out" to find and promote women, and in private practice, where firms have been willing to craft creative solutions for women lawyers in the child-bearing years. She also believes that women judges can make significant, and at times unique, contributions to jurisprudence. She told me, "As a state court judge once said, at the end of the day, a wise old woman and a wise old man reach the same decision. But there is always a need for diversity of backgrounds to permit a fuller discussion of the issues presented to the court. Women, because of their life experiences, bring that something extra to the discussion."

Unlike forty, or even ten, years ago, challenging part-time legal work in big law firms is now available, particularly for women lawyers with young children. In the Washington, D.C., office of my law firm, Paul, Hastings, for example, both of the young women I mentor, Michelle Cohen, a communications lawyer, and Jenny Wu, an employment law specialist, work less than full-time schedules. Each is managing to do it all and do it exceedingly well. Michelle and Jenny were recently promoted to Of-Counsel status, the last step before partnership consideration in my firm.

Harvard Law School, which came late to opening opportunities for women students and faculty members, has creatively and enthusiastically embraced and even led the changes. It is a much better place as a result. The stern centuries-old portraits of English judges in their robes and wigs have mostly been relocated to the Caspersen Room, the school's portrait gallery and rare-book room. For a while one classroom even had framed photographs of women judges and professors looking out benignly on coeducational classes, but that classroom was converted into library space when Langdell was renovated in 1997. Perversely, none of them held a Harvard Law degree, although at least one, Justice Ruth Bader Ginsburg, deserves, at the minimum, an honorary J.D. in recognition of her extraordinary career, including the distinguished years she spent at Harvard Law School as a student and a visiting professor. There are now ladies' rooms in Langdell Hall and every other classroom building, although, until the summer of 2001, the one in the basement of Austin Hall remained a time warp, right down to the plumbing fixtures and the asbestos wraps on the sagging overhead pipes we came to know so well. There are even separate facilities for women faculty members. There are no ladies' days anymore. In sharp contrast to our era, when I was called on to state and discuss salacious cases for the edification, and presumed amusement, of the men in my class, Harvard Law School now offers the courses Battered Women and the Law, Sex (an analysis of the law of sexual injury), and Employment Discrimination Law. Students no longer have dinner at the dean's house—which is a shame.

Professor Dan Coquillette, Harvard Law School's official historian, reminds us that American legal education was essentially invented at Harvard. From the grading system, examination requirements, postings of class ranking, and Socratic methodology, instituted by Dean Christopher Columbus Langdell in the 1870s, "as a badly needed counterbalance to a world that was divided by wealth and social class," to the LSAT, invented by Vice Dean and Admissions Director Louis Toepfer in the 1950s to enable the selection of a more diverse student body, Harvard Law School has been in the forefront of legal education for over a century.[1] It has a lot of spirited competition from great schools like Stanford, Yale, Columbia, NYU, Georgetown, Michigan, Chicago, and Virginia, among others, and is no longer automatically ranked number one every single year. But it is always in the very top tier and continues to lead the way in cutting-edge research, technology, prominence of the faculty, and overall qualifications of its students. The 690 dormitory rooms now on campus are open to men and women alike. Langdell Hall, renovated in 1997 under the dynamic leadership of Dean Robert Clark, still contains the largest private collection of law books and legal materials in the world. Starting in the fall of 2001, for the first time since the Civil War,

1-L sections were reduced from 140 students each to 80, with each section having designated faculty leaders who are charged with responsibility for students' intellectual and social activities outside the classroom. It may even be that Harvard Law School is becoming less Darwinian, although one can never be completely sure about that.

As former Law School dean and Harvard president Derek Bok acknowledges, the school is a much better place now, for both men and women, than it was forty years ago: "When I was there, the law school had relatively few student organizations. The faculty paid a lot of attention to the law review and virtually none to any other organization. That was bad. It is incomparably better now. There are lots of law reviews and clinical activities so that everybody can find a small niche that he or she is interested in, can make a difference in, and be part of the meaningful community. Then it was not so bad, of course, with the Board of Student Advisors and the Legal Aid, but after that—the top 9 percent of each class—there was nothing specific for the other 91 percent of the students. There was such an emphasis on work and hierarchy, and a lot of that was overdone. The trouble is that the pendulum had to go way over to the other side before it could move to some sensible middle, which is where I believe the school is now."

Of course, most of the women in my class thought the Harvard Law School was pretty terrific when we were there forty years ago. And, of course, even today Harvard is still Harvard. It *is* great. And it is not exactly humble about it. On April 13, 2001, the dean wrote to the five justices of the United States Supreme Court who had attended the school about the new methodology the school would employ in continuing Harvard's long tradition of having a Supreme Court justice preside at the annual finals of the Ames Moot Court Competition. It was a modest proposal "to make participating in this tradition as easy and as agreeable as possible for you":

> We have in mind a 5-year plan whereby [you] can, by seniority on the Supreme Court, choose one year of the next five years most convenient to [your] November schedule to sit on the Ames Court. After the most senior Justice chooses a year, the next Justice in line of seniority would decide on a year, and so on down the line. Thus no one Justice would be asked to take part in the Ames Final more than once in a 5-year period. To keep delays to a minimum, we are sending a similar letter simultaneously to all five relevant Justices.

The great judge and legal scholar Learned Hand attended Harvard Law School and taught there before becoming a judge first on the federal trial bench in the Southern District of New York, then on the U.S. Court of

Appeals for the Second Circuit. His concluding words at Harvard's Holmes Lectures echo our sentiments, our recollections, and our gratitude for the extraordinary training and education we received:

> More years ago than I like now to remember, I sat in this building [Austin Hall] and listened to—yes, more than that, was dissected by—men all but one of whom are now dead. What I got from them was not alone the Rule in Shelley's Case, or what was one's duty to an invited person—as we then called him—or what law determined whether a contract has been made, or how inadequate was the common law of partnership before the advent of Cory on Accounts, or in what jurisdictions a corporation is "present." True, I did get those so far as I was able to absorb them, but I got much more. I carried away the impress of a band of devoted scholars; patient, considerate, courteous and kindly, whom nothing could daunt and nothing could bribe. The memory of those men has been with me ever since. Again and again they have helped me when the labor seemed heavy, the task seemed trivial, and the confusion seemed indecipherable. From them I learned that it is as craftsmen that we get our satisfactions and our pay. In the universe of truth they lived by the sword; they asked no quarter of absolutes and they gave none. Go ye and do likewise.[2]

In our professional lives, we have tried to follow that exhortation, and by and large, it has proved out for us. We would add only that we also found each other at Harvard Law School. And that has made all the difference.

Closing Legal Brief:
Harvard and Law School Today for Women

Kathleen M. Sullivan, Dean, Stanford Law School

Having graduated from Harvard Law School in 1981 and, from 1984 to 1993, having served as the seventh woman to join the faculty there, I can scarcely imagine living life with the pluck, creativity, and determination of the women Judith Richards Hope brings to life in this beautifully rendered, often heart-wrenching book. Like virtually every woman ever connected with the Law School, I had heard the folklore, passed down from one class of women to the next, about "the early days," including flabbergasting stories about ladies' days and dinner at the dean's. It was hard to believe them, but now they are documented, testimony to the courage and wit of the early women law students at Harvard, and to the enlightenment that has come to law schools and the legal profession at large over the last four decades.

Women of my era, twenty years later, have their own stories of difficulty and challenge. I remember being flattered when, after a summer clerkship in 1980, a leading Manhattan law firm offered me a full-time job, promising that "if you join us, you can be our first woman litigation partner." I later found out that they'd been telling women associates that for ten years before and would for ten years after.

Being one of only five women on Harvard Law School's faculty from 1984 to 1993 was exhilarating but daunting: the teaching alone was demanding enough, but with so few women professors, the nonteaching requirements were particularly heavy. Every faculty committee seemed to need at least one woman member, and many of the more than three hundred women students sought counseling, particularly from the five of us. A number of the older male professors couldn't get used to having women col-

263

leagues around: they seemed to call all of us Martha, lumping us together with Martha Field, Harvard Law's second tenured woman professor, and Martha Minow, who arrived a short time later. We also had to deal with what I now realize was a traditional absence of ladies' toilets there. The faculty library had two small bathrooms, but neither was marked Women. We managed to rectify that only after we suggested that one be marked Men and the other Martha.

There has been a sea change in the law school environment for women in the twenty years since I graduated from Harvard, and women entering the profession today do so with options and opportunities unimaginable to those in Judy Hope's class. Women now make up 48 percent of Harvard's Law School students, and 23 percent of the faculty; at Stanford, 52 percent of the students and 25 percent of the faculty are women. The first and most senior woman professor at Stanford is Barbara Babcock, who started out with Judy at Williams & Connolly in 1964 and has her own hair-raising stories about those early days of women trial lawyers.

Today's women law graduates are not all postponing pregnancy as so many women of my generation did, often until too late. During the 2000–2001 law school year, there were so many births to Stanford's women law students that we reconfigured one of our (many) women's bathrooms to add a "nursing room" so that student mothers can nurse their babies between classes and when they are studying late at the library.

If I have one concern today for women in law, it is that they probably still cannot do it all, at least not all at the same time. The demands of our profession for hard work, long hours, and meticulous accuracy are in tension with family life, especially when small children are involved. But the basic rule for women lawyers starting out today hasn't changed much from twenty or forty years ago. We still have a heavier burden of persuasion than our male counterparts. The age-old solution is still the best: work hard and always be excellent. That will see us through, no matter what difficulties we encounter. That, plus the legacy of respect and achievement left to us by the women of this book, who carried all of us on their shoulders.

Palo Alto, California
June 2002

Appendix: Excerpts from the Archives of Harvard University Regarding the Admission of Women to Harvard Law School

MEMORANDUM

To: The Faculty   April 15, 1949
From: The Committee on the Admission of Women

We transmit to you herewith a Report of the Committee to the Faculty. It is anticipated that the recommendation of the Committee will soon be submitted to the Faculty for its consideration.

REPORT OF THE COMMITTEE ON THE ADMISSION OF WOMEN

In 1869, in the course of his Inaugural Address, President Eliot remarked that "the world knows next to nothing about the natural mental capacities of the female sec". Forty years later a distinguished graduate of the Harvard Law School, speaking as lawyer and historian, indicated confidence that in the intervening years the boundaries of knowledge had been extended. In 1910 Brooks Adams pronounced that women "as an intellectual being . . . has only the importance of a degraded boy". Perhaps such superciliousness was not surprising that one year before the publication of Brooks Adams's discouraging reflection the Harvard Corporation reaffirmed an earlier decision that women should not be admitted to the Law School.

In his Address, President Eliot suggested that the University's policy with respect to the admission of women should be developed cautiously. "Only after generations of civil freedom and social equality will it be possible to obtain the data necessary for an adequate discussion of woman's natural tendencies, tastes, and capabilities." He urged, however, that the University's policy should be "expectant". The note of hopefulness suggested by that expectancy was derived from his conviction that "Americans, as a rule, hate disabilities of all sorts, whether religious, political, or social". In the years since 1869 the American people by many signs—by custom, by legislation and by constitutional amendments—have indicated that President Eliot's estimate of their persuasion was accurate. In numberless ways the nation has shown its dislike for those traditional discriminations by which women had been denied political rights and professional opportunities as nearly as possible equal to those offered to men.

Within the University, policy in this matter has followed that of the nation. At the present time women are admitted to all the graduate departments of the University, with the exception of the Business School and the Law School. The recent readjustments of the relationships between the College and Radcliffe, and the recent determination that women should be admitted to the Medical School strikingly indicate the University's conviction that time has shown, as President Eliot believed that it might, that woman's tendencies and capabilities entitle her to equality of educational opportunity within the Harvard community.

With national policy clear and University action consistent with that policy, any department of the University which continues to enforce a rule of exclusion on grounds of sex alone, has the burden of justifying that rule. The Committee to which the question of admitting women to the Law School was referred has considered the justifications for the continued exclusion of women and is persuaded that those justifications are insufficient.

It would be idle to pretend that if women are admitted to the Law School significant qualities in its traditional atmosphere may not be altered. Students coming here from co-educational colleges have undoubtedly found its relative monasticism a stimulating contrast to the atmosphere of their undergraduate experience. One member of the Committee, for instance, believes that if he could recapture his youth and thus regain the occasion of choosing a law school, he would select a good law school from which women are excluded in preference to a bisexual Harvard. He is, though, cheerfully ready to recognize as significant the less austere view of others who find in recent years a demonstration that the most significant traditions of the School are strong enough to thrive in an unmonastic climate. Even with wives in lecture rooms and reading rooms, and with children at nursery school in Hastings Hall, the students have continued to observe the highest standards of achievement. There seems little reason to fear, therefore, that if the relatively small group of qualified women applicants who might be expected to apply for admission should be admitted to the School its effectiveness would be appreciably jeopardized.

Perhaps the most serious justification for the exclusion of women is based upon the probability that a relatively small proportion would make professional use of their training for a significant period of time, and that for each woman admitted a qualified man, somewhat more likely to use his training in his career, would have to be excluded. Statistics made available to us by other comparable law schools following a co-educational policy, have not, for the most part, thrown much light on the predictable fate of women lawyers. The most significant figures are those obtained from the Law School of Columbia University. They show that approximately half of the seventy-eight women who graduated there between 1936 and 1943 discontinued their careers in employment within five years. There is, of course, no way of telling whether some such mortality rate as that is likely to continue in the future, but it may fairly be used as a rough measure of probability. Accepting it as such, the Committee is not persuaded that that mortality rate justifies the complete exclusion of qualified women from the Law School. Dean Burwell, of the Medical School, in answering the Committee's inquiry as to the grounds upon which his school determined that women should be admitted made the following statement: "We anticipated that a large proportion of our women graduates might not practice medicine for any great length of time, but in spite of this we believed it was unfair to deny properly qualified and selected women applicants the privilege of getting a Harvard M.D. degree." It seems clear to the Law School Committee that in principle it is indefensible for Harvard's admissions policy to be non-discriminatory as to medicine and discriminatory as to law.

It is, of course, true that the women at the bar has always faced special difficulties and obstacles. It is likely that that situation will continue for some time to come and that on graduation she will find the initial problems of placement and the later problems of advancement far more difficult to solve than will her male classmate. There are, to be sure, occasional signs that employers in recent years have found an unexpected utility in women lawyers. Some months ago, before the appointment of the present Committee, a distinguished graduate of the School, practicing in New York City, in replying to a questionnaire with respect to the profession, wrote to Professor Fuller as follows: "Since you ask for criticisms, I venture one. . . . Our experience during recent war years with about a half a dozen or so carefully selected women lawyers has opened our eyes to their very real value as members of our staff. We took on as 'replacements' for the duration but have ended keeping them all, although practically all our service men have come back to us, and we are much inclined to believe that in future there is likely to be a female section of our staff on the basis of merit. . . . There is of course the question whether accommodations could be found for women at the Harvard Law School, but apart from that I think the day will come when the School will admit them." Elsewhere, Mr. Harrison Tweed of the New York bar, has spoken of the "abundant opportunity" which women lawyers have for useful work in legal aid, in Bar Association activities, and in the American Law Institute, and has voiced his "strong belief that women can accomplish great things at the bar". Theses opinions are, quite possibly, exceptionally optimistic. Yet they seem to the Committee to bespeak a point of view which is likely to become increasingly representative as the responsibilities of the lawyer in private practice, in government, and in scholarship expand and change. The fact that the woman lawyer is under special handicaps in securing the fullest opportunity for professional success is hardly sufficient justification for the preservation of a rule of exclusion which forbids her from attempting to overcome them and denies her the right to secure what we like to consider the best education in the law which the nation offers.

The cumulative effect of these considerations leads the Committee to recommend that beginning in the Fall of 1950 qualified women be admitted to the Law School. Earlier initiation of this policy seems undesirable, partly because of the fact that until that time there will still be a substantial number of qualified veteran applicants to whom we owe a special obligation, and partly because as a practical matter, the effective date for applications for admission in the Fall of 1949 would have passed before action on the matter could be expected from the Corporation. It is, furthermore, the recommendation of the Committee that in the first years of executing the new policy admission of women should be on a separately planned selective basis. Time may show that it is either unnecessary in fact, inadvisable as a matter of policy, or unworkable as a matter of administration to have one standard of qualifications for women applicants and another for men. Until we learn how many women will apply for admission and until we have had some experience in evaluating the records of women's colleges, we must proceed by gradual stages. The Committee prefers to make no recommendation as to a maximum number of women to be admitted in the first years of the new policy, feeling that that decision if it has to be made should be made on the advice of the Admissions Committee after applications have been received and evaluated.

With respect to housing, medical, and other similar problems which the admission of women to the Law School would present the Committee, appreciating their seriousness, is persuaded that their dimensions are not such as to justify the continuation of our policy of exclusion. One of the minor problems is capable of easy solution: the Building and Grounds Department has advised the Committee that toilet and rest room facilities can be installed in the basement of Austin Hall for an estimated cost of $11,000. The Committee realizes that it will be impossible for the University to provide housing, and medical and athletic facilities to women students. That impossibility will doubtless present administrative difficulties of some seriousness. Yet the Committee believes that if women applicants are made aware in advance that they are largely on their own in Cambridge, the problem will not be serious. There is, furthermore, some reason to hope that in the course of a few years Radcliffe, which is already concerned with the problem of providing dormitory accommodations for a number of its own graduate students as well as for women at the Harvard Architectural School and the School of Education may be as able as it is willing to offer dormitory accommodations, athletic facilities and medical services to women in the Law School. The Committee, therefore, is hopeful that with time desirable arrangements of that sort, and not involving large expense to the Law School, may be worked out with President Jordon and the Radcliffe administration.

The Committee, accordingly, recommends to the Faculty

that it recommend to the Harvard Corporation that beginning in
the Fall of 1950 qualified women applicants be admitted to the Law
School as candidates for our degrees upon a selective basis to be
developed on the advice of the Admissions Committee.

> Austin W. Scott
> John M. Maguire
> Ernest J. Brown
> Louis Toepfer
> Mark DeW. Howe, Chairman

Law School of Harvard University

Cambridge 38, Mass.

OF RECORD

JUN 22 1949   May 11, 1949

Dear President Conant,

I am writing this letter to transmit to you a vote taken by
the Faculty of the Law School at a meeting held on May 10, 1949.
The Faculty voted to recommend to the governing boards that
beginning in the fall of 1950 qualified women applicants be admitted to the Law School as candidates for our degrees upon a selected
basis to be developed upon the advice of the Admissions Committee.

This matter has been under discussion in the Faculty for
some time. Late in January, a committee was appointed, consisting
of Professor Howe as chairman and with Professors Scott, Maguire,
and Brown, and Assistant Dean Toepfer as members. This committee unanimously reported in favor of the admission of women,
and it was this report which was adopted by the Faculty at its
meeting yesterday. I am enclosing copies of the committee's report
with this letter.

The vote of the Faculty was 22 in favor of the recommendation, and 2 opposed.

It will be noted that the proposal is for admission of women
effective in September 1950, and not in September 1949. Applica-

tions for our first year class next fall have already closed, and we are still receiving a substantial proportion of applications from veterans. It has seemed to us best that the actual admission of women should not occur until a year from this fall. For this reason, too, it would be desirable not to make any announcement of the change, if it is adopted, until next fall. It would be convenient, however, to be able to make the announcement as early in the fall as possible, so that it could be included in the printed "Instructions for Applicants" which we prepare each year for distribution to those who are seeking admission to the School.

Very truly yours,

Erwin N. Griswold
Dean

President James B. Conant
Massachusetts Hall

Enclosures

Notes

PART ONE

1. At the farewell dinner given for me in the spring of 2000, when I retired from the Corporation, I recounted this story of my first few minutes as a Fellow. My successor in the Flynt chair, Herbert S. "Pug" Winokur, told me he knew no more than I did about where to sit at his first meeting, and no one told him either. Solving the riddle of seating, I decided, must be a gentle hazing rite, passed down through the generations by Harvard Fellows.
2. R. Cox, letter to Rosemary's parents, October 20, 1960, Mount Holyoke College Archives and Special Collections.
3. Ibid.
4. S. E. Morison, ed., *Development of Harvard University*, lxx.
5. J. J. White, "Women in the Law," *Michigan Law Review* 65 (April 1967): 1051.
6. C. Grant Bowman, "Bibliographical essay: Women and the legal profession," *American University Journal of Gender, Social Policy & the Law* 7 (1998–99): 149.
7. Archives, Harvard University, Eliot Papers #462, box 124.
8. Archives, Harvard University, 15.160.9, vol. 1, p. 159.
9. Archives, Harvard University, Lowell Papers, 1909–14, UA15.160 #959.
10. *Harvard Law Bulletin* (summer 1988): 5.
11. Archives, Minutes of Meetings, the President and Fellows of Harvard College, October 11, 1909.
12. Archives, Harvard University, Lowell Papers, 1909–14, UA15.160 #959.
13. Archives, Minutes of Meeting, Harvard Law School Faculty, August 19, 1947.
14. E. Brown, personal interview, April 16, 1998.
15. E. N. Griswold, *Ould Fields, New Corne*, 170.
16. Archives, Minutes of Meetings, Harvard Law School Faculty, January 11, 1949.
17. Ibid.
18. E. J. Brown and L. Toepfer, personal interviews, July 6, 1998, and August 9, 1999, respectively.
19. Report of the Committee on the Admission of Women, Archives, Harvard University, April 1949.
20. Approved June 22, 1949.
21. R. Rosenbaum, "The Great Ivy League Nude Posture Photo Scandal: How scientists coaxed America's best and brightest out of their clothes," *New York Times Magazine*, January 15, 1995, 26.

22. N. Banerjee, "Some 'Bullies' Seek Way to Soften Up; Toughness Has Risks for Women Executives," *New York Times*, August 10, 2001, C-1.

23. R. G. Gettel, inaugural address as President of Mount Holyoke College, November 9, 1957, Mount Holyoke College Archives and Special Collections.

PART TWO

1. C. Trillin, *New Yorker*, March 26, 1984, 53.

2. E. N. Griswold, *Ould Fields, New Corne*, 171

3. Report of the Committee to Study the Admission of Women Students to the Harvard Law School, Archives, Harvard University, April 1949.

4. R. Cox, letter to Rosemary's parents, September 18, 1961, Mount Holyoke College Archives and Special Collections.

5. A. Pasachoff, "University Considers Fate of Gracious Living," *Cornell Daily Sun*, 1961.

6. Archives, Minutes of Meetings, Harvard Law School Faculty, January 11, 1949.

7. Memorandum to the Faculty, from the Committee to Study the Admission of Women, Archives, Harvard University, April 15, 1949.

8. *Harvard Law School Yearbook*, 1964, 19.

9. *Harvard Law School Yearbook*, 1962, 116.

10. *Harvard Law School Yearbook*, 1964, 21.

11. R. Cox, letter to Rosemary's parents, October 19, 1961, Mount Holyoke College Archives and Special Collections.

12. *Harvard Law School Yearbook*, 1965, 28.

13. Ibid.

14 R. Cox, letter to Rosemary's parents, October 31, 1961, Mount Holyoke College Archives and Special Collections.

15 Ibid.

16 W. B. Leach, letter to Rosemary Cox, June 6, 1962.

17. R. Cox, letter to Rosemary's parents, October 18, 1961, Mount Holyoke College Archives and Special Collections.

18. Ibid.

19. J. Murphy, personal interview, September 15, 1998.

20. N. K. Kirkpatrick, personal interview, September 8, 2001.

21. R. Cox, letter to Rosemary's parents, October 19, 1961, Mount Holyoke College Archives and Special Collections.

22. E. N. Griswold, *Ould Fields, New Corne*, 173–74.

23. R. Rogers and O. Hammerstein, "There Is Nothin' Like a Dame," *South Pacific*.

24. R. Cox, letter to Rosemary's parents, January 19, 1962, Mount Holyoke College Archives and Special Collections.

25. R. Cox, letter to Rosemary's parents, March 11, 1962, Mount Holyoke College Archives and Special Collections.

26 Reavis Cox, letter to Rosemary's parents, March 18, 1962, Mount Holyoke College Archives and Special Collections.

27. *Griswold vs. Connecticut*, 381 U.S. 479, 485 (1965).

28. Ibid.

29. Ibid.
30. R. Cox, letter to Rosemary's parents, February 1962, Mount Holyoke College Archives and Special Collections.
31. *Harvard Law School Yearbook,* 1962, 14.
32. *Harvard Law School Yearbook,* 1964, 185.
33. E. Borgeson, personal interview, July 6, 2001.
34. E. Dole and R. Dole, *The Doles,* 73.
35. C. Fuchs Epstein, *Woman's Place,* 22–24, passim, quoting in part Hunt, "The Direction of Feminine Evolution," in S. M. Farber and R. H. L Wilson, eds., *The Potential of Women,* 260.
36. *Harvard Law Record,* 37, no. 1 (September 26, 1963): 5.
37. *Harvard Law Record,* 37, no. 1 (September 26, 1963): 6.
38. *Harvard Law Record,* 37, no. 1 (September 26, 1963): 4–5.
39. *Harvard Law Record,* 37, no. 1 (September 26, 1963): 6.
40. D. P. Levitt, "In Memoriam. John F. Kennedy." *Harvard Law School Yearbook,* 1964.

PART THREE

1. "Women Have a Handicap," *Harvard Law Record,* 37, no. 9 (December 12, 1963): 14.
2. R. Cox, letter to Rosemary's parents, November 2, 1963, Mount Holyoke College Archives and Special Collections.
3. *Washington Post,* page C-4, November 27, 1994.
4. E. Thomas, *Robert Kennedy,* 288.

PART FOUR

1. L. Hughes, "Mother to Son" (1922).
2. P. Schroeder, *Champion of the Great American Family,* 8.
3. T. P. Cameron Wilson, *Waste Paper Philosophy,* 21.

PART FIVE

1. M. Ezzard, "Elizabeth Dole Quit Without Showing What She Had to Offer," *Atlanta Journal-Constitution,* October 24, 1999, 1B.
2. G. Dullea, *New York Times,* July 11, 1977, 30.
3. M. Coleman, "Barry Appoints Corporation Counsel; Mayor Selects Judith Rogers to Be New Corporation Counsel," *Washington Post,* April 12, 1979, C-1.
4. J. Berlau, "IRS Commissioner Rossotti's Conflict of Interest: A Taxing Dilemma," *National Institute for Tax Education,* April 4, 2001, 6.

CODA

1. D. Coquillette, Speech to the Combined Reunion Classes, Harvard Law School, October 27, 2001.
2. L. Hand, *The Bill of Rights*, 77.

Bibliography

Abramson, Jill, and Barbara Franklin. *Where Are They Now: The Story of the Women of Harvard Law.* New York: Doubleday, 1974.

Apter, Terri. *Working Women Don't Have Wives: Professional Success in the 1990s.* New York: St. Martin's Griffin, 1993.

Cameron Wilson, T. P. *Waste Paper Philosophy.* New York: George H. Doran, 1920.

Cox-Fill, Olivia. *For Our Daughters: How Outstanding Women Worldwide Have Balanced Home and Career.* Westport, Conn.: Praeger, 1996.

Cushman, Clare, ed. *Supreme Court Decisions and Women's Rights.* Washington, D.C.: CQ Press, 2001.

Dolan, Jill. *The Feminist Spectator as Critic.* Ann Arbor: University of Michigan Press, 1988.

Dole, Bob, and Elizabeth Dole. *The Doles: Unlimited Partners.* New York: Simon & Schuster, 1988.

Drachman, Virginia G. *Sisters in Law: Women Lawyers in Modern American History.* Cambridge, Mass.: Harvard University Press, 1998.

Epstein, Cynthia Fuchs. *Woman's Place.* Berkeley: University of California Press, 1971.

———. *Deceptive Distinctions: Sex, Gender, and the Social Order.* New Haven, Conn.: Yale University Press, 1988.

———. *Women in Law* (2d ed.). Urbana and Chicago: University of Illinois Press, 1993.

Farber, David, ed. *The Sixties: From Memory to History.* Chapel Hill: University of North Carolina Press, 1994.

———. *The Age of Great Dreams: America in the 1960s.* New York: Hill and Wang, 1994.

Farber, S. M., and R. H. L. Wilson, eds. *The Potential of Women.* New York: McGraw Hill, 1963.

Forbes, Malcolm. *Women Who Made a Difference.* New York: Simon & Schuster, 1990.

Friedan, Betty. *The Feminine Mystique.* New York: W. W. Norton, 1963.

Galbraith, John Kenneth. *The Affluent Society.* Boston: Houghton Mifflin, 1958.

Gitlin, Todd. *The Sixties: Years of Hope, Days of Rage.* New York: Bantam Books, 1987.

Glendon, Mary Ann. *A Nation Under Lawyers: How the Crisis in the Legal Profession Is Transforming American Society.* Cambridge, Mass.: Harvard University Press, 1994.

Graham, Katharine. *Personal History.* New York: Alfred A. Knopf, 1997.

Griswold, Erwin N. *Ould Fields, New Corne: The Personal Memoirs of a Twentieth-Century Lawyer.* St. Paul, Minn.: West Publishing Company, 1992.

Guinier, Lani, Michelle Fine, and Jane Balin. *Becoming Gentlemen: Women, Law School, and Institutional Change.* Boston: Beacon Press, 1997.

Hand, Learned. *The Bill of Rights: The Oliver Wendell Holmes Lectures.* Cambridge, Mass.: Harvard University Press, 1958.

Harrington, Mona. *Women Lawyers: Rewriting the Rules.* New York: Plume, 1993.

Hickey, Mary C., and Sandra Salmans. *The Working Mother's Guild Guide.* New York: Penguin Books, 1992.

Holcomb, Betty. *Not Guilty!: The Good News About Working Mothers.* New York: Scribner, 1998.

Kahlenberg, Richard D. *Broken Contract: A Memoir of Harvard Law School.* New York: Hill and Wang, 1992.

Kirshner, Ralph. *The Class of 1861: Custer, Ames, and Their Classmates After West Point.* Carbondale: Southern Illinois University Press, 1999.

Kotter, John P. *The New Rules: How to Succeed in Today's Post-Corporate World.* New York: The Free Press, 1995.

Laiou, Angeliki, ed. *Consent and Coercion to Sex and Marriage in Ancient and Medieval Societies.* Washington, D.C.: Dumbarton Oaks Research Library and Collection, 1993.

Law, Lisa. *Flashing on the Sixties.* San Francisco: Chronicle Books, 1987.

Lewis, Deborah Shaw, and Charmaine Crouse Yoest. *Mother in the Middle: Searching for Peace in the Mommy Wars.* Grand Rapids, Mich.: Zondervan Publishing House, 1996.

Margolis, Jon. *The Last Innocent Year: America in 1964.* New York: William Morrow, 1999.

Matusow, Allen J. *The Unraveling of America.* New York: Harper & Row, 1984.

McCarthy, Mary. *The Group.* New York: Harcourt Brace, 1963.

Metropolitan Museum of Art, New York. *Jacqueline Kennedy: The White House Years.* New York: A Bulfinch Press Book/Little, Brown, 2001.

Morello, Karen Berger. *The Invisible Bar: The Woman Lawyer in America: 1638 to the Present.* New York: Random House, 1986.

Morrison, S. E., ed. *Development of Harvard University, 1869–1929.* Cambridge, Mass.: Harvard University Press, 1930.

Nercessian, Nora N. *Worthy of the Honor: A Brief History of Women at Harvard Medical School.* Boston: President and Fellows of Harvard College, 1995.

Rampersad, Arnold, ed. *The Collected Poems of Langston Hughes.* New York: Vintage Classics, 1995.

Rimm, Sylvia. *See Jane Win: The Rimm Report on How 1,000 Girls Became Successful Women.* New York: Three Rivers Press, 1999.

Roat, John Carl. *Class-29: The Making of U.S. Navy Seals.* New York: Ballantine Books, 2000.

Schroeder, Pat. *Twenty-four Years of House Work . . . and the Place Is Still a Mess: My Life in Politics.* Kansas City, Kan.: Andrews McMell, 1998.

———. *Champion of the Great American Family.* New York: Random House, 1989.

Seligman, Joel. *The High Citadel: The Influence of Harvard Law School.* Boston: Houghton Mifflin, 1978.

Sorel, Nancy Caldwell. *The Women Who Wrote the War.* New York, HarperCollins, 1999.

Sullivan, Patricia. *Day of Hope: Race and Democracy in the New Deal Era.* Chapel Hill: University of North Carolina Press, 1996.

Sutherland, Arthus E. *The Law at Harvard: A History of Ideas and Men, 1817–1967.* Cambridge, Mass.: The Belknap Press of Harvard University Press, 1967.

Thomas, Evan. *Robert Kennedy: His Life.* New York: Simon & Schuster, 2000.

———. *The Man to See: Edward Bennett Williams, Ultimate Insider; Legendary Trial Lawyer.* New York: Simon & Schuster, 1991.

Trumpbour, John, ed. *How Harvard Rules: Reason in the Service of Empire.* Boston: South End Press, 1989.

Turow, Scott. *One L: An Inside Account of Life in the First Year at Harvard Law School.* New York: G. P. Putnam, 1977.

Tuttle, William M., Jr. *Daddy's Gone to War: The Second World War in the Lives of America's Children.* New York: Oxford University Press, 1993.

Unger, Irwin, and Debi Unger, eds. *The Times Were a Changin': The Sixties Reader.* New York: Three Rivers Press, 1998.

U.S. Marine Corps, Command and Control, Washington, D.C., United States Government as represented by the Secretary of the Navy, 1996.

Walsh, Elsa. *Divided Lives: The Public and Private Struggles of Three Accomplished Women.* New York: Simon & Schuster, 1995.

Wells, Rebecca. *Divine Secrets of the Ya-Ya Sisterhood.* New York: HarperCollins, 1996.

Whalen, Charles, and Barbara Whalen. *The Longest Debate: A Legislative History of the 1964 Civil Rights Act.* Cabin John, Md., and Washington, D.C.: Seven Locks Press, 1985.

OTHER SOURCES

Harvard Law School Class of 1964: Twenty-fifth, Thirtieth, and Thirty-fifth Anniversary Reports. Cambridge, Mass.: 1989, 1994, 1999.

Harvard Law School Yearbook. Cambridge, Mass.: 1962, 1963, 1964, 1965.

Legenda (Wellesley College Yearbook). Wellesley, Mass.: 1961.

Panorama (Defiance High School Yearbook). Defiance, Ohio: 1953, 1957.

Wellesley College Reunion Reports for the Class of 1961. Wellesley, Mass.: 1981, 1986, 1991, 1996, 2001.

Women at Harvard Law School: Celebration 35, 40, and 45. Cambridge, Mass.: 1988, 1993, 1998.

Index

Page numbers in *italics* refer to illustrations.